globalisation and labour mobility in china

Globalisation and labour mobility in China

edited by

Ingrid Nielsen, Russell Smyth and Marika Vicziany

Monash University Press
Clayton

Monash University Press
Building 11
Monash University
Victoria 3800, Australia

www.monash.edu.au/mai

All Monash University Press publications are subject to double blind peer review

National Library of Australia cataloguing-in-publication data:

Globalisation and labour mobility in China.

Bibliography.
ISBN 9781876924478 (pbk.).

1. Labor mobility - China. 2. Globalization - China. I. Nielsen, Ingrid (Ingrid L.), 1969– .
II. Smyth, Russell L. (Russell Leigh), 1969– . III. Vicziany, Marika. IV. Title.

331.127951

Cover design by Minnie Doron.
Printed by BPA Print Group, Melbourne, Australia - www.bpabooks.com

contents

contributors

Professor Amiya Kumar Bagchi, Director of the Institute of Development Studies at Kolkata University, has received many international awards, culminating in the 2005 Padma Shri, awarded in recognition of his outstanding contribution to the study of Indian political economy. His most recent work is *The developmental state in history and in the twentieth century* (2004).

Cai Fang is the Director of the Institute of Population and Labour Economics, Chinese Academy of Social Sciences. His research interests span several aspects of economic reform in China, including development theory and policy, agricultural policy, labour economics and population economics.

Gao Wenshu is an associate professor at the Institute of Population and Labour Economics, Chinese Academy of Social Sciences. His research interests include macroeconomic aspects of migrant labour shortage, effects of population aging, and labour markets in China.

Sukhan Jackson is a senior lecturer at the School of Economics, University of Queensland, Australia. She has published extensively, on health financing in China, the economics of disease control in China, and the economics of ageing in Australia.

Serena Lillywhite is the Manager of Ethical Business, Brotherhood of St Laurence, Australia. Her research and practical interests focus on principles surrounding ethical investment in China, including promoting responsible supply chain management and improving labour conditions in enterprises.

Liu Xi-Li is the Doctor-in-Chief at the Henan Centre for Disease Control and Prevention, Zhengzhou, China. He has published widely on malaria control, tuberculosis and community health.

Ingrid Nielsen is a senior lecturer in Organisational Behaviour in the Department of Management at Monash University, Australia. Her main research interest is Chinese off-farm migration—in particular the social psychological implications of migration, including migrant–urbanite inter-group processes, subjective quality of life and job satisfaction amongst migrant workers.

Kenneth Roberts is a professor and holder of the Hugh Roy and Lillie Cullen Chair in the Department of Economics, Southwestern University, United States. His research interests are in population economics and in particular mass migration in developing countries such as China and Mexico.

Adrian C Sleigh is a professor of Epidemiology at the National Centre for Epidemiology and Population Health, Australian National University. He has published research on health effects of dams, parasitic infections, tuberculosis and viral diseases, including SARS.

Russell Smyth is a professor and Deputy Head of the Department of Economics and Director of the Asian Business and Economics Research Unit in the Faculty of Business and Economics, Monash University, Australia. His research interests include Asian economies, Chinese economic reform, law and economics and applied time series econometrics.

Dorothy Solinger is a professor of Political Science at the University of California, Irvine, United States. She has published extensively on internal migration in China and is now focusing her research efforts on the topic of urban exclusion in China.

David Treisman is a PhD candidate at the Monash Asia Institute, Monash University, Australia. He is completing his thesis on the political economy of ASEAN integration.

Marika Vicziany is a professor of Asian Political Economy and the Director of the Monash Asia Institute, Monash University, Australia. She works on mass poverty and security in India, Pakistan and western China.

Wang Dewen is an associate professor at the Institute of Population and Labor Economics, Chinese Academy of Social Sciences. His research interests include migrant labour shortage, social security reform urban labour markets and urban poverty in China.

Wang Guo-Jie is an associate doctor-in-chief at the Henan Centre for Disease Control and Prevention, Zhengzhou, China. He works in tuberculosis control and regularly publishes his research on tuberculosis.

Guibin Zhang is a research associate of the Monash Asia Institute, Monash University, Australia. His research is focused on the emergence of informal stock markets and private enterprises in Chengdu, China.

James Xiaohe Zhang is a lecturer in the Faculty of Business and Economics, University of Newcastle, Australia. His research interests include international business, international trade and economic reform in China.

chapter one

Movement of the masses in the global economy

Ingrid Nielsen, Russell Smyth and Marika Vicziany

Introduction

On the eve of market reforms in the late 1970s China's economy was crumbling. A decade of havoc wreaked by the Cultural Revolution (1966–76) had brought the country to its knees. In response, in 1978 Deng Xiaopeng initiated a series of economic reforms beginning with the household responsibility system in rural areas that increased the role of markets and kick-started a long process of integrating China into the global economy. China's economic reforms have been a spectacular success. Over the past quarter century China has had the highest rate of economic growth of any country in the world. Put simply, China has gone from a basket case of near economic collapse at the time of Mao Zedong's death in 1976 to be, along with India, one of the two emerging economic superpowers of the 21st century. Estimates by the consulting group Consensus Economics, published in 2005, suggest that by 2015 China will overtake the United States as the world's largest economy and India will move past Japan to occupy third place (Eslake 2006). And there is a lot of potential for further economic expansion. An article in the *New York Times* predicted that the 21st century would be China's century, given its potential for future growth (Fishman 2004).

An almost immediate result of the reform process has been the geographic motility of China's population. Since the 1980s, China's policy on restricted human movement—embodied in its strict application of the household registration (*hukou*) system that prohibited both rural–urban migration and migration between the provinces—has been progressively relaxed. The government's rationale behind the relaxation of this policy was that cheap peasant labour could be used in the cities to drive manufacturing growth (Solinger 1993). The result of this policy shift has been the largest movement of people in China's history and possibly in the history of the world. Conservative estimates are that since the 1980s, 120 to 150 million people have migrated from rural to urban areas (Roberts 2001). The scale and impact of this can perhaps be best appreciated by considering that a mere 53 million Europeans moved to the New World over a period of 110, years from 1820 to 1932 (UN 2004; Thomas 1959). In other words, in a mere 20 years three times as many Chinese people have migrated internally within China; and all this movement has occurred in about 20% of the time taken by Europeans to move. In March 2006 Liu He, a senior official in the Central Leading Group of Financial and Economic Affairs, predicted that over the next two decades another 300 million Chinese farmers would migrate to urban areas in search for jobs (Xinhua 2006). Again, this anticipated movement of Chinese people will exceed the mass European migrations of the 19th century by no fewer than six times.

The migrants who have flooded into the cities along China's eastern seaboard have been the fuel for the engine room of China's high growth rate. Migrants have made China the world's factory by working long hours for low wages that has made it possible for China to produce cheap manufactured exports that are super competitive in international markets. However, despite their contribution to China's economic success, migrants remain the 'outsiders' in China's cities (Solinger 1999). Migrants do not receive the same basic rights such as access to social insurance as those with an urban registration (Nielsen, Zhang et al 2005). There is much evidence that those with an urban registration 'look down' on migrants (Nielsen, Zhang et al 2006). The negative perceptions those with an urban registration have of migrants are based on widely-held views among urban residents that migrants are to blame for most of the problems of urban life.

According to one survey conducted in the mid-1990s in Shanghai, 74% of those with an urban registration blamed migrants for at least three of the following four problems: crime, transportation difficulties, unemployment and environmental degradation. Migrants are particularly singled out as being responsible for rising crime rates in China's cities. Another survey, of residents in Beijing, Guangzhou and Shanghai in the mid-1990s found that poor social order has become the 'number one public enemy'. Respondents considered migrants to be the 'root cause' of their insecurity and rising crime rates (Solinger 1999). Statistics for some specific localities suggest that migrants commit a disproportionately high level of crime in some big cities. According to official statistics, in Beijing 44% of crimes solved by the police in 1995 were committed by transients (Xu 1995). In Guangzhou 80% of burglaries in the mid-1990s were recorded by the police as being committed by transients. And in Guangdong as a whole, 90% of those charged with drug trafficking and prostitution were recorded as migrants (Chen & Luo 1995). However, as Roberts (2001) noted 'knowledgeable observers think migrants are scapegoats'. Solinger (1999) has argued that official statistics on crimes committed by migrants are often unreliable. Not all crimes attributable to them in the official statistics can reliably be attributed to migrants because authorities are often prejudiced against them and record crimes committed by urban vagrants as being committed by migrants.

The essays in this edited volume collectively provide an overview of how China is responding to the difficulties raised by mass internal migration, while simultaneously meeting the challenges of globalisation. Section I, which consists of the next four chapters, examines the 'big picture' issue of the relationship between economic restructuring, labour market reform and China's integration into the global economy. The chapters in this section look at the emerging and paradoxical phenomenon of a shortage of migrant labour; the effect of phasing out the household responsibility system on China's economic welfare; the role of migrant entrepreneurs in reducing the income gap between East and West and the role of labour mobility in a proposed ASEAN–China free trade area. Section II, which covers Chapters 6 to 9, shifts the focus to examine the emerging issues that migrants are facing in their everyday lives. The chapters in this section examine the working conditions, social insurance rights, health status, leisure activities and basic living conditions of migrants in China's cities. The final section provides a comparative perspective of the migration experiences in China, India and Mexico as well as the differing ways in which the labour markets of China, France and Mexico have been restructured.

Section I: International integration, economic restructuring and the effect on labour mobility

While official government estimates suggest that there are still 150 million surplus rural workers (*China Daily* 2006c), in 2004 China began to experience a shortage of migrant labour for the first time (Nielsen, Smyth & Guo 2006; Shao et al 2006). According to one study by China's Ministry of Labour and Social Security conducted in late 2004, there was a shortage of two million migrant workers in the Pearl River Delta, amounting to 10% of the workforce. The report found Fujian had a shortage of 200,000 workers and in Changzhou in Jiangsu the number of vacancies was 2.7 times the number of job seekers (*SCMP* 2005). In Chapter 2 Wang Dewen, Cai Fang and Gao Wenshu argue that the shortage of migrant labour is due to a structural imbalance and that the shortage coincides with the rapid expansion of exports, acceleration of economic growth and the shift in industrial concentration that occurred after China joined the WTO. The shortage means that factories in the worst affected regions must increase wages and improve working conditions to attract and retain staff. These changes suggest that China might be moving up the economic ladder as migrant workers see opportunities beyond being unskilled assemblers of the world's goods, but the challenge is to move out of lower-end manufacturing such as sporting goods, textiles and toys into higher value added production (Barboza 2006).

One pressing issue that has emerged from the shortage of migrant labour in the coastal provinces is the need to improve the flow of labour from China's central and western regions. A key conclusion Wang, Cai and Gao draw is that to achieve this objective there is an urgent need to further reform the household registration system to create an integrated rural and urban labour market. In Chapter 3 James Zhang estimates the economic impact of Chinese labour market liberalisation on aggregate economic welfare in China and the rest of the world through simulating a simple two-sector general equilibrium model. Previous similar studies have found that net benefits of China's membership of the WTO will be maximised if China adopts a policy of gradually relaxing restrictions on rural-urban migration in conjunction with further labour market reform (Fan & Wang 2002). Supporting Wang, Cai and Gao's call for further labour market integration, Zhang finds that freer labour mobility between rural and urban areas would increase economic welfare in China and the rest of the world with the gains unevenly distributed across regions. He finds that China, NAFTA and Australasia would benefit the most from labour market liberalisation in China, while the European Union and most of the ASEAN member countries would face more fierce competition.

Chapter 4 by Marika Vicziany and Guibin Zhang focuses on the role of minority entrepreneurship in facilitating economic integration between eastern and western China. Vicziany and Zhang consider the movement of Uygurs from Xinjiang into the cities of eastern China and western/central Asia and show how labour mobility is related to the establishment of Uygur businesses in Shanghai and Tashkent. They argue that there is a close relationship between Uygur migration and Uygur entrepreneurship, largely because discrimination against migrant labour in the eastern provinces of China makes it very difficult for Uygurs to find employment outside of the Uygur community. Using three detailed life histories, the chapter reports on the growing prosperity of the Uygur entrepreneurs who have looked beyond Xinjiang and followed their traditional 'Silk Road' instincts to travel and build business connections beyond their homelands. There is, however, nothing inevitable about this window of prosperity. The authors argue that more needs to be done by state authorities to create an economic climate conducive to minority entrepreneurship in order for them to match mounting and severe competition from traders in central Asia and beyond. In addition to fostering regional integration, promoting minority entrepreneurship by the Uygurs simultaneously promises to improve social integration. As China's largest Muslim minority, located on the sensitive border regions of western China, affirmative action by the state will help to reduce Uygur alienation which in turn will help to stabilise Xinjiang and reduce the risks of insurgency.

While Vicziany and Zhang focus on the role of entrepreneurial migration in facilitating economic integration between cities and regions within China and neighbouring countries such as Pakistan, in Chapter 5 David Treisman examines the role of labour in an ASEAN–China free trade area. Treisman's chapter focuses on international migration and in particular skilled migration within Asia. Although there is much unskilled internal migration within China, China is an important source for skilled migration to the rest of the world. According to the United Nations in 2005 China sent 35 million people abroad, the largest group of migrants leaving any country in the world. The remittances which Chinese migrants abroad sent home in 2004 totalled US$21.3 billion (*China Daily* 2006e). The prospects for increased trade with China that would come with a Free Trade Area have been widely anticipated in ASEAN member countries such as Laos, Malaysia and Thailand (*Bangkok Post* 2005; Xinhua 2005; *BDMN* 2005). Treisman recognises the potential benefits from such a free trade area in terms of promoting gains from trade, but he argues that the issue of labour and labour mobility has not been adequately dealt with within the ASEAN–China free trade area agreement. In reality, labour mobility under an ASEAN–China free trade area is likely to be restricted to limited categories of skilled labour with the wide scale movement of unskilled labour unacceptable given that it would exacerbate unemployment. Even as it stands, as Treisman points out, the similarities in the industrial bases of ASEAN and China are expected to cause short-term unemployment and rationalisation of industries. The effect on labour markets is an issue that needs to be handled sensitively in light of recent large-scale labour shedding from China's state-owned enterprises or, as Dorothy Solinger emphasises in her contribution, it has the potential to contribute to social unrest.

Section II: Emerging issues for China's floating population

In Section II of this volume authors consider a range of issues facing off-farm migrants in their quest to live and work in China's major cities. Recent media reports have documented a range of obstacles and difficulties faced by migrants, including labour-specific issues such as working conditions and social insurance rights (*China Daily* 2006b); general and occupational health problems (*Beijing Review* 2005; *Shanghai Daily* 2005a); and the living conditions of migrants. Among these reports there are some state-sponsored media 'good news' stories (*China Daily* 2005), but many more independent reports of a migrant housing system in disarray (*New York Times* 2003), with workers and their families forced to live in crowded and unsanitary conditions (*UNESCO Courier* 1999).

In Chapter 6, Serena Lillywhite documents the many forms of employment discrimination and social inequality that are faced by off-farm migrant workers. Chief amongst these are low—and sometimes unpaid—wages, long working hours, and limited access to social security entitlements. Lillywhite explains that while China's Labour Law clearly stipulates minimum wage rates, penalty and overtime rates, minimum wages are rarely paid to migrant workers and on average, migrant workers earn roughly 80% of the wages of local urban workers with equivalent levels of human capital. Benefits such as social insurance that naturally accrue to urban workers are regularly denied to migrants. As Ingrid Nielsen and Russell Smyth explain in Chapter 9, despite some recent steps to improve migrant workers' access to social insurance, there is still a long way to go. Migrant workers are often paid irregularly, or not at all. However, with little or no labour protection, the practical reality is that the majority of migrant workers have no recourse against such illegal practice. However, evidence of a growing awareness among workers of their legal entitlements and their willingness to seek assistance from lawyers and paralegals might suggest that the tide is about to turn.

In the meantime though, migrants are faced with the reality of a struggle between growing demands for fair and decent working conditions that are at odds with output demands. Such demands translate into long working hours and excessive overtime for migrants. As Lillywhite explains, China's Labour Law stipulates that workers should work eight hours a day and 40 hours per week, but most migrants usually work 70—and up to 100—hours a week. Such long and demanding labour schedules make migrant workers vulnerable to a range of occupational diseases and significantly impact on migrant workers' physical well-being. Sukhan Jackson, Adrian Sleigh, Wang Guo-Jie and Liu Xi-Li discuss a startling example of the latter in Chapter 8. Beyond physical symptoms, migrant working conditions have also been linked to psychological symptoms, with sadness and depression a result of the long working hours, frustration over the inability to raise grievances, and social isolation. Physical and psychological problems are often exacerbated by harsh living conditions, with migrants commonly living in cramped and crowded dormitories with little or no privacy, poor food and substandard sanitation.

While Lillywhite paints a vivid picture of labour discrimination against migrants, in Chapter 7 Ingrid Nielsen and Russell Smyth's analysis points further to social discrimination against migrants, in terms of access to adequate housing and leisure consumption. Faced with life in a city of strangers, with demanding labour and few comforts, China's migrants commonly experience 'psychological poverty' (*China Daily* 2003b) due to loneliness, isolation and social exclusion.

Nielsen and Smyth report that living conditions of migrants contrast markedly with that of urban locals. A large percentage of migrants live in dormitory style housing. This type of housing has been documented elsewhere as being cramped and with providing little or no private space (Jacka 2005). The actual accommodation usage area enjoyed by migrants is about half that enjoyed by those with an urban *hukou*, yet nearly 85% of migrants live in households with more than two other people, while the comparable figure for those with an urban *hukou* is fewer than 10%, further attesting to the comparatively crowded living conditions of migrant workers.

With the oppressiveness of their general living and working conditions, one strategy for migrants to improve their quality of life might be to engage in leisure activities. But while leisure consumption in urban China has been steadily on the rise since the advent of the economic reforms, Nielsen and Smyth's analysis suggests that this is largely concentrated within the local urban population. The vast majority of migrants surveyed in this chapter reported that they had undertaken no basic leisure activities in the past three months. Of those few migrants who did undertake some leisure activity, the most popular were going to the park or the library. Notably, these are activities that attract no charge. Rarely did migrants report attending venues for which they had to pay, such as nightclubs, video arcades or the cinema. The leisure profile of urban locals was rather different though, with urban locals engaging in a wider range of leisure activities than migrants and also visiting paying venues, such as cinemas or nightclubs much more frequently than migrants.

The positive effect of leisure on psychological well-being has been well documented (Lu & Hu 2002) and the engagement in more, and more regular, leisure activities would likely benefit migrants and alleviate their feelings of loneliness and social isolation. Nielsen and Smyth argue that migrants' apparent reluctance to engage in leisure activities may reflect a current mismatch between leisure demand and supply. They argue that the development of demographically tailored pools of leisure choices in urban China might even further fuel China's economy, with the positive effects of migrants' leisure consumption contributing to a happier and more productive migrant workforce.

Beyond the need to address the commonly observed negative psychological symptoms among migrants, in Chapter 8 Sukhan Jackson, Adrian Sleigh, Wang Guo-Jie and Liu Xi-Li discuss the frequently concomitant physical morbidity that exists in migrant communities and its impact on families. They argue that disease prevalence is routinely higher among migrants than urban locals in China's cities and this in part can be attributed to the poor living conditions experienced by many migrants, as discussed earlier by Lillywhite and by Nielsen and Smyth. In particular, overcrowded housing increases exposure to infectious air-borne diseases such as tuberculosis. While rates of tuberculosis in developed countries have rapidly fallen due to improved sanitation and immunisation programs, there remain 4.5 million Chinese tuberculosis patients—the second highest number in the world after India.

Acknowledging that rapid industrialisation and resultant demographic change tend to predict changes in disease pattern, Chapter 8 explores the issue of whether Chinese off-farm migration can account for changes in the prevalence of tuberculosis in rural China. Specifically, they argue that housing and labour conditions endured by migrants in the cities facilitate the spread of infectious diseases such as tuberculosis, but when migrant workers become too sick to work, they are sent home to their villages—hence carrying the disease back to their rural home town.

Working with data from four counties in Henan, Jackson, Sleigh, Wang and Liu found support for this argument. Nearly half the tuberculosis cases had out-migrated for work compared to fewer than a third of controls (non-tuberculosis cases). The cost of tuberculosis disease is a heavy burden on families, accounting for up to 55.5% of annual household income. Jackson, Sleigh, Wang and Liu note that while there has been much publicity about the plight of migrant workers, scarce attention has been paid to the often dire consequences of poor working and living conditions as the focus is mostly on unpaid wages, discrimination and the absence of legal rights. Furthermore, there also seems to be a lack of focus on the sending communities now bearing the cost of tuberculosis brought in from the cities.

In the final chapter of Section II, Ingrid Nielsen and Russell Smyth revisit the issue of labour discrimination amongst migrants, focusing specifically on migrants' social insurance coverage. Against the backdrop of Shanghai's forthcoming Expo 2010, with its theme 'Better city—better life', Nielsen and Smyth pose the question 'for whom'? In particular, they question whether the millions of migrants who have toiled to make Shanghai the hotspot of modern China, will ever reap the longer-term social protection benefits that their local counterpoints already enjoy.

Nielsen and Smyth note that while China has a comprehensive social insurance scheme for individuals with an urban *hukou*, most migrants in China's cities have little or no social insurance coverage at all. Most migrants are unable to obtain an urban *hukou* and hence they have to rely on social insurance schemes that are specifically designed to provide coverage for migrant workers. While social insurance payments to migrants in Shanghai are prescribed by the *Interim Procedures on Comprehensive Insurance for External Labour Forces in Shanghai*, Nielsen and Smyth explain that employer non-compliance with social insurance obligations in Shanghai is high. While the official figure was that 2.26 million migrants were covered by Shanghai's social insurance scheme in November 2005 (*Shanghai Daily* 2005c), in reality the number of migrants receiving social insurance is smaller than this figure suggests because of low compliance rates.

Using interview data from two case studies to illustrate differing attitudes of firms in Shanghai towards paying social insurance to migrants, Nielsen and Smyth uncover two differing approaches to paying social insurance to migrant workers. The first, and typical, approach is to pay nothing at all. The second approach is to pay a 'migrant comprehensive package' with a total value of about 1500 RMB a month. While this sounds attractive to the average migrant, in reality it is an amount for which most people with an urban *hukou* would not work.

While improved monitoring and enforcement is helping, Nielsen and Smyth argue that such 'top down' approaches can only go part of the way to addressing the problem of non-payment, or under-payment, of social insurance to migrants. They argue instead that a better long-term solution can only come on the back of a 'bottom-up' response, where migrants start to shun organisations with poor working conditions.

Section III: Comparative perspectives

Dorothy Solinger's essay opens the third section by shifting the focus to a new kind of movement—the movement of workers from being employed members of the workforce to the ranks of the unemployed. Her analysis of China's experience is a comparative study with the experience of French and Mexican labour, taking as her starting point the decision that the three governments in these countries made to join the global economy in 1980. According to Solinger, the pressures of globalisation gave these governments no choice but to embark on a process of economic liberalisation that saw the creation of mass unemployment regardless of the configuration of the domestic political system.

In the case of Mexico, the pressure came from NAFTA and the GATT: for France from the EU; and for China from the WTO. Solinger has mapped out a depressing scenario, as the implication is that nothing can save governments from the inexorable pressures of market rationality—it makes no difference whether they are socialist states, democracies, authoritarian regimes, advanced capitalist countries or developing economies, once they signed up to these international trading agreements they all had to submit to globalised production norms and the attendant unemployment.

Solinger goes on to compare the extent of unemployment generated by the anti-labour policies of Mexico, France and China. In all three cases the governments did a U-turn away from previous strategies in order to shore up the long-term strength and competitiveness of their economies. But as John Maynard Keynes said in his now famous quip: in the long run we are all dead. So in the final section of her chapter, Solinger addresses the question of how the labourers themselves stood up for their rights to employment, given that they had been abandoned by their governments and labour unions. Worker discontent eventually led to street demonstrations and strikes in all three cases, compelling varying reactions from governments promising to do something to alleviate problems associated with joblessness. The more muted the labour opposition to unemployment, the less willing the governments appear to be to reinstitute welfare measures. In the case of China, despite the many gaps, the need for welfare measures has been taken more seriously perhaps because the Communist Party recognises the connection between labour instability and the continuation of its dominance. If Solinger has a policy prescription it is addressed to labour—act now, act strongly and you might just have a chance of alleviating the insecurity that is attached to unemployment.

Amiya Bagchi takes the international comparisons one step further by looking at how India, the second biggest peasant society in the world after China, has fared on employment in the past two hundred years. As with China, India has always had a segmented labour market, but the nature of its segmentation is different from that of India. The abusive inequalities of caste in particular, have produced an especially degraded category of low-cost labour for centuries. The British abolished slavery, but not the fundamental cultural and economic rationale that has supported the persistence of this group, the 'untouchables'. Today's unemployment therefore sits on top of persistent traditional forms of labour exploitation which are hard to match anywhere else in the world. Certainly the discrimination faced by today's untouchables and tribal people cannot be found in any part of contemporary China where the Maoist revolution, despite its many tragic consequences, set up a new value system that asserts equal opportunity for all. Despite persistent and increasing GDP growth rates, unemployment in India has soared since the economic liberalisation of the economy in 1991. Indeed, the rate of employment growth has been shrinking with every percentage increase in macroeconomic performance. This is an especially depressing scenario because India did experiment with labour-intensive production by supporting the small-scale cottage industries sector for the first 50 years of its independence. That experiment left no positive legacy and has been increasingly corroded as India has adopted tougher and tougher market-driven economic rationalities. New research has not affirmed the value of small-scale industries for their labour-absorbing capacities, and there is no sign yet that the failure of earlier policy measures in this area can be reversed. Of course, as Bagchi argues, the failure of the small-scale sector has been driven by institutional obstacles that prevent them from accessing new technology, capital, bank loans and entrepreneurial talent. In rural India, the labour situation is even more desperate owing to the power of landlords over land, the bondage of impotent labour, the violence of landlord armies and above all else, peasant indebtedness. None of the growth areas in the Indian economy have affected this. The new jobs in the IT sector cannot make good the lack of opportunity in the rural sector and international migration of Indians cannot remove sufficient numbers of people to alleviate domestic pressure on a scale that can reverse the tendency towards a massive army of unemployed people—an army of unprecedented magnitude, even for India.

The Indian example is a compelling one for China—it presents the face of what happens to labour under a political economy that had some aspirations to socialist values but always operated within a capitalist economy that was integrated into the global economy to an extent not matched by China's autarchic preferences before 1980. In contrast, China has witnessed massive discontinuities in its labour market structures and practices. Until the 1980s it was common for international observers to note that China had none of the slums and street dwellers of India. But what appeared to be a virtue to outsiders was hotly contested by Indian scholars who countered that the lack of movement in China was the result of authoritarianism. Indians moved, because Indian democracy allowed people to move—if and when they wanted—and move they did into the vast and ever growing cities.

As Bagchi notes, with the establishment of communes under Mao, China's pre-existing labour market vanished—not to reappear until the reforms of Deng Xiaoping in the late 1970s. The classical symptoms of third world under-employment also vanished. With rural-to-urban migration banned and controlled through a stringent registration system, the familiar slums, pavement dwellers, vagrants and beggars that characterise Indian cities vanished. Five decades later the symptoms of rural poverty and urban hope have reappeared on the streets of China's cities. Behind the obvious manifestations of new competition and new poverty there stand the hidden pressures of much more unemployment and labour insecurity. Only some of this is driven by rural-to-urban migration; an equally important factor contributing to social insecurity, as Solinger's chapter makes clear, is the privatisation of state-owned enterprises over the past decade.

It is paradoxical to note that after fifty years of divergent economic policy, China is increasingly facing the predicaments that have bedeviled Indian public policy since independence in 1947. At the same time, Bagchi, in line with most international commentators, is convinced that China has a basic endowment that is better able to cope with the international pressures for competition—higher literacy, rapidly growing secondary and tertiary education, massive inward foreign investment and greater socioeconomic equity in the opportunities open to its people. These endowments are all legacies of the earlier period of socialist development. Other important legacies include China's resistance to financial liberalisation and the long history of central and regional government commitment to some kinds of social welfare, a point on which Bagchi agrees with Solinger. Even if the latter has been pared back, important elements remain in a way that has not been evident in India.In the final chapter Ken Roberts returns us to the question of labour migration, this time from a comparative framework that considers the momentum behind the movement of people in China relative to the experience of Mexican migrants moving to the United States in the past four decades. Roberts notes the common attributes: migration involved relatively short distances between place of origin and destination, migrating rural workers remained attached to plots of land which by law could not be sold. And on top of this asymmetric relationship between people, land and rights came liberalising trade agreements that placed agriculture under enormous pressure. Beyond this, however, the pattern of migration, its sequencing and its consequences for rural and urban dwellers in the two societies varied as much as it shared some commonalities. An enduring similarity, possibly a universal one, is that rural migrants into Chinese and US cities have suffered social discrimination at the hands of the local urbanites. Citing Tamara Jacka, Roberts argues that this 'constitutes a form of ethnicity'. Given discrimination, it is perhaps a good thing that the socio-economic networks that facilitated the rapid growth and diversification of Mexican migration into the US are still relatively immature in the case of China. However, as noted earlier in this chapter, the next 20 years will see a great acceleration of rural-to-urban drift, no doubt driven by the elaboration of the networks currently lagging behind the Mexico–US experience. Roberts confirms the likelihood of this latter migration explosion, driven perhaps as in the Mexican case, by the widening economic pressure on rural China.

Roberts explores the comparative experience of Mexican and Chinese migrants under various headings that together suggest some powerful convergences that indicate the likelihood of Chinese migration gathering momentum, tapping into increasingly diversified sources and destinations, diversification of the occupational backgrounds of migrants from unskilled into skilled workers, and shifting from temporary to permanent migration quite rapidly. Perhaps the most compelling similarity is the feminisation of migration, and it is the feminisation that also pushes migrants into taking up more permanent residence in cities. This feminisation, however, is also a source of difference—Chinese women, appear to be much bolder than their Mexican counterparts: they are moving earlier in the migration sequence, faster, with or without husbands, and are more determined to settle in the glittering cities of eastern China that increasingly challenge US economic hegemony.

Conclusion

Human history can be written as a story about migrations. Migration is simultaneously a story about the hope of those that leave their homelands and the discrimination that they face in their new abode. What distinguishes the migrations of contemporary Chinese people is the astonishing speed with which migration is occurring and the involvement of millions of people—soon to be hundreds of millions of people. Another distinguishing feature of contemporary Chinese migration is that it is all happening within China: the population is displacing itself from rural areas to cities and towns.

The contours of Chinese migration and its impact on social wellbeing is an untold story, compared with the level of attention given to Asian migration into Europe where the arrival of foreigners has become a political issue. Despite the great European debate on migration, a new report from Germany reveals that of the 26 million migrants living in the 15 states of the European Union, only a fraction are from Asia. A stocktake of the most significant Asian migrant communities in the EU demonstrated that in 1999 the total Asian migrant population was under one million (about 777,900 from the largest Asian migrant communities). The largest group was from India living in the UK—some 153,000 (DGAP 2004:table 1, 5). These Indian estimates are on the low side, with British reports giving a figure that is closer to half a million (IPPR 2006; MIS 2001). But even this is a small story compared to the total population of India and the 6.3 million foreigners who were living in India in 2000 (UN 2004:30).[1]

In contrast to Indian migration, all available accounts agree that the number of Chinese migrants to Europe is small: Italy 47,100;[2] Germany 42,900; Spain 24,700; France 14,000; Netherlands 8,000 and Sweden 4,200 (DGAP 2004: table 1, 5). These overseas Chinese communities total some 140,900 people—an infinitesimally small number compared to those of people moving in China. Another estimate suggests that in 2000 there were about 200,000 legal Chinese migrants in Europe (Laczko 2003). Of course, Chinese migration to the New World has involved greater numbers than these because of a much longer history. But the figures are far short of the mass migration of Europeans to the US in the era leading up to the First World War. In 1980 the Chinese diaspora in America numbered only 286,000 despite the long history of migration dating from the gold rushes of the nineteenth century. In the 20 years after 1980, there was a great increase in numbers to about 1.5 million (Newland & Patrick 2004). Today, the growing momentum of Chinese migration to the US is largely an undocumented one because it takes the form of people smuggling. For example, the dramatic arrival of the 'Golden Venture' boat in New York on 6 June 1993 focused attention on the 10,000 illegal Fujian migrants who annually arrive in

Manhattan (Liang & Ye 2001). New York has about 100,000 Fujians who have fled from rural southern China (a mountainous province located on the shore facing Taiwan) and now find themselves living in the heart of one of the most sophisticated cities in the world.[3]

These stories of international Chinese migration make for dramatic headlines but they need to be kept in perspective because the real story of Chinese migration in the 20th and 21st century is the flooding of millions of peasants and rural workers into the urban centers of China. This volume addresses the multifaceted dimensions of that extraordinary human process: the relationship between domestic Chinese migration and economic liberalisation at the national and international levels; the conditions migrant labourers face in their new host societies; and the characteristics of the fragmented labour markets that are rising up in China today compared with India, Mexico and France. And as population projections suggest, the flood has only just begun. The present volume therefore seeks to capture some of the important trends that have started to emerge at the start of the 21st century. These trends are likely to exert extraordinary pressures on Chinese governments at all levels, and in particular on the Communist Party of China. Domestic population movement could well turn out to be the single most important catalyst for political change in China. These pressure points have little possibility of external release: Europe, America and Australia have adopted a 'fortress' mentality towards international migration despite the relatively small numbers involved until now and into the foreseeable future. Of course, what constitutes small numbers for China and India does have a disproportionate impact in Europe simply because of the demographic imbalance between Asia and the EU. Thus in 2003, the population of the UK was 59.3 million of whom only 2.87 million were foreign-born; and of these only some one million came from South Asia. For the UK this small number by Asian standards represented a doubling of the foreign-born population since 1984 (Sriskandarajah & Hopwood Road 2005) and has given birth to 'rising anxieties'.

International migration today comes nowhere near replicating the scale of mass European migration to the New World in the period 1820–1932. Nor is such replication likely. It is China, therefore, that must solve the problems thrown up by the movement of her people. We must therefore hope for enlightened policies to ease the burdens on raw migrants, ethnic minorities, and rural workers in China's cities and towns. These burdens also place special responsibilities on the international community to ensure that China can accommodate the needs of her people through fair international trade policies that will create rather than destroy jobs.

Notes

1 In the same year, 2000, foreign residents in China, including Hong Kong, numbered about 2.7 million (UN 2004:30).

2 The Chinese population in Italy, for example, has attracted attention perhaps because about 20,000 live in Prato, where they have become the key workers and entrepreneurs in the local silk industry. Such concentration in a small town gives the Chinese migrants greater visibility.

3 Fujians are also arriving in Europe through illegal/forced means (Gao 2004:4–5).

Section I

International integration, economic restructuring and the effect on labour mobility

chapter two

Globalisation and the shortage of rural workers: a macroeconomic perspective

Wang Dewen, Cai Fang and Gao Wenshu

Introduction

China is the most populous country in the world. Its per capita GDP reached US$1,067 in 2003, breaking through the US$1,000 ceiling for the first time, and in 2004, it increased to US$1,162. Although China has had rapid economic growth for more than 20 years, its income level still places it in the world's low-income group. During this development stage, its labour supply, especially of unskilled rural labour, has appeared infinitely endless. However, by the end of 2003, the phenomenon of a rural labour shortage emerged in the southeast coastal region. In 2004, the shortages were concentrated mainly in the Pearl River area of Guangdong Province and Fuzhou and Xiamen cities in Fujian province near Taiwan. The labour shortage intensified in 2005 and spread to the Yangtze River Delta area and the northern coastal region. Even in traditional major centres of rural labour such as Hunan and Jiangxi provinces, enterprises experienced difficulties hiring rural workers.

This phenomenon appears to be a simple issue of the dynamic adjustment of the regional labour market, but the underlying forces are much more complex. It is in fact a response of the domestic labour market to the rapid expansion of the export industry, the acceleration of economic growth and the shift in the concentration of economic centres. With China's accession to the WTO, fierce international competition has changed China's regional relative advantages and shifted the spatial concentration of economic activities, shaping a pattern of multiple economic growth poles. As the inland regions catch up in economic terms, the demand for rural workers will expand and possibly worsen the shortage of rural workers in coastal areas. The shortage of rural workers therefore symbolises to a large extent a transition of China's surplus rural labour from the previous situation of unlimited supply to limited surplus. From the perspective of resource allocation, these structural changes have important implications for China's labour market integration and shifting industrial focus.

In this chapter we first discuss the nature of labour shortage and examine why the shortage of rural workers has occurred mainly in coastal areas. We then investigate the transition in the rural labour surplus, analyse the relationship between regional competition and changes in the pattern of labour mobility and explore labour market conditions for a regional industry shift. The final section concludes with policy implications.

What is labour shortage?

Labour shortage can be defined as a situation in which its supply cannot meet labour demand at a given market wage rate. In a competitive labour market, the relationship between the supply and demand for labour is determined by the wage rate. Figure 1 demonstrates two situations of dynamic adjustment of a labour market. Figure 1-a assumes that the supply of labour is inelastic for a short time period. Figure 1-b assumes that the supply of labour is elastic over a longer time period. In both cases, assume that there is a rapid expansion in the demand for labour that comes from accelerated economic growth, export expansion, labour-intensive industrial development and a rise in the prices of other factors of production. The shift in the labour supply curve will then depend on the length of time of labour market adjustment and changes in the wage rate.

Figure 1: Dynamic adjustment of the labour market

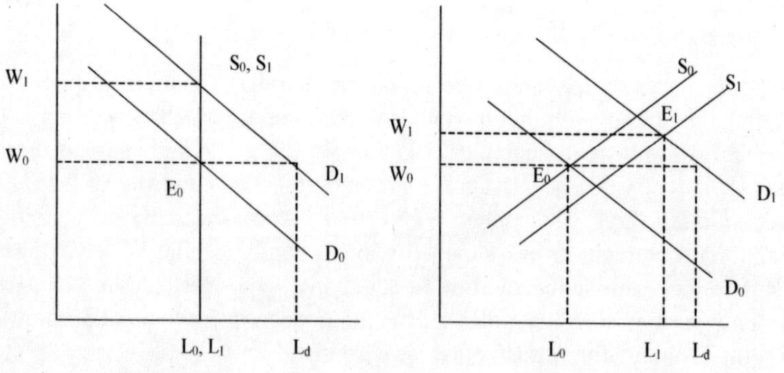

Fig. 1-a Fig. 1-b

Generally speaking, labour market adjustments have a certain time lag. The rapid increase in the demand for labour leaves no time for labour supply to adjust in the short-run as illustrated in Figure 1-a. If the wage rate remains unchanged, a large gap between the demand and supply of labour will be generated because labour supply is vertical and inelastic in the short-run. When demand shifts from D_0 to D_1, the new quantity of labour demanded at the previous wage rate will be L_d. Therefore, a gap between L_d and L_0 will exist due to the rigidity of labour supply. Even if firms were willing to increase the wage rate from W_0 to W_1, the vertical supply curve cannot provide more labour to meet the increasing demand for labour. A rise in wage rates only contributes to the increase in the cost of labour and a reduction in profits. Market competition for labour will force firms to increase wage rates. For example, if Firm A is not willing to increase the wage rate while Firm B does, workers in Firm A will leave and choose to work in Firm B, thus the pressure from the reallocation of labour between the companies also provides an incentive for them to increase their wage rates to retain their workforce.

Over a longer period as illustrated in Figure 1-b, labour supply is elastic. A rise in the wage rate, resulting from the growth in the demand for labour, will stimulate the supply of labour, giving rise to a downward shift in labour supply. In Figure 1-b, although the magnitude of the shift in the demand for labour is larger than that in Figure 1-a, the rise in the wage rate is smaller due to elastic supply. With an increase in the wage rate, a rise in the cost of labour will reduce firms' willingness to hire more workers, thus the labour market will reach a new equilibrium at a new wage rate. In Figure 1-b, the corresponding labour demand at the new equilibrium point E_1 is L_1 and the point where the previous wage rate W_0 intersects the new labour demand curve is L_d. The difference between L_d and L_1 is much less than the corresponding magnitude in Figure 1-a. Therefore, the issue of labour shortage refers to the specific relationship between labour demand and labour supply at a given wage rate, which will finally be replaced by a new equilibrium as the labour market adjusts over time.

Why is the shortage of rural workers mainly concentrated in coastal areas?

The geographic concentration of exports and manufacturing industries in a few key locations is one factor that caused the shortage of rural workers in coastal areas. Table 1 presents exports and manufacturing employment in major coastal provinces and provincial level cities. Exports in Guangdong and the Yangtze River Delta area account for one-third of total exports in the eight provinces (cities). The share of exports in the eight provinces (cities) is 83%, and their share of employment is nearly half of China's total employment in manufacturing. Sub-sectors of manufacturing industry with high gross output are highly geographically concentrated. For example, textile manufacturing in Shanghai, Zhejiang and Jiangsu accounted for 49.3% of total gross output value and 35.8% of total employment. In Guangdong and in Fujian it accounted for

13.3% of total gross output value and 10.8% of total employment. Because of rapid export growth in coastal areas, the expansion of production in labour-intensive manufacturing has increased the demand workers from the rural sector.

Table 1: Shares of exports and manufacturing employment and export growth in major coastal provinces and provincial cities

	Share of manufacturing					
Province	Share of export (%)	Employment (%)	Export growth (%)			
	2004	2004	2001	2002	2003	2004
Beijing	3.5	1.8	-1.5	7.0	33.9	21.8
Tianjin	3.5	1.5	10.0	22.5	23.4	45.4
Hebei	1.6	7.0	6.6	16.1	29.0	57.6
Shanghai	12.4	3.2	9.0	16.0	51.2	51.7
Jiangsu	14.7	9.0	12.1	33.2	53.7	48.0
Zhejiang	9.8	9.4	18.2	28.0	41.4	39.8
Fujian	5.0	3.9	7.9	24.7	21.7	39.1
Guandong	32.3	9.4	3.8	24.1	29.0	25.3
Total	82.7	9.4				
Average			7.2	23.6	36.2	36.2

Source: NBS (2002a; 2003a; 2004a; 2005)

The increase in demand for rural workers in the service sector has also intensified the shortage of rural workers available for the manufacturing industry. The service sector is more sensitive to labour demand than the manufacturing industry for younger workers, especially females. The upsurge in employment opportunities in the service sector lowers young workers' willingness to be employed in manufacturing industries where jobs are sometimes dirty or dangerous, low paid and where working conditions are inferior.

The structure of the labour force also plays a role in the shortage of rural workers. Manufacturing enterprises, particularly in the textile and food processing sectors, lack rural workers aged 20–30 years and especially younger women. Since the family-planning policy was first implemented in the mid 1970s, the birth rate has dropped significantly. This has caused a drop in the cohort aged 20–30 two to three decades later (Figure 2). In 2003, the share of the population aged 20–24 was only 7.6%, 1.6 percentage points fewer than those aged 15–19 and the share of population aged 25–30 was only 7.4%, 2.1 percentage points fewer than those aged 30–34. When the economy booms, export growth increases the demand for young workers in manufacturing industries. But the relatively lower share of the population aged 20–30 magnifies the structural imbalance between labour supply and demand.

Figure 2: China's demographic age structure 1982—2005

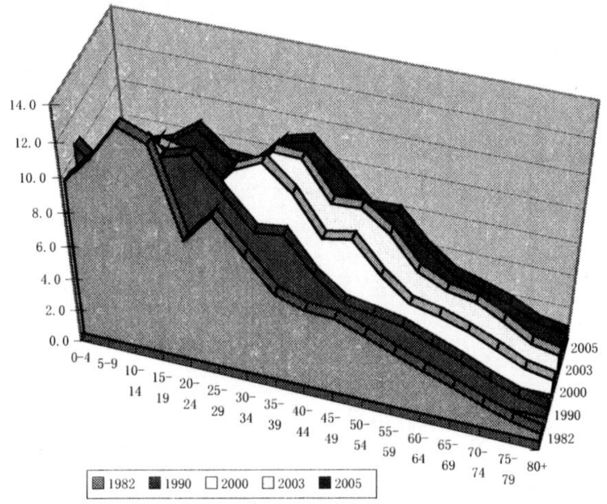

Source: NBS (1986; 1993b; 2002b; 2004a; UN 2005a)

The supply transition of surplus rural labour

The shortage of rural workers has been attributed to an increase in the opportunity cost of migration. Increases in grain prices coupled with subsidies for grain producers and the abolition of agricultural taxes have increased the opportunity cost of rural–urban migration in recent years. If returns from out-migration cannot compensate for the increase in the opportunity cost, the willingness of rural labour to migrate will decrease. If non-agricultural wage rates remain unchanged, the increased opportunity cost will reduce the expected returns of rural migrants and depress their enthusiasm to migrate, causing a reduction in the number of rural–urban migrants and leading to a shortage of rural workers in the cities.

According to data from the Rural Fixed Survey Network of the Ministry of Agriculture, however, rural migration has been increasing not only in absolute overall numbers but also on an annual basis. Table 2 presents statistics on the migration of the rural labour force between 1993 and 2004. Outward migration was about 3.75 million from 1995 to 1997, reflecting a slowdown in economic growth, but increased to 4.14 million over the period 2001 to 2004 because of rapid economic growth. This suggests that the increase in agricultural returns did not slow the outflow of the rural labour force in 2004. If the increase in opportunity cost can be compensated by returns from migration, it will not affect the total amount of rural migration. The ratios of the average wage of workers in township enterprises to rural net income from 2000 to 2004 was relatively stable at around 2.5:1, inferring that the equilibrium labour market did not change and that the shortage of rural worker is not an aggregate issue.

Table 2: Migration of rural labour force 1993–2004

Year	Outflow from townships (10,000)	Annual increment (10,000)	Share of inter-provincial migration (%)
1993	6,200	800	-
1995	7,000	400	-
1996	7,223	223	-
1997	7,722	499	38.3
2001	8,961	348	46.9
2002	9,430	479	46.4
2003	9,820	390	41.0
2004	10,260	440	41.9

Source: SGMA (2005)

From the perspective of a dynamic adjustment of the labour market, the rural labour shortage phenomenon is consistent with the depiction in Figure 1-b. Rural migration is increasing, but there is also expanding demand for rural migrants from the manufacturing and export sectors. And the magnitude of the former is less than that of the latter, so we observe a rise in the wage rate, meaning some firms have difficulties recruiting workers. According to an enterprise survey conducted by the Guangdong Bureau of Statistics in the spring of 2005, one-third of enterprises in Guangdong province offered higher wages in an attempt to solve their recruitment problems, but there was still a recruitment gap of one million. This suggests that some firms had to face the shortage issue if they did not adjust their wage offer in time.

A rise in wage rates is not only a response of the labour market to changes in the relationship between labour supply and demand, but also reflects compensation for the increase in the opportunity cost of migration as agricultural returns increase. While the size of the surplus rural labour force was estimated to be about 150 to 170 million over the period from 1997 to 2000, (equivalent of 30–35% of the rural labour force (Liu 2003)), the emergence of a shortage of rural workers indicates a change in supply of China's surplus rural labour.

In development economics, the classic Lewis (1954) model is often cited to explain rural–urban migration in developing countries. The Lewis model divides the economy into two sectors: the modern industrial sector and the traditional agricultural sector. According to the Lewis model there is a pool of surplus rural labour in the agricultural sector. Assuming that the marginal productivity of surplus rural labour is almost zero, the supply of surplus rural labour is unlimited, providing cheap labour for the expansion of the modern industrial sector. When development of the industrial sector reaches the point that it exhausts the reservoir of surplus rural labour, a further expansion in the demand for rural labour will place upward pressure on wage rates. Thus, there is only one turning point in the Lewis model. The Lewis model was developed by Fei and Ranis (1965) into a two-turning-point model that is a better representation of the transition in the labour market in developing countries.

Figure 3: Supply Transition of Rural Surplus Labour Consistent with the Fei and Ranis model

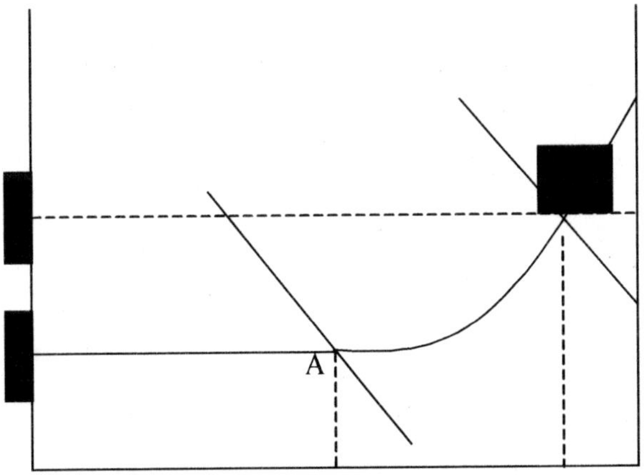

As shown in Figure 3, there are two turning points in the supply transition of rural surplus labour in developing countries. The first one is at the stage of transition of the rural labour force from unlimited supply to limited surplus, i.e., point A in Figure 3. Before this point, the supply of rural surplus labour is unlimited and there is no pressure for wage adjustment. The second turning point is at the stage where the rural wage equals the urban wage, which is when the rural surplus labour force is totally absorbed by the expansion of the urban non-agricultural sector, i.e. point B in Figure 3. Between points A and B, the supply of rural surplus labour becomes limited with a certain elasticity. If enterprises do not adjust wage rates at this time, they can expect to face difficulties in hiring rural workers.

In China, 1991 is an historical turning point for agricultural employment, after which the absolute number employed in agriculture began to drop gradually. Rapid economic growth from 1992 to 1996 moved millions of rural labourers into the non-agricultural sector, causing a decline of the share of agricultural employment from 59.7% in 1991 to 49.9% in 1997, the first time that the share of agricultural employment fell below 50% since the foundation of the People's Republic. The share of agricultural employment lingered around 50% from 1998 to 2002, decreased to 49.1% in 2003, and significantly dropped to 46.9% in 2004.

The appearance of a supply transition of surplus rural labour is further supported by the following observations. First, China's economy experienced rapid economic growth following Deng Xiaoping's famous 'southern tour' speech in 1992, but enterprises did not experience a shortage of rural workers at that time. Second, the low wage rates received by rural workers have recently come under upward pressure, although there was almost no change in rural workers' wages in the past. For example, a survey by the National Statistical Bureau reported that the wage rate for rural workers increased by 6.5% in 2003, and 11.1% in 2004.

Regional competition and changes in the pattern of labour mobility

The mobility of the rural labour force from the Pearl River Delta area to the Yangtze River Delta area reflects a new trend in migration patterns, which is a response of the labour market to the shift in regional economic concentration with trade liberalisation, following China's accession to the WTO. During the process of open expansion, regional competition increased the mobility of production factors. Changes in the spatial distribution of trade and investment have not only created multiple economic poles, but also produced differences in employment opportunities that have altered the pattern of rural-urban migration in China.

As illustrated in Table 2, the share of inter-provincial migration decreased by 5.4 percentage points in 2003 from the previous year which largely reflected concerns over the infectious disease SARS. In 2004, the share of inter-provincial migration rose slightly to 41.9%, but was still a lower figure than 2002. This indicates that as the inland provinces catch up economically, more employment opportunities for the rural labour force have been created within these provinces, forming a co-existing pattern of inter- and intra-province migration.

The shift in economic concentration

We categorised 31 provinces, cities directly under the jurisdiction of the central government and autonomous areas into eight regions according to similarities in geography and industrial structure.[1] They are: the north-east region, the north coastal region, the middle Yellow River region, the east coastal region, the south coastal region, the middle Yangtze River region, the north-west region and the south-west region. We use these regions to observe the impact of changes in the spatial shift of economic concentration on migration patterns.

The share of trade in GDP reveals the extent to which an economy is integrated into the global market. In China the share of trade in GDP has shown an upward trend since 1990, with a rapid increase since 2001. However, there have been substantial variations from region to region within China. Table 3 shows regional openness and concentration of trade in the eight regions over the period 1990 to 2004. Compared with the base year 2001, the increase in openness in the east coastal region has been the largest, followed in turn by the south coastal region, the north-west region, the north coastal region, the north-east region, the middle Yangtze River region, the south west region, and the middle Yellow River region.

Table 3: Regional openness and concentration of trade 1990–2004

	Openness (%)			Trade concentration index (%)		
Region	1990	2000	2004	1990	2000	2004
Northeast	19.4	20.9	26.3	9.9	5.2	4.4
North coastal	15.6	45.2	40.9	11.6	20.5	14.2
Middle Yellow River	5.9	7.4	9.2	2.9	1.8	1.7
East Coastal	22.0	55.3	101.0	15.6	27.0	37.8
South Coastal	90.3	99.8	130.4	53.2	41.0	37.5
Middle Yangtze River	6.3	6.8	9.4	3.9	2.3	2.1
Northwest	5.6	9.9	15.7	0.9	0.7	0.8
Southwest	4.6	6.6	9.6	2.0	1.5	1.5
National	30.0	43.9	70.0	100.0	100.0	100.0

Source: NBS (1991; 2001; 2005)

Accession to the WTO has not only provided enhanced opportunities for China to increase exports, but has also readjusted the regional pattern of trade concentration. As shown in Table 3, the coastal share of trade has accounted for more than 80% of total trade since 1990. The trade concentration index, which is the regional ratio of trade-to-total-trade, can be used to examine changes in the pattern of trade concentration within the coastal regions. From 1990 to 2004, the trade concentration index rose from 15.6% to 37.8% in the east coastal region, declined from 53.2% to 37.5% in the south coastal region, and initially increased but subsequently dropped in the north coastal region. This indicates that the trade centre has shifted from the Pearl River Delta area to the Yangtze River Delta area.

The shift in the pattern of trade concentration reflects changes in the direction of product mobility that comes from the movement and agglomeration of production and investment. Generally, products and capital have higher mobility. With changes in regional relative advantage, capital will move from regions with low expected returns to regions with high expected returns. The mobility of capital drives the movement of investment and this, in turn, gives rise to changes in the spatial pattern of investment concentration.

Table 4: Regional concentration index of investment: 1990–2004

	Total investment in fixed assets (%)			State-owned invesment in fixed assets (%)			FDI (%)		
Region	1990	2000	2004	1990	2000	2004	1990	2000	2004
Northeast	11.4	8.5	8.2	15.1	9.2	7.7	9.1	6.7	9.7
North coastal	18.6	19.6	20.2	19.1	19.3	20.8	15.8	16.1	23.8
Middle Yellow River	11.5	9.4	11.3	11.0	11.3	10.7	2.1	2.9	1.6
East Coastal	20.4	21.3	22.1	14.6	18.2	22.7	10.9	27.8	34.1
South Coastal	14.8	15.8	13.4	15.9	13.3	14.2	59.4	38.8	20.1
Middle Yangtze River	10.6	11.5	11.5	9.9	12.8	11.1	1.8	5.4	9.2
Northwest	4.3	4.1	3.7	5.4	5.1	3.4	0.2	0.2	0.2
Southwest	8.4	9.8	9.6	9.0	10.8	9.4	0.7	2.1	1.3
National	100.0	100.0	100.0	100.0	100.0	100.0	100.0	100.0	100.0

Source: NBS (1991; 2001; 2005)

From 1990 to 2004, the concentration indices of state-owned investment in fixed assets in four regions: the north coastal region, the east coastal region, the middle Yangtze River region, and the south-west region went up, while those in the other four regions declined. Changes in the FDI concentration index are much more significant. In the early 1990s, nearly 60% of FDI was concentrated in the south coastal region, but FDI has shifted to be largely concentrated in the east coastal region due to decreasing capital returns in the Pearl River Delta area. From 1990 to 2004, the FDI concentration index in the east coastal region increased by 23.2 percentage points, while that in south coastal region decreased by 39.3 percentage points. The FDI concentration indices in the middle Yangtze River region and the south-west region increased by 7.4 percentage points and 0.6 percentage points respectively, indicating the emergence of a new region of economic growth along the Yangtze River valley area.

Table 4 shows the concentration index of investment for the eight regions over the period 1990 to 2004. The three coastal regions have the highest investment concentration, accounting for 54% of total investments in fixed assets. Since 1990 there has been an upward trend in the concentration index of total investment in fixed assets in five regions: the east coastal, the north coastal, the middle Yellow River, the middle Yangtze River, and the south-west. In the same period there has been a downward trend in the south coastal region, the north-east region and the north-west region. In terms of total investment in fixed assets, the share of state-owned investment and foreign direct investment (FDI) (including investment from Hong Kong, Taiwan and Macau) are 40% and 10%, respectively. Therefore, these two indicators can largely explain the major changes in the regional pattern of total investment in fixed assets.

Employment creation and changes in the pattern of mobility

Since the start of market reforms in the late 1970s, the coastal region has played a leading role in China's economic growth, but this has changed over time. In the 1980s, the Pearl River Delta area took the lead in initiating reform and opening up, making it the engine room of China's high rate of economic growth through the 1980s and the first half of the 1990s. From the beginning of the 1990s, the east coastal region gradually replaced the south coastal region and become the engine of growth, thanks to the opening of the Yangtze River Delta area. The opening up of China after its accession into the WTO has brought about multiple economic poles that promote China's economic growth.

Table 5 presents statistics on regional economic growth and employment growth over the period 1990 to 2004. Table 5 indicates that the south coastal region had the highest rate of economic growth, followed by the east coastal region and the north coastal region in the first half of the 1990s. Growth rates were similar in three coastal regions during the second half of the 1990s. After China joined the WTO, economic growth in the east coastal region was the highest followed by the north coastal region and the south coastal region.

Table 5: Regional economic growth and employment growth: 1990–2004 (%)

	Annual GDP growth			Annual growth, non-agricultural employment	
Region	1990–95	1995–2000	2000–04	1995–2000	2000–04
Northeast	9.7	8.9	11.1	-4.1	3.5
North coastal	14.6	10.9	12.8	0.3	4.8
Middle Yellow River	11.2	9.7	12.8	0.6	3.3
East coastal	16.8	11.2	13.1	-0.5	7.2
South coastal	18.6	10.4	11.6	1.2	5.9
Middle Yangtze River	12.9	10.3	10.8	0.4	4.8
Northwest	10.1	8.7	10.5	0.2	4.8
Southwest	10.7	8.9	10.9	2.4	5.5

Source: NBS (1991; 1992; 1993a; 1994–2001; 2002a; 2003a; 2004a; 2005)

Table 5 indicates that the inland regions have undergone similar economic growth trajectories since the middle of the 1990s, speeding up after China's accession to the WTO. Both trade expansion and investment growth have not only shaken off the constraint of sluggish domestic demand, but also stimulated China's economic growth.

The imbalance in economic catch-up and industrial restructuring has also generated differences in employment opportunities. The annual growth in non-agricultural employment including employment in secondary and tertiary industries in Table 5 shows that employment opportunities have indeed had an important impact on the pattern of labour mobility. From 1995 to 2000, non-agricultural employment growth was positive in the south coastal region, but negative in the north coastal region and the east costal region. From 2001 to 2004, non-agricultural employment growth in the three coastal regions was positive. Among the three coastal regions, the east coastal region experienced the highest growth in employment opportunities, followed by the north coastal region and the south coastal region. There is a similar trend in the inland regions. Rapid economic growth from 2001 to 2004 promoted employment growth in the inland areas. Given stable relative wages and regional differences in employment opportunities, information in the local labour markets is transmitted through the national labour market, guiding changes in the pattern of labour mobility.

Labour mobility and regional industry shift

The phenomenon of the shortage of rural workers reflects the increasing integration of the labour market between rural and urban areas and between regions. This trend indicates that there is a link between comparative advantage across regions and a maturing of China's labour market. With further openness, trade liberalisation has resulted in inter-regional industrial restructuring in accordance with the principle of comparative advantage to improve resource allocation. In the meantime, the integration of the labour market provides a good basis for effectively solving the issues of local and structural labour shortages.

China faces fierce international competition and whether its manufacturing industry can maintain its competitiveness depends on the relative advantage of its labour costs and the speed of industrial restructuring and the industrial shift between regions. If the increase in labour costs can be overcome by regional industrial shifts, China's manufacturing industry will be able to keep its labour cost advantage for a longer term.

International comparison of labour costs in the manufacturing industry

Maintaining low wages is a key factor for China to retain its international competitiveness. Table 6 shows a comparison of the international cost of labour in manufacturing industries using International Labour Organisation (ILO) statistics. Compared with most other countries, China has an absolute advantage in terms of labour cost in manufacturing, but the gap has dramatically been narrowed due to the rapid growth of wage rates in China. From 1995 to 2002, the annual growth rates of wages in manufacturing in China, Japan, the United States, the United Kingdom, South Korea, Singapore and Hong Kong were 11.6%, -2.8%, 3.1%, 4.3%, 2.5%, 2.2% and 3.3% respectively. China's labour cost advantage in the manufacturing industry will face challenges from its Asian neighbours who have experienced fast economic growth such as Malaysia, India, Thailand and Vietnam. According to Table 6, India's labour cost in manufacturing in 1995 was about 70% of China's, and this gap has been widening over the last decade. With exports of manufacturing products from neighboring countries increasing, China will face a more competitive environment. If the labour cost of China's manufacturing products continues to increase, China's competitive advantage in manufacturing exports and hence its role as the world's factory will be weakened.

Table 6: International comparison of the annual average manufacturing wage: 1995–2002 (US$)

	1995	1996	1997	1998	1999	2000	2001	2002
China	619	679	716	853	941	1,057	1,181	1,329
Japan	35,569	31,296	28,485	26,547	30,667	32,638	29,376	28,366
US	25,667	26,520	27,331	27,976	28,808	29,786	30,701	31,803
UK	25,997	29,902	29,319	31,588	32,139	31,345	31,530	34,412
South Korea	17,486	18,813	16,729	10,999	14,894	16,993	15,824	17,812
Singapore	18,264	19,740	20,097	19,474	19,844	21,132	20,876	21,137
Malaysia	4,801	5,318	5,161			4,383	4,835	
India	434	402	367	345	429	336		

Notes: (1) Figures in this table are expressed in US$ according to the currency exchange rate of individual countries

(2) Because of differences in how wage statistics are expressed, hourly wages in the US and UK are multiplied by 40 hours per week and 52 weeks to get the annual wage; monthly wages in other countries are multiplied by 12 to get the annual wage.

Source: International Labour Organisation, http://laborsta.ilo.org/

The possibility of regional shifts of manufacturing industry

From the viewpoint of industrial policies, the phenomenon of the shortage of rural workers has further manifested the pressing issue of regional industrial shift. The increase in labour costs has changed the relative price of labour to capital, and market competition has forced the adjustment and upgrading of regional industrial structures. The increasing extent of production specialisation (Cai, Wang & Wang 2002) has also mirrored the on-going industrial restructuring of China's manufacturing industry in the face of international competition.

Certain conditions are required for the shift of labour-intensive industry from coastal regions to inland regions. With rising wages in coastal areas, whether labour-intensive industries can be shifted to inland regions will be determined by the cost savings from so doing. Table 7 shows provincial comparative advantage in textile manufacturing, which is the largest source of employment among manufacturing industries in China. In Table 7, average wages in inland areas are relatively lower, but the share of enterprises making losses is higher and profit rates are lower. In contrast, profit rates are higher and the share of enterprises making losses is lower in coastal provinces such as Jiangsu, Zhejiang and Fujian. In some developed coastal provinces and provincial-level cities, profit rates are relatively lower and the share of loss-making enterprise is relatively higher, such as in Guangdong and Beijing.

Table 7: Regional comparative advantage of textile manufacturing in China

Province	Average enterprise size, 10,000 RMB	Share of loss-making enterprises	Rates of profit to cost[2]	Average wage	Labour productivity	Relative advantage co-efficient[3]
National	47.0	18.6	2.7	8,079	38,198.2	4.7
Beijing	39.0	25.0	-0.1	11,505	35,237.0	3.1
Tianjin	22.3	42.8	4.0	10,056	22,324.6	2.2
Hebei	48.8	12.5	4.3	6,890	32,359.9	4.7
Shanxi	39.6	31.0	-3.1	5,056	14,833.3	2.9
Inner Mongolia	97.4	19.0	3.3	7,386	56,451.6	7.6
Liaoning	36.7	40.1	1.7	5,933	23,507.2	4.0
Jilin	52.9	31.1	-1.0	5,242	21,309.2	4.1
Heilongjiang	43.1	28.6	1.4	7,152	18,455.4	2.6
Shanghai	32.2	20.9	2.4	14,649	41,912.0	2.9
Jiangsu	44.5	17.0	2.3	9,211	48,851.4	5.3
Zhejiang	55.2	9.4	3.7	11,577	48,072.2	4.2
Anhui	38.4	37.1	0.3	6,502	25,563.9	3.9
Fujian	42.8	16.8	4.3	11,281	45,032.6	4.0
Jiangxi	24.4	25.2	1.8	6,837	22,323.0	3.3
Shandong	61.0	12.0	4.6	7,574	40,803.9	5.4
Henan	36.5	19.2	2.2	6,735	25,371.4	3.8
Hubei	42.9	21.2	0.8	6,240	29,600.5	4.7
Hunan	30.2	30.3	0.0	6,366	21,388.0	3.4
Guandong	49.8	23.8	1.0	10,681	48,004.7	4.5
Guangxi	31.9	45.6	-0.2	6,969	17,527.8	2.5
Hainan	84.4	42.9	2.2	9,943	61,304.3	6.2
Chongqing	40.1	28.7	-1.7	6,797	14,083.7	2.1
Sichuan	37.4	24.4	1.4	6,672	21,137.1	3.2
Guizhou	17.5	43.5	-6.6	5,960	8,000.0	1.3
Yunnan	19.6	50.0	-9.0	6,944	7,696.3	1.1
Shaanxi	52.0	55.3	-4.7	7,657	14,574.7	1.9
Gansu	18.2	29.9	-1.7	6,632	20,149.3	3.0
Qinghai	18.3	25.0	-0.9	6,132	26,451.6	4.3
Ningxia	97.8	6.3	5.2	10,037	148,958.3	14.8
Xingjiang	48.6	51.4	-5.1	7,642	19,751.5	2.6

Source: NBS & MLSS (2004); NBS (2004c)

The relative advantage coefficient in Table 7 is defined as labour productivity divided by average wages. This coefficient shows that the coastal provinces still have certain relative advantages. For example, the relative advantage coefficients in several coastal provinces such as Hebei, Jiangsu, Shandong and Hainan are greater than the national average. But there are also signs of a shift in labour-intensive industry to the inland provinces. For example, the relative advantage coefficient in Inner Mongonia, Hubei and Ningxia are near to, or greater than, the national average.

Linking the relative advantage coefficient with profit rates and enterprise size, we observe that profitability has a positive relationship with enterprise size. For example, the average enterprise size in Ningxia province is the largest as are the relative advantage coefficient and profit rate. In the Yangtze River Delta area, average enterprise size and profit rate are the largest in Zhejiang province, but its share of loss-making enterprises is relatively low.

The key to the shift in labour-intensive industry from coastal areas to inland areas is to improve backward production technology and management systems. In the long run, the improvement in the profitability of labour-intensive industries in the inland provinces will definitely offset the impact of increasing labour costs on China's international competitiveness and maintain the labour cost advantage of China's manufacturing industry.

Labour market efficiency and industry shift

The improvement in labour market efficiency has important implications for industrial restructuring and industry shift. From the viewpoint of employment, labour market efficiency comes from mobility efficiency and matching efficiency. Mobility is a precondition for the effective operation of the labour market. If institutional barriers in the labour market exist, the mobility of labour will be impeded and if information in the labour market is not transmitted efficiently, the wage signal will lose its function in regulating labour supply and demand.

Using data on manufacturing wages from *China Labour Statistical Yearbook*, Du & Cai (2004) verify that the extent of China's regional labour market integration has been increasing. This finding reflects the fact that the labour market is producing spatial matching. However, the existence of institutional barriers such as the *hukou* system has caused geographic separation between labour supply and demand. The supply of rural workers is mainly located in inland areas, whereas the demand for rural workers is largely located in coastal areas. The geographic separation of the labour market hinders the immediate transmission of labour market information where there is a mismatch between demand and supply, which amplifies the effects of unexpected shocks and magnifies fluctuations in the labour market.

To illustrate, assume that at a given wage rate, exports and economic growth increase demand for rural workers in coastal areas, but the institutional constraints on mobility and matching hinder the instant flow of surplus labour from inland areas. This outcome implies that labour supply in coastal areas is rigid in the short term. Enterprises cannot recruit the needed number of rural workers at the given wage rate and thus face a shortage of labour. If enterprises attempt to increase wage rates, this will only increase the wage rates of current on-job workers, increase labour costs and reduce profits, but leave the added demand unsatisfied.

If labour markets between rural and urban areas and between regions are integrated, flexible and effective, the supply of surplus rural labour will become more elastic. When increased exports and growth generate an increasing demand for labour, rural labourers will migrate to the coastal areas to meet the excess demand if there is surplus labour in inland rural areas.

Conclusion and policy implications

The new pattern of labour mobility demonstrates that the previous conditions governing the operation of the labour market are insufficient to meet the new challenges. The *hukou* system reform needs to be deepened and the reforms to the labour market strengthened to facilitate rural migration, speed up the integration of regional labour markets and improve efficiency.

Increase labour market integration

With structural adjustment and industrial shift, the integration of the labour market requires an efficient allocation of the urban and rural labour forces. Strengthening the construction of the employment information system and the employment service system is an important policy measure to regulate the supply and demand of labour. On the one hand, we need to collect information on the situation of rural employment in different regions. And on the other, we need to collect information on the demand for labour in coastal and urban areas. Through employment information and employment service systems, we can effectively match the supply and demand for labour between rural and urban areas and between regions. Timely adjustments to the supply of, and demand for, labour according to the prevailing economic situation, can be made to maintain the stability of the labour market.

Deepen the hukou system reform

Since a series of institutional hindrances attached to the *hukou* system still exist, rural workers face widespread discriminatory treatment. Deepening the *hukou* system reform should focus attention on the abolition of welfare attached to the *hukou* system, i.e. separating rights of employment, housing, education, social security and welfare from the *hukou* system to remove institutional barriers to labour mobility. Institutional design should encourage equal employment. Government management of migrants in those regions where they end up should address issues of employment, housing, labour protection, social security, and education for rural workers. This will pave a smooth path for rural migration and non-agricultural employment.

Enhance the quality and skill of rural migrants

Industrial restructuring introduces new requirements for quality and a higher skill base in the rural labour market. To address this need the government needs to develop vocational skill training through a rural vocational education system and the relevant programs designed for rural migrants to improve their employment capability. Examples of the latter are the National Training Plan for Rural Workers 2003 to 2010 and the Sunlight Project for training of rural migrants.

Strengthen the construction of labour market institutions

Younger workers are more interested in development opportunities that go beyond wage rates. They have higher expectations of their work conditions and place more emphasis on job stability. These expectations will inevitably bring about more incidents of conflict between employers and employees as attention is focused on insufficient labour protection for rural workers. If these conflicts are not addressed properly, it will lead to social instability.

In the long run, institutional reform is the key in ensuring the effective operation of the labour market. Major policy measures include strengthening relevant legislation and execution of laws and regulations for labour protection to address the problem of wage arrears of rural workers, expand the coverage of the social security system to provide more support for rural workers, and reforming the trade union system to increase migrant representation.

Notes

1 North east region: Heilongjiang, Jilin, Liangning; North coastal region: Beijing, Tianjing, Hebei, Shandong; Middle Yellow River region: Inner Mongolia, Shanxi, Henan, Shaanxi; East coastal region: Shanghai, Zhejiang, Jiangsu; South Coastal region: Fujiang, Gaungdong, Guangxi, Hainan; Middle Yangtze River region: Anhui, Jiangxi, Hunan, Hubei; North west region: Gansu, Qinghai, Ningxia, Xinjiang; South west region: Chongqing, Sichuan, Yunnan, Guizhou, Tibet.

2 Rates of profit to cost are the arithmetic average of monthly data from April 2004 to May 2005, available from the China Economic Information Network (www.cei.gov.cn).

3 The relative comparative coefficient is labour productivity divided by average wage.

chapter three

Labour market liberalisation in China and its impact on the world economy

James Xiaohe Zhang

Introduction

With an annual average GDP growth rate of more than 8% over more than two decades, China has become a new economic power in the world economy. A number of factors can be attributed to this spectacular economic performance. These include pragmatic market-oriented economic reform, *de-facto* privatisation of public enterprises and other economic assets, a dramatic change in its external economy characterised by encouraging exports of labour intensive goods and attracting tremendous foreign direct investment inflows. Given that all these factors have contributed to the rapid growth in GDP and international trade in China, more attention should be paid to its internal structural change, particularly the change in its labour markets. This is because with the world's largest labour force of over 700 million workers, any change in China's labour market affects production, trade and employment in many other countries around the world.

The purpose of this chapter is to estimate the economic impact of the liberalisation of the Chinese labour market on aggregate economic welfare for China and the rest of the world. The liberalisation of the labour market is characterised by the abolition of the household registration system that prohibited permanent migration from rural areas to urban areas. This restriction on migration, which has been maintained for more than 50 years, is being gradually relaxed on a trial basis and is going to be abolished in the near future. It is expected that making it easier for China's rural surplus labour to work in China's urban industrial sector will have a significant impact on production, employment and trade patterns in China and the rest of the world, particularly in labour-intensive industries. This will result in a large-scale restructuring of the world economy in line with regional specialisation and the pattern of comparative advantage.

The chapter is organised as follows. The next section introduces some characteristics of the Chinese labour market, followed by a theoretical discussion of the possible consequences of removing the household registration regime, and its likely impact on production and trade in the rest of the world. Some propositions are derived from a theoretical two-sector model. These propositions are tested tentatively using a well known general equilibrium model (the GTAP Model). The simulation results are reported and discussed in Section 4. Conclusions and policy implications are summarised in the final section.

Labour market reforms in China

The labour market in China has been seriously distorted since the 1950s when the restriction policy on rural-urban migration was implemented. China is one of the few countries in the world that uses a household registration (*hukou*) regime to prohibit migration not only from rural to urban areas, but also from one province to another. Starting in 1955, the *hukou* regime virtually prohibited inter-sector migration (Cheng & Selden 1994). Chinese citizens were thus divided broadly into two groups: rural and urban residents. Since the *hukou* regime differentiated not only rural and urban residents, but also urban residents in different provincial administrative units, the mobility among different provincial units was also prohibited. The *hukou* regime, in conjunction with an elaborate rationing mechanism that restricted food and housing supply to urban dwellers, froze and formalised each individual's job position and eliminated possibilities of changes in residential status. This created a hierarchical economic structure with big cities at the apex, provincial and smaller cities in the middle, and the poorest rural areas at the base.

As part of China's industrialisation strategy, the *hukou* regime was developed with the objective of establishing a strong industrial base in the urban areas at the expense of the rural sector. The regime was further reinforced by a 'reverse migration' of city youth to rural areas when they graduated from high schools in the late 1960s and early 1970s. It is reported that more than 48 million people were sent to the countryside during the period 1960–76 (Selden 1993:166). This de-urbanisation process ceased only after the Cultural Revolution ended in 1976.

This policy has never been officially abolished though its impact has been greatly reduced since the 1980s when market-oriented reforms commenced. The farmers who have flocked into the cities and towns since the 1980s in order to find temporary jobs in urban areas are known as 'blind floating people', a term referring to people who are physically resident in the cities and who do not have an urban *hukou*. Without an urban *hukou*, the floating people would neither have access to employment opportunities in state-owned enterprises, nor enjoy state subsidies for housing, health care or schooling for their children. The total population of blind floating people reached 80 million in the late 1980s (Chai & Chai 1997:1040) and is now about 120 million.

It is only in the past few years that the government has started to openly address the challenges posed by rural–urban migration. Some smaller and middle-sized cities are relaxing *hukou* restrictions. Since 2001 China has started to introduce reforms to the *hukou* system in specific provinces. The reforms enable qualified migrants to register as urban residents and obtain the benefits of urban registration including social insurance entitlements. The reforms have been implemented at the provincial level in Anhui, Guangdong, Hebei, Jiangsu, Shandong and Zhejiang as well as several large cities including Beijing, Chongqing and Shanghai. Nevertheless, for most new migrants—obtaining an urban registration and the entitlements that come with it—is still a remote possibility. The reason is that in order to obtain an urban *hukou*, a migrant first has to typically meet certain conditions such as having a stable job, owning property worth a specified amount or having investments to a certain value. The value of the property and/or investments varies from city to city depending on its perceived desirability as a place to live, but in most cases it is outside the reach of the average migrant. To be eligible for a city *hukou* in the big cities like Beijing, Shanghai and Shenzhen, the migrant requires extremely high educational levels, skills and income levels. Some cities, such as Zhengzhou had to restore residence rules after tentatively relaxing the *hukou* regime due to a flood of immigrants into the city to take advantage of the urban welfare and social security system (Carter & Estrin 2005).

The labour market liberalisation, reflected in the relaxation of controls on rural to urban migration, has led to several significant changes in China's labour market. First of all, the long history of labour market segmentation between the rural and urban sectors has virtually ended. Rural migrants are now able to work in the cities and towns as long as they can finance their own living expenses. Secondly, the lifetime employment and subsidisation of privileged urban workers (maintained in state-owned enterprises for more than 40 years) no longer exists. A variety of employment modes, including temporary, casual and fixed-term employment contracts are concurrently used. In some provincial cities in the South, residential status plays no role in recruitment, working compensation and prospects for promotion. Thirdly, segmentation in labour markets and consequential wage differentials between the two sectors has created a phenomenon known as *rural industrialisation* in China. Manufacturing activities have mushroomed in almost all rural villages and towns since the 1980s. These rural enterprises as a whole have been the largest economic entity in employing non-agricultural workers in China, overtaking total employment in state-owned enterprises since 1996 (Zhang 1999; 2000b).

The change in the landscape of the labour market in China seems significant and irreversible. According to Cai (2003) there were about 77 million rural migrants working temporarily in cities in 2000. In addition to this, there were 151.6 million rural labourers working in manufacturing or service activities in the rural areas. Altogether there were about 230 million rural workers working in non-farming activities, which accounted for about one third of the total labour force of the country.

Another event that accompanied labour market liberalisation was the dramatic increase in foreign direct investments (FDI) in the 1990s. By 2003, China had absorbed US$54 billion in FDI, making it the largest destination for FDI in the world. FDI in China is mainly directed into urban manufacturing activities. Two particular areas—the high-tech industry and industries with strong export-orientation—have greatly benefited from preferential government treatment designed to expand FDI including measures such as tax concessions and subsidised land use fees (Zhang 2000a).

A theoretical framework

Economic dualism in the development literature is defined as a dichotomy between a modern industrial sector, in which workers are hired at an institutional wage in numbers that rise with the growth of the industrial capital stock, and a traditional agricultural sector, in which workers subsist at an income level that is somewhat below the industrial wage and is linked to their average rather than marginal productivity (Lewis 1954; Ranis & Fei 1961). In such a dual economy, factor rewards will not equal either their marginal productivity or their opportunity cost, and factor price differential exists for the same factor used in different sectors.

According to this theory, dualism between a capital intensive industrial sector and labour surplus agricultural sector implies a misallocation of resources since more can be produced through additional investment in agriculture and the use of less capital-intensive industrial technology in the industrial sector. However, if labour were mobile, the modern sector would absorb surplus labour from the traditional sector until the marginal products in the two sectors were equalised. At this point dualism would end and the entire economy would allocate labour and other resources in such a way that their respective marginal products were equalised across sectors. This would result in industrialisation (and urbanisation), a key stage of development in all less developed countries (Bhattacharya 1993:243).

The economic impact of dualistic development in the Chinese labour market can be described by a simple two-sector model. We assume that a standard dual economy produces two goods and allocates its labour between two sectors. Manufactured goods are produced using labour and capital (but not land), while food is produced using land and labour (but not capital). Labour is therefore the only mobile factor and the other two factors (land and capital) are assumed to be specific. If there were no restrictions placed on labour mobility, then labour would move between sectors until the value of the marginal product of labour in each sector was equal to the wage rate.

This model is described using the beaker-shaped diagram in Figure 1. The two vertical axes indicate the wage rates in the urban manufacturing sector and rural food sector respectively. The total labour force is represented by the horizontal axis. While manufacturing employment is measured from left to right, rural agricultural employment is measured from right to left. Two negatively sloped demand curves for the labour in the two sectors, D_m and D_f, are determined by the marginal productivity of labour employed in the two sectors respectively. The equilibrium wage rate and employment (L^e and W^e respectively) will be reached when the marginal productivities of labour in the two sectors (D_m and D_f) are equalised.

Figure 1: The impact of rural–urban migration restriction

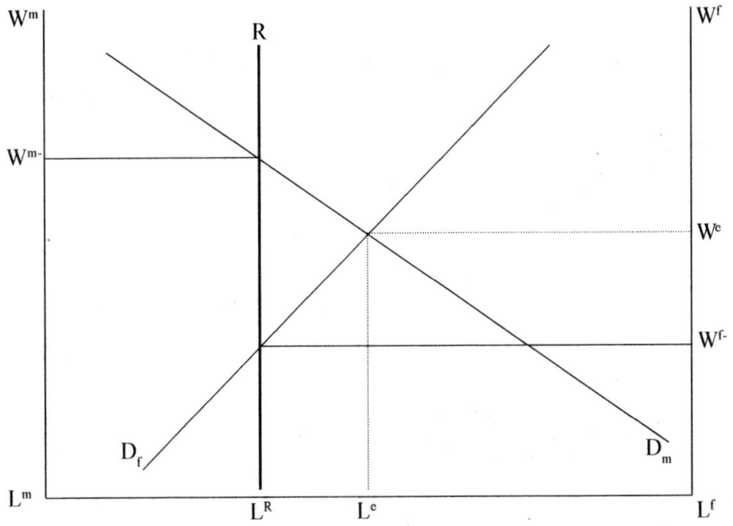

Assuming now that the government implements a restriction on labour mobility, a vertical line denoted by R is inserted to the left hand side of the equilibrium. This will create a gap in the wage rate between the two sectors (W^m and W^f) equal to Wm- minus Wf-, a contraction in urban manufacturing employment (from L^m L^e to L^m L^R) and an expansion in rural employment in the food sector (from L^f L^e to L^f L^R).

Labour market liberalisation in China, characterised by removal of the migration restriction between the rural agricultural sector and urban manufacturing sector, will restore the initial equilibrium (L^e and W^e in Figure 1), and lead to an increase in employment in the urban manufacturing sector, a fall in employment in the rural food sector, and a convergence in wage rates between the two sectors.

A more realistic dual economic model of the Lewis-type may incorporate the concept of surplus labour. In this case, the initial equilibrium is reached when the marginal productivity of labour in the urban manufacturing sector and the *average productivity* of rural labour in the rural food sector are equalised. This setting of the labour market is based on a well-observed fact in developing countries that when a capitalist marketing mechanism dominates the production and employment pattern in the modern sector, the rural sector remains as a traditional community where income is shared among all of the members. The income has to be shared because the supply of labour in the rural traditional society is virtually unlimited. When some of the surplus labour is removed from the rural sector, the output in this sector does not fall. In fact, when surplus labour migrates from the rural food sector to the urban manufacturing sector, the overall productivity of labour could even increase. It is hypothesised that this is exactly what has happened in the Chinese labour market since the late 1980s.

The following propositions can be derived directly from the model:

1. When the restriction on migration between the two sectors is removed, urban manufacturing production, employment and exports will increase in the way that the Rybcynski effect in international trade theory predicts. There will be an absolute expansion in labour intensive manufacturing activities, and a contraction in land intensive food production.

2. If labour intensive manufacturing production represents a source of comparative advantage in China, labour market liberalisation, along with the opening of the economy, will shift the demand curve for urban manufacturing labour to the right. This will result in a higher equilibrium wage rate, and larger urban employment (urbanisation).

3. If there is an external increase in capital in the urban manufacturing sector, the expansion of manufacturing activities and contraction of food production will be magnified.

4. The increase in the share of labour intensive manufacturing exports from China in the world market will lead to large-scale restructuring of the world economy in line with regional specialisation and comparative advantage. Specifically, most, if not all, of the labour intensive manufacturing activities in the industrialised economies will tend to contract, while their capital intensive and natural resources intensive production will expand; this assumes that Chinese firms are more competitive in labour intensive manufactured products and less competitive in land intensive and resource based products.

The above propositions are the major hypotheses that this chapter attempts to test. To carry out such a multi-national and multi-sector analysis, a well-known computable general equilibrium model, the Global Trade Analysis Project (GTAP) model, is used.

Model, data, scenarios and results

The Global Trade Analysis Project (GTAP) is a globally applied general equilibrium project based at Purdue University. Since its inception in 1993, GTAP has rapidly become a common 'language' for many conducting global economic analysis. GTAP offers a variety of products, including data, models and software for multi-region and multi-sector applied general equilibrium analysis of global economic issues. In this study Version 5 of GTAP is used. To capture the regional and sectoral impact of the change, the world economy is divided into ten regions and ten sectors. The method of this aggregation is detailed Tables A1 and A2 at the end of the chapter.

Three policy scenarios are simulated. The first scenario assumes that there is a net increase of 25% in unskilled labour endowment in five of the 10 sectors in China, which in turn will greatly increase labour intensity in these industries. These five sectors, namely textiles and clothing, machinery, construction, services and other light manufactured goods, are considered conventionally as labour intensive (Leamer 1984; Zhang 1992; 1994; Song 1996). A quarter of the labour force in these industries (46 million workers), which accounts for about half of the floating population in the late 1990s, is assumed to be rural surplus labour. This experiment is therefore a standard test of the surplus labour theory: the transfer of rural surplus labour into either urban manufacturing activities or rural non-farm industries will not affect the *effective* labour force and output in the agricultural sector.[1]

The second scenario assumes that there is no surplus labour in China so the increase in the labour force in the manufacturing sector must result in a corresponding reduction of the same amount of labour in the agricultural sector. Assuming that the floating population is about 100 million, i.e. about one fifth of the total rural employment of 493 million rural labourers in 1997 (NBS 1999:137), 20% of the rural labour force is therefore removed from the rural agricultural sector.[2] As a result production and employment in the rural agricultural sector are expected to decline.

Table 1: Changes in production and employment in China (%)

	Scenario 1 (surplus labour)	Scenario 2 (labour mobility)	Scenario 3 (labour & capital)
Output			
Food	1.81	-5.28	-4.23
Other primary goods	1.57	1.38	3.20
Textiles	11.02	9.69	12.30
Petroleum and coal	4.39	3.19	6.98
Metals	4.25	4.58	8.56
Machinery	10.74	11.48	16.29
Utilities	5.00	3.91	7.98
Construction	6.00	4.44	9.76
Other manufactures	8.78	8.17	11.48
Service	8.91	7.58	11.46
Factor price (sector average)			
Land	6.84	5.77	9.66
Unskilled labour	6.87	6.89	9.16
Skilled labour	1.13	-0.44	1.41
Capital	2.10	0.55	4.36
Natural resources	5.25	3.78	6.99
Employment (sector average)			
Land	0.46	-2.83	-4.18
Unskilled labour	1.21	-0.73	-0.83
Skilled labour	1.59	3.25	3.42
Capital	0.92	2.14	1.51
Natural resources	-0.01	-0.01	-0.02

To capture the impact of the dramatic increase in FDI inflows in the late 1990s in China, the third scenario combines the second scenario with the application of capital augmenting technology in all sectors except for the food sector. Given that the US$45 billon actually utilised FDI in China contributed to about 10%

of the total investment in fixed assets in 1997 (NBS 1999:185, 595), and that FDI was mainly used in the manufacturing, construction and service industries (Lai 2002:280), a 10% increase in all of the sectors except for the food sector is projected.

The simulation results of the key economic variables for the three scenarios are summarised in tables 1, 2, 3 and 4.

Changes in production and employment in China

Table 1 shows a significant increase in output in almost all industries except for food in China in each of the three scenarios. While textiles, machinery, service and other light manufactured goods achieve the greatest gain, the decline in food output in the second and third scenarios is an expected consequence because we assume that 20% of the *effective labour force* is deducted from the food sector. Factor prices are increased for the factors of land, labour, capital and natural resources in all cases with the only exception being that when unskilled labour is transferred from the food sector into the five labour intensive industries, the return to skilled labour falls. The owners of unskilled labour, land and natural resources gain the most. The result in employment is mixed. When demand for the scarce factors of skilled labour and capital increases, demand for the abundant factors, land, and unskilled labour declines in two of the three scenarios. The demand for natural resources decreases in each of the three scenarios.

Changes in regional GDP

Table 2: Changes in value of regional GDP (%)

Regions	Scenario 1 (surplus labour)	Scenario 2 (labour mobility)	Scenario 3 (labour & capital)
NAFTA	-0.20	-0.16	-0.28
China	4.68	3.84	6.97
ANZ	0.02	0.20	0.13
East Asia	-0.27	-0.30	-0.41
Japan	-0.32	-0.33	-0.56
EU15	-0.29	-0.26	-0.45
ASEAN	-0.21	-0.11	-0.20
South Asia	-0.38	-0.28	-0.45
Non-EU Europe	-0.20	-0.17	-0.34
ROW	0.00	0.08	0.00

Table 2 shows the change in the growth rate of GDP in the ten regions for the three scenarios. It is clearly shown in the table that in the three scenarios the growth of GDP in China is the most significant. However, this high economic growth in China is achieved at the expense of almost all other regions with the only exceptions being Australia and New Zealand (ANZ) as well as the region classified as rest of the world (ROW). Among the three scenarios, the labour and capital augmenting scenario generates the largest output gain, followed by the surplus labour scenario and labour mobility scenario for the Chinese economy. The second scenario brings the largest output gains for Australia and New Zealand, and to a lesser extent for the ROW region.

Changes in international trade

Table 3: Changes in regional exports and imports (%)

	Scenario 1 (surplus labour)	Scenario 2 (labour mobility)	Scenario 3 (labour & capital)
Exports			
NAFTA	0.19	0.09	0.33
China	4.54	4.49	5.37
ANZ	0.11	0.18	0.30
East Asia	0.00	-0.12	-0.08
Japan	0.01	-0.15	0.13
EU15	-0.21	-0.23	-0.30
ASEAN	-0.25	-0.32	-0.44
South Asia	-0.21	-0.18	-0.11
Non-EU Europe	-0.10	-0.14	-0.16
ROW	0.11	0.09	0.18
Imports			
NAFTA	0.26	0.25	0.25
China	1.14	4.16	7.59
ANZ	0.16	0.37	0.31
East Asia	0.53	-0.13	-0.17
Japan	0.52	-0.11	-0.31
EU15	0.19	-0.21	-0.41
ASEAN	-0.13	-0.39	-0.59
South Asia	-0.18	-0.35	-0.56
Non-EU Europe	0.20	-0.14	-0.33
ROW	-0.06	0.19	0.09

Table 3 shows the changes in international trade which mirrors the change in production reflected in Table 2. China, Australia and New Zealand, and to a much lesser extent the NAFTA countries, gain from increased trade in all scenarios. Trade is also created by Japan and the other East Asian economies in some scenarios, but is decreased for all other regions and scenarios.

Economic welfare

The GTAP program has the capacity to decompose the sources of economic welfare into a group of components. These components include allocation efficiency, technical efficiency, the terms of trade and the investment-saving balance effect. Allocation efficiency is achieved when the marginal productivities of all factors in all sectors are equalised. Technical efficiency is achieved when the production cost is minimised through the optimal usage of labour and capital. The terms of trade effect, as well as the balance between investment and saving, offset each other between different regions.

The equivalent variation (EV) which shows the change in utility measured by real income change is used as an indicator of the changes in economic welfare. In terms of the change in EV, Table 4 shows that the third scenario (a combination of labour and capital augmenting technology) generates the largest welfare gain. This is followed by the surplus labour scenario and the labour mobility scenario. This result seems to suggest that labour and capital are co-operative. In other words, the increase of one factor will significantly increase the productivity of the other, and *vice versa*.

Despite the large welfare gains to the world as a whole that are generated by labour market liberalisation in China, these gains are not evenly distributed across regions. As expected, China gains the most in all of the three scenarios, followed by NAFTA, ANZ, ASEAN, non-EU members in Europe and the countries in the ROW, whereas Japan, the EU15, the East Asian countries and South Asian countries are the losers. This seems to indicate that there is a *complementary* relationship between China and its Australian, New Zealand, ASEAN, non-EU and American trading partners, and a *competitive* relationship between China and its East and South East Asian neighbors, as well as the EU15.

Through the GTAP de-composition method, the major sources of these welfare gains can be identified. For China, the welfare gains are mainly created by improvements in allocation efficiency and technical efficiency. For the other beneficiaries, the gains are created by improvement in their terms of trade.

Table 4: Changes in economic welfare (US$ million)

	Scenario 1 surplus labour	Scenario 2 labour mobility	Scenario 3 labour & capital
NAFTA	2,361	2,491	3,306
China	94,440	67,105	117,689
ANZ	412	496	619
East Asia	-252	-845	-846
Japan	-599	-1,456	-2,076
EU15	-313	-387	-1,216
ASEAN	117	126	266
South Asia	-236	-219	-285
Non-EU Europe	430	322	339
ROW	3,242	3,043	3,968
World	99,603	70,675	121,763

Conclusion

Based on a brief review of the dualistic nature of the Chinese economy and a theoretical discussion of a simple two-sector economic model, this chapter examines the economic impact of free labour mobility between a traditional rural agricultural sector and a modern urban manufacturing sector in China on the world economy. Through simulating general equilibrium experiments on the basis of three different assumptions about the economy, most of the theoretical propositions and hypotheses generated from the theoretical discussions are confirmed.

Though still very tentative, the findings of this chapter are informative. First, the net impact on economic welfare of labour market liberalisation in China is positive for the world as a whole in general and for the Chinese economy in particular. Second, the welfare gains are magnified when labour market liberalisation is accompanied by foreign capital inflows into China. Third, these gains are not evenly distributed across countries or sectors. While China, NAFTA and the Australasian countries benefit from the labour market liberalisation in China, the EU15 and the rest of Asia, perhaps with the only exception of the ASEAN countries, are more likely to face greater challenges due to more fierce competition.

Table A1: The aggregation of the ten regions

	Region code	Economies	Description
1	NAFTA	USA, Canada, Mexico	North American Free Trade Area
2	China	China	China
3	ANZ	Australia, New Zealand	Australia, New Zealand
4	East Asia	Korea, Hong Kong, Taiwan	Korea, Hong Kong, Taiwan
5	Japan	Japan	Japan
6	EU15	Australia, Belgium, France, Netherlands, Luxembourg, Italy, Germany, UK, Ireland, Denmark, Greece, Spain, Portugal, Sweden, Finland	The 15 countires that comprised the European Union in 1997
7	ASEAN	Singapore, Malaysia, Vietnam, Indonesia, Thailand, Philippines	ASEAN members in 1997
8	South Asia	India, Pakistan, Bangladesh	India, Pakistan, Bangladesh
9	Non-EU Europe	Turkey, the former Soviet Union, Hungary, Poland, and the rest of the Central European Association	Non-EU member countries in Europe
10	ROW	Rest of the world	All countires not included in the other groups

Table A2: The aggregation of the ten sectors

	Sector code	Industries	Description
1	Food	Paddy rice, wheat, cereal grain, vegetables, fruits, nuts, oil seed, sugar cane, sugar, beet, crops, cattle, sheep, goats, horses, animal products, raw milk, fishing, meat, dairy products, tobacco, beverages	Primary production, land and resource intensive
2	Other primary goods	Plant-based fibres, wool, silk, forestry, coal, oil, gas, minerals	Primary production, land and resource intensive
3	Textiles	Textiles, apparel, leather	Labour intensive
4	Petroleum and coal	Petroleum, coal, chemicals, rubber, minerals	Resource-based and capital intensive
5	Metal	Ferrous metals, metal products	Resource-based and capital intensive
6	Machinery	Motor vehicles and parts, transportation equipment, electronic equipment, machinery	Capital or labour intensive
7	Utilities	Electricity, gas distribution, water	Capital intensive
8	Construction	Construction, dwellings	Labour intensive
9	Other manufactures	Shoe polish and other manufactures	Labour intensive
10	Service	Trade, transport (sea, air, land), communication, financial services, insurance, recreation, public administration, education	Labour intensive

Notes

1 Bhattacharyya and Parker (1999) estimated that in 1995, between 35% and 40% of the agricultural labour force was redundant in China. Cook (1999) also found that the marginal productivity of farm labour is very low in China.

2 This is consistent with Carter and Estrin's (2003) estimate that WTO membership and complementary labour market reforms will result in a 25% decline in the agricultural labour force.

chapter four

Minority entrepreneurs on the move—the Uygers

Marika Vicziany and Guibin Zhang

Introduction

The typical image of China's Uygurs is of a minority besieged in their own homeland: in 1940–1941 they represented some 60% of the population of the Xinjiang Uygur Autonomous Region relative to the Han with 4%; today this has declined to 45.2% with the Han population almost equal at 40.6% in the 2000 census (Mackerras 2004:table 2; Gladney 2003:8).[1] So when it comes to the mobility of labour in western China, research has focused on the mobility of Han workers into Xinjiang in response to government encouragement to settle the wild frontier during the Maoist era from 1950 to 1976 and then on the 'Go West' development strategy during the late 1990s. Periods of 'planned' migration oscillated with spontaneous migration (Qiang & Xin 2003:95–7). In addition to these civilian labour movements into Xinjiang, the Chinese paramilitary known as the Xinjiang Production and Construction Corps (XPCC or Bingtuan) has actively recruited temporary and permanent labourers from the 1950s to the present. The XPCC functions as a parallel government with a central subvention that allows it to do whatever the central government believes to be necessary for the stability of Xinjiang (Becquelin 2000:80)—in the past this included recruiting labourers without work permits although work permits were required in the civilian sector (Becquelin 2000:76). Where the question of the mobility of the Uygur has been discussed it has taken two forms: the movement of Uygurs within Xinjiang and in particular into the southern parts of Xinjiang where a powerful, distinctively Uygur–Islamic culture survives (Rong 2003; Tsui 2003) and their migration abroad to form part of the small Uygur diaspora (Gladney 2003:11).[2] The present chapter moves beyond these concerns. We consider the movement of Uygurs into the cities of eastern China and western/central Asia and how that labour mobility is related to the establishment of Uygur businesses in Shanghai, Tashkent and other cities. We argue that there is a close relationship between Uygur migration and Uygur entrepreneurship, largely because ethnic prejudices make it difficult for Uygurs to find employment outside the Uygur community. Even within Xinjiang, finding a job typically depends on relying on

Uygur networks (Tsui 2003:129).[3] Using three detailed life histories, this chapter reports on the growing prosperity of the Uygur entrepreneurs who have looked beyond Xinjiang and followed their traditional 'Silk Road' instincts to travel and build business connections beyond their homelands. Studies about the mobility of labour and capital *out* of Xinjiang are likely to become more important now that the Chinese government has started to reassess its 'Go West' development strategy. More importantly, understanding how minority entrepreneurs have survived and prospered provides insights into the kind of policies needed to promote the wellbeing of important groups such as the Uygur who not only remain economically disadvantaged relative to the Han but whose socioeconomic status has slipped during the last five decades (ADB 2002:27–8).

Uygurs migration in China

Little research has been undertaken on the trends and reasons for labour migration into and out of Xinjiang, and even less is known about labour migration amongst the Uygur, a distinctive Muslim minority that numbers about 8.6 million people as per the 2000 Chinese Census (Gladney 2003:7) living mainly in Xinjiang Uygur Autonomous Region.[4] One study of labour migration out of western China by the Ministry of Agriculture in 2002 provides some general hints about what has been happening. According to a survey of 5,805 rural families in 116 villages in western China in late 2002,[5] of the 16,416 rural labourers, just under 20% had migrated out of their home provinces in search of jobs (Zhang 2003). Extrapolated to general population estimates, the Ministry calculated that perhaps some 33.5 million labourers from Western China had migrated in that year. A breakdown of the industries into which these western migrants were absorbed is provided in Table 1. It shows that the largest number of migrants, about a quarter, end up working for the construction industry. This is hardly surprising for the construction industry in India is also one of the largest employers of displaced rural labour. After that, manufacturing accounted for some 22% and restaurants and related service industries for almost 19%. This particular report does not break down the findings by provinces or nationalities of origin ('nationalities' is the word used by the Chinese government to describe the minorities). However, if we assume that these proportions are roughly true of Uygur labour, the results are not surprising. If jobs in the hard working and highly unstable construction industry cannot be had, one would expect minority workers to drift towards industries such as these. In the case of the Uygurs, they must find employment that is compatible with their cultural preferences. Even amongst secular Uygur middle class families there is a strong taboo against eating or working with pork or pork products.[6] The taboo is even stronger amongst the Uygur working class who therefore prefer to work for Uygur entrepreneurs in, for example, the leather goods industry or Uygur restaurants and food manufacturing that use only *halal* ingredients. The domestic market for these products is small for the total Muslim population of China numbers only some 20 million people. But there is also a rising international market for these goods, in particular across the landed borders of Xinjiang where significant Muslim populations inhabit the now Islamic republics of the former USSR. There is also a growing interest in Uygur customs, including culinary tastes, amongst the majority Han population who are to be found in large numbers as patrons of Uygur restaurants and consumers of Uygur chocolates in Ürümqi, Beijing and Shanghai.

Table 1: A break down of the migrant labourers from Western China by industries

Industry	Percentage of total
Construction	25.0
Manufacture	22.0
Food, restaurants and services	18.6
Transportation	7.3
Trade and commerce	6.7
Agriculture	3.3
Hospitality and nursing	1.6
Others	15.5

Source: Based on Zhang (2003).

According to the same study by Xiao Hui Zhang, the migration of labour in western China has the distinctive characteristic of being predominantly short rather than long distance migration: some 64.5% of migrants moved *inside* the province of their origin and of these a minority of 29% moved between counties. As many as 35.3% of labour moved *inside* the county of origin. Inter-provincial migration accounted for about 35.5 % of the movement of labour in this sample. In other words, inter-provincial (long distance) and intra-county (short distance) migration were roughly of the same order (Table 2). If this characteristic is true of the general migrant population of western China, it could mean a number of things:

1. that the costs and risks of long distance migration are too high for the people of western China;
2. that potential migrants from western China have few socio-economic networks to sustain long distance migration;

3. that the opportunities for casual labour within home counties and provinces is *perceived* to be higher than in provinces at a greater distance from home.

We are not in a position to comment on the applicability of any of the above, but these trends do appear to support the conclusions reached by Ingrid Nielsen and Russell Smyth in chapter 8 in this volume, on the fragmented labour market of China as a whole.

Table 2: Geographical breakdown of the migrant labourers from Western China.

Inter-provincial migration	35.5%
Intra-provincial migration	64.5%
Inter-country migration	29.2%
Intra-country migration	35.3%

Source: Based on Zhang (2003)

The labour from western China that does engage in long distance migration prefers to move to the industrial hub of Guangdong and Fujian. This region absorbed about 46% of the inter-provincial migration recorded by the Ministry of Agriculture report. After that, with 17% migration to other provinces *within* western China was the next most popular destination (about 17%), followed by 8% who went to Shanghai, Jiangsu and Zhejiang, and a further 6% who migrated to Beijing. Of those who migrated into another part of western China, the preferred provinces were first Yunan, then Xinjiang, Tibet, Shanxi, Guizhou and Gansu.

Another survey of migration in western China suggests a much lower level of movement than the report by Xiaohui Zhang. In a sample of 1,550 rural families in Xinjiang (representing some 4,000 labourers), 2.44% travelled in search of employment, and the majority were male (66.10%) (Yi & Yang 2004). These migrants tended to remain inside Xinjiang, were mainly employed in the tertiary sector (79%) and were aged between 19 and 40 years (76%).

Clearly these patchy surveys are giving conflicting impressions about the extent of labour mobility within, and out of, western China. They are also confined to rural households, and so we learn nothing about migration from urban households or how migratory patterns differ between the two groups. The official literature also gives an unwarranted importance to the role of the state in facilitating inter-provincial migration. For example, there is a tendency to focus on the creation of special minority villages in the cities of the eastern seaboard. According to one report on Uygur migration into Beijing (Mu 2003), the arrival of the Uygur minority in that city occurred in response to the Chinese government's policy of building a Uygur village in the centre of town as part of the Xiyuan Hotel complex in the early 1950s. The central government recruited Uygur chefs and cooks to work in the hotel, and they in turn brought their families and relatives with them. Slowly the 'village' grew into two dense communities located in the suburbs of Ganjiakou and Weigongcun, north and northwest of central Beijing.[7] In the 1970s, the central government also hoped that Uygur villages of this kind would help to bridge the gap between the Islamic minorities and the general population. In reading this report, it is hard to escape the impression that Yi Mu based it largely on interviews with government officials. Ma and Xiang reported that by the mid-1990s the larger village of Ganjiakou had about 1,000 residents employed largely in 32 Uygur restaurants and bakeries; the small village of Weigongcun had about 800 residents and 15 restaurants (Ma & Xiang 1998:566). These populations swelled in the lead up to the *Haj*, when some 3,000 Uygurs arrived in Beijing *en route* to Mecca (Ma & Xiang 1998:567). Ma and Xiang note that some 80% of the Uygur restaurateurs in Beijing come from the cities of Xinjiang, but until now no detailed biographies of these entrepreneurs have been written. Nor does it seem that the Uygur enclaves in the cities of eastern China represent the typical 'peasant communities' described by Solinger amongst others (Solinger 1999).[8] Rather Uygur migration into Beijing and Shanghai, for example, seems to involve mainly people and families from the urban centres of Xinjiang. The case studies in the following section are based on interviews conducted in Kashgar, Ürümqi and Shanghai. At this stage, our project has not yet extended to Beijing. But already it is obvious that the Uygur entrepreneurs who have migrated to the eastern seaboard of China have also expanded their commercial networks with central and south Asian towns on the far western borders of China. Thus, the opportunities for cross-border trade need to figure in accounts of Uygur entrepreneurship and migration. In the following sections we look at the numbers of Uygurs currently living in Shanghai, Beijing and the cities of central Asia. This is followed by case studies of three Uygur businessmen from the western city of Kashgar and the relationship between trade, entrepreneurship and migration.

According to the 2000 Chinese census, the Uygur community of Shanghai numbered only about 1,701 persons (Table 3). The Uygur community of Beijing was slightly larger—about 3,129. As a proportion of the 53,771 Uygurs living outside of Xinjiang, this amounted to a relatively low percentage given the importance of Shanghai and Beijing in the national economy: about 3% and 6% respectively, or a total of only 9% (Table 3). However, as a proportion of the permanent and temporary migrants from Xinjiang who live in these two cities, the Uygurs are well represented: 11.37% and 25.76% in Shanghai and Beijing respectively (Table 3). Given that the Uygurs also represent about half of the population of Xinjiang, the proportion of Uygur migrants is well below what might be expected had the opportunities for Uygur migration been as extensive as those for non-Uygur migrants. A major problem exists with the figures for Uygur migrants. We really do not know what these figures represent—whether temporary or permanent or new arrivals in the year of the census. As Ma and Xiang have noted, there are three types of migrants: permanent, temporary/floating migrants who register, and temporary/floating migrants who do not register (Ma & Xiang 1998:554). The importance of these distinctions is that the total population of China's cities remains undetermined with the vast bulk of migrants probably preferring to come and go as they please without any registration process attached to their periods of residence. By 1994, the unregistered temporary population of Beijing had 'exceeded 50%' of the registered temporary population (Ma & Xiang 1998:557). In particular, under-reportage of Uygur migrants can be expected not only because of the itinerant nature of these migrants with movement backwards and forwards to and from Xinjiang but also because this community is under heavy surveillance by the Chinese government, especially since 9/11 and the assumption that Xinjiang has an active terrorist movement.

Given the millions of migrants who live in Shanghai and Beijing, whichever way one consider the figures on Uygur migration into the cities of the eastern seaboard of China, this is not a big story when it comes to the numbers involved. Even if this were ten times larger, it would still not constitute a big statistical impact. But Uygur migration—whether temporary or permanent—is a big story in terms of the significance it holds and the potential of Uygur entrepreneurship. The optimistic life histories described below show how the constraints of Islamic culture also provide economic opportunities. The linguistic skills of the Uygur facilitates their trade with the countries to the west of the Chinese borders; the strictures of *halal* enable them to specialise in Islamic foods which have large domestic and international markets. Their custodianship of Uygur music, poetry and history places them in a unique position from which China can respond to international curiosity about the 'old Silk Road' and its cultural secrets. The critical thing in all this is to ensure that Uygur entrepreneurship is encouraged and not crowded out by making it easier for Han entrepreneurs to obtain the necessary licenses and approvals for starting up businesses in fields where Uygurs should remain the cultural specialists.

In the following section we look at the chief characteristics of cross-border trade between Xinjiang and the Islamic republics of the former Soviet Union, before turning to a discussion of the case studies of Uygur entrepreneurship. Table 6 shows that estimates of the Uygur population of the central Asian region are that it is over 500,000, which is very large compared with the number of Uygurs in the main cities of the eastern Chinese seaboard. But one common characteristic that the migrant Uygur communities share is that they are largely an urban people. Another feature that applies equally to the cities of eastern China and those in central Asia is that a large floating population of Uygur merchants drifts in and out of the towns and cities—few, if any, of these people are recorded in the censuses.

Table 3: Migrants in Shanghai and Beijing: Xinjiang migrants and Uygur migrants (2000 Census of the PRC)

		Shanghai	Beijing	% of total migrants Shanghai	% of total migrants Beijing
1	Permanent migrants from Xinjiang 2000	2,197	1,253	1.0%	0.7%
2	Temporary migrants from Xinjiang	12,762	10,892	0.4%	0.4%
3	Those born in Xinjiang who migrated to Shanghai or Beijing from another province (permanent or temporary not known)	5,472	2,182		
4	Total Xinjiang migrants to Shanghai and Beijing (rows 1 + 2 + 3)	20,431	14,327		
5	Permanent as % of total (row 1/row 4)	10.75%	8.75%		
6	Uygur migrants	1,701	3,129[9]		
7	Total Uygur migrants to all provinces	53,771	53,771		
8	Uygur migrants to Shanghai and Beijing as % of total Uygur from Xinjiang to all provinces (row 6/row 7)	3.16%	5.82%		
9	Uygur as % of total migrants from Xinjiang to Shanghai and Beijing (row 6/row 4)	8.33%	22.84%		

Source: NSB (2002:730–4, 20, 26, 1797–812)

Cross-border trade and the Uygurs

In 2001, the authors were part of an international team that was appointed to devise a strategy for the Asian Development Bank (ADB) and the State Council of China to develop western China. It was at the height of the 'Go

West Development Strategy' and the brief from the Chinese government and the ADB was to consider the role of cross-border trade as a way of accelerating the development of China's western regions. As the final report noted, the potential for such cross-border trade was considerable and a number of border ports had, therefore, already been opened by the Chinese government in the preceding decade. As Table 4 shows, by the 1990s between 40% and 50% of Xinjiang's international trade already took the form of cross-border trade. From the late 1990s this continued to rise and was closer to 60% of Xinjiang's international trade.

Table 4 also shows a dramatic growth in the total value of Xinjiang's cross-border trade between 1993 and 2003 when the value of that trade increased fivefold. Table 5 supports this by showing that the value of trade with Xinjiang's largest commercial partner, Kazakhstan, also increased by about five; cross-border trade with Kazakhstan accounts for some 75% of the total cross-border trade of Xinjiang. A large volume of this trade is organised by Chinese state-owned enterprises, yet despite this many opportunities exist for private entrepreneurs too. Pakistan is another rapidly growing market. Although still small compared to Kazakhstan, Pakistan is now Xinjiang's third largest trading partner. Cross-border trade with Russia and Pakistan is also more conducive to the involvement of the private sector because it is not dominated by energy imports. Trade with Pakistan is especially important for the southern city of Kashgar where the twice-weekly flights between Islamabad and Kashgar facilitate the movement of merchants and entrepreneurs.

Table 4: Xinjiang cross-border trade volumes 1993–2003 in US$ millions

Year	Total imports and exports	Exports	Imports	% of cross-border trade/total international trade
1993	577	289	288	63.3
1994	512	239	273	50.1
1995	694	275	418	52.6
1996	731	186	544	52.1
1997	749	229	520	51.8
1998	869	325	291	40.5
1999	1,023	573	449	58.0
2000	1,319	580	739	58.3
2001	980	214	796	55.4
2002	1,543	472	1,071	57.3
2003	3,039	1,604	1,435	63.6

Source: Calculated from Xinjiang Statistical Yearbook (2004:523).

Table 5: Xinjiang's Total Imports and Exports with Bordering Countries from 1997–2003 in US$ millions ranked by order of importance in 2003

	1997	1998	1999	2000	2001	2002	2003	% of total cross-border trade
Kazakhstan	550.1	560.23	888.89	1,182.45	904.26	1,365	2,546.13	74.0
Russia	51.21	76.17	66.93	67.7	122.53	215	274.53	8.0
Pakistan	13.98	21.16	46.38	22.52	8.73	69.4	255.39	7.5
Kyrgyzstan	112.41	202	111.73	171.37	99.22	154	230.94	6.8
Uzbekistan	4.22	3.87	2.1	9.52	5.55	19.1	37.73	1.1
Turkmenistan	19.78	6.1	10.7	2.43	0.96	9.9	24.72	0.72
India	2.48	2.16	4.09	17.8	2.06	10.97	22.6	0.66
Mongolia	17.93	12.81	11.05	7.11	8.6	4.2	8.78	0.26
Tajikstan	72.25	60.18	5.81	10.28	7.06	4	8.73	0.26
Afghanistan	0.25	0	0.37	0.02	0.25	0.117	1.27	0.04
Total							3,410.82	100.00

Source: Invest China (2005); Xinjiang (2004).

Table 6: The Uygur populations of the central Islamic republics of the former USSR

Provinces	Kazakhstan	Tajikstan	Krygyzstan	Uzbekistan	Total Uygurs Shanghai and Beijing
Uygur population estimates*	213,265	73,208	52,138	200,000	4,830
Gladney estimates**	185,000	n/a	37,000	36,000	

Sources: * as cited in the text below; ** Gladney (2003:21)

Cross-border trade was reinvented by Deng Xiaoping in the 1980s, but it entailed a return to a pattern of economic and cultural interchange that had existed for millennia before that. Evidence for this is reflected in the minority Uygur populations that live in the central Asian republics of the former Soviet Union (Table 6). In Kazakhstan, 1.4 % of the population are Uygur (CIA 2006a) and in Tajikistan about 1% (CIA 2006b). Small Uygur groups are to be found throughout Central Asia: Kyrgyzstan has about 50,000 but unofficial estimates are twice as high (Ibraimov 2004). Official estimates in 1989 suggested that about

35,700 Uygurs lived in Uzbekistan but unofficial estimates range from 200,000 up to 500,000 (Tarimi 2004). Official policy towards these Uygur minorities has varied greatly, but until 1996 the Kyrgyz government had the most liberal attitudes and even tolerated the existence of a Uygur organisation called Ittipak (Unity) (Laumulin 2005). These foreign Uygur communities on the borders of Xinjiang provide associations and links that give Uygur traders living in China the confidence to do business with these Central Asian republics, the regimes of which often create a business atmosphere that Uygurs regard as harsh.

Case studies

The following three case studies are based on interviews conducted in Ürümqi, Kashgar and Shanghai during the three years 2004–2006. We have changed the names of the Uygur entrepreneurs to protect their privacy. These case studies show that the merchants of the Kashgar region have developed trade and business links with cities on the eastern seaboard of China and on the other side of the country's far western borders. The last case study is especially interesting because this particular entrepreneur's business interests stretch all the way from Shanghai to Tashkent, mediated by his home town, Artush, which forms part of the Kashgar county. This long distance trade by Uygur entrepreneurs has been commented on by Gladney who noted that electronic goods from Hong Kong were purchased by Uygurs in Guangzhou and Shenzhen and then resold in Almaty, the closest large Kazak town to Ili in northern Xinjiang (Gladney 2003:11). Despite these observations, we are not aware of any systematic study of the trade and entrepreneurial links forged by the Uygurs of modern China. These case studies make a modest contribution to this issue and also show that Uygur migration is not a new phenomenon. Again, our third entrepreneur left Xinjiang during the Cultural Revolution and is now regarded as one of Shanghai's most sophisticated Uygur leaders.

The first case study is of a wealthy Kashgar merchant who was initially involved in cross-border trade with the USSR but then gave up this sugar exporting business in order to concentrate on importing cloth from Shanghai and then diversifying into the Uygur restaurant business in that city. The second case study is of another successful Uygur merchant who lives in the town of Artush, famous for its centuries-old tradition of entrepreneurship. Again, the business of importing modern textiles from Shanghai for the Xinjiang markets was an important factor in building that success. From that base, he has diversified into cross-border trade with Pakistan and Kyrgyzstan importing leather for further processing in Kashgar and Shanghai. The idea of cross-border trade was based to a considerable extent on three years of international travel that showed him how other people were living in Europe and the Middle East and expanded his view of what constituted a modern market.

These three case studies throw up a new hypothesis: that the mobility of the Uygur minority is directly related to Uygur entrepreneurship. The development of trade links with the eastern seaboard and cross-border countries provides opportunities for entrepreneurial growth and the development of small migrant communities attached to those business interests. The capacity of poor Uygurs currently living in Xinjiang to move beyond their homelands is much more limited outside these small cultural enclaves. This probably explains why even today, the Uygur communities of Shanghai and Beijing are so small. Table 3 shows that the Uygur population of these two cities is under 2,000 and just over 3,000 respectively and the proportion of Uygurs to total migrants from Xinjiang is well below the proportion of the Uygur population of Xinjiang which is 49% (Table 3, Row 9).

Case study 1: A rich merchant of old Kashgar

Hasim's father began a textile business in Kashgar but the family originally came from Ili, in northern Xinjiang. This Ili connection was maintained by Hasim's father when he began exporting sugar to the USSR. The sugar export business pre-dated Deng Xiaoping's policies because the USSR was a socialist state and so an acceptable trading partner. For many years Hashim's father travelled backwards and forwards between Kashgar and Ili. Now the USSR is no more and he is also no longer in the sugar business although the two incidents are not related. In addition to sugar, Hasim's father had a considerable business importing cloth from Shanghai into Kashgar. Buyers come by air from Islamabad to Kashgar and stock up for the Pakistani and middle-eastern markets.

As China emerged as one of the world's leading textile producers during the 1990s, his extensive business travel to Shanghai gave rise to the idea of setting up a Uygur restaurant in that city. His sons now manage this restaurant. It is highly profitable because Uygur food is popular amongst the Han in Shanghai and other cities. Shanghai currently has about 100 Uygur restaurants plus many smaller eateries and food vendors. The restaurant business then gave Hashim's father the idea of establishing a *halal* butchery in the Shanghai area—this butchery currently services the Muslim restaurants and communities of that city. In eastern China, the Muslim community is predominantly Hui. China has about 9.2 million Hui, according to the 2000 census, in addition to some 8.6 million Uygurs and just over 1.3 million Kazak (Gladney 2003:7). This constitutes an important domestic market of some 20 million people.[10]

In the shops of modern Kashgar one can see other opportunities for exporting the culturally specific goods and services of Xinjiang—the locals make an excellent *halal* chocolate that has potential markets throughout the Islamic world. All that is needed is a bit of government and corporate encouragement to ensure that the bureaucratic obstacles to trade are lightened, in particular by making it easier for Uygurs to obtain licenses to set up factories and trade internationally.

Today Hasim lives in a large, three-storey house built in traditional Uygur style in 'old Kashgar', which is situated on a hill that dominates the new part of Kashgar city. He is prosperous and proud of Uygur traditions. He is a highly respected member of the local Uygur community. The women in this extended household observe various forms of *purdah* or veiling, but that is largely because this is a wealthy family where the women do not go out to work. Kashgar as a whole has a liberal culture in which only women of high status or older women veil themselves—and the popular veil in the latter case is a short brown, shoulder length scarf that can be readily flipped back over the head when the women go to market and need direct eye contact with the sellers to strike a good bargain.

What does this case study say about our hypothesis that the mobility of the Uygur minority is directly related to Uygur entrepreneurship? Hashim's father has generated employment for about 100 Uygurs in Shanghai, based on the assumption that the restaurant and butchery each employ about 50 persons (a reasonable number for private, medium-sized establishments of this kind). That employment is directly related to the investments by this Kashgari family in Shanghai. But the number of persons who share in this prosperity is larger than this figure of 100. First because, a proportion of the Shanghai workforce would return to Kashgar on a regular basis and be replaced by new workers (there appears to be considerable job hopping amongst the Uygurs). Second, because the older workers in Shanghai (those in their thirties and forties) typically bring their wives with them. If those older workers then have children, these children are reared in a complex and fast moving environment—the experience of being brought up in cosmopolitan Shanghai might well lead to enhanced economic opportunities for the next generation.

Case study 2: A rich merchant of Artush

Salim is one of the most successful Uygur merchants in the Kashgar region, living in a village on the outskirts of Artush famed for its long history of clever traders and merchants. The small town of Artush is about an hour's drive north of Kashgar. Some 25 years ago Salim was a farmer like everyone else in this area but he studied and followed the economic policies promoted by Deng Xiaoping from 1979 onwards. Artush has a long tradition of learning, and in the early 20th century was the heart of an educational reform movement that stressed modern, scientific and secular education. The debate between this school of thought and the traditional Islamic approach to education continues in modern Xinjiang.

Salim was encouraged by Deng Xiaoping's attitudes and began to import textiles from Shanghai into Kashgar. Then in the 1990s, the inland borders of China were opened and he started to import semi-processed skins from neighbouring Pakistan and Kyrgyzstan in 1996. He still owns 7 *mu* of land, but this is insufficient to sustain his family so he was compelled like others in the area to diversify. The origin of his family business depended on him making the first lot of money as there was no previously inherited wealth. In addition to importing skins and selling them to leather manufacturers and shopkeepers in Kashgar and Shanghai, in 2004 he opened a cotton factory in Artush to clean and bale cotton. Some of his entrepreneurial drive stems from the three years he spent travelling in the Middle East and Europe in the early 1990s. Today his entrepreneurial diversification has made his family so prosperous that he owns two expensive cars. His wife is articulate, ambitious for her children and dresses in the typical Uygur style of the region—boots, skirt, blouse/jumper and a short headscarf—and like her husband is ferociously proud of the liberal education of the Artush area. Salim and his wife are patrons of Uygur culture and the local artisans. This sits comfortably alongside their liberal attitudes to other aspects of modern living. His wife wears a headscarf but is not veiled and she freely engaged in conversations with our research team without any hesitation. At the same time, she deferred to her husband and left it to him to explain the nature of their business and building ventures.

Again we ask the question: how does this case study support our hypothesis that the mobility of the Uygur minority is directly related to Uygur entrepreneurship? In this instance, Salim and his wife did not migrate out of Artush but managed their extensive business dealings from that town. This decision was driven by practical necessity: as Salim's business grew, importing skins from south and central Asia became more important than importing textiles from Shanghai. That lucrative import trade was easier to manage from his home base in Artush which is close to the Kyrgyzstan border (only 300 kilometres) and close to Pakistan via air and by road along the Karakoram highway. There was, therefore, no point in moving to Shanghai. The Shanghai end of the family business could be managed well enough through short visits to source textiles in eastern China. Those short visits were also useful in planting the idea of cleaning and baling raw cotton in Kashgar. The size of the Shanghai textile market no doubt gave Salim confidence in the long-term demand for Xinjiang cotton. He had the connections in the textile business to make the right investment decision but again, that decision did not indicate any benefit in migrating to the eastern seaboard. Hence the employment that Salim has generated through his entrepreneurship has remained in Xinjiang. We have included this case study in this chapter because it stresses the rational thinking behind decisions about whether and when to migrate. Migration is not always the only or best option.

Case Study 3: A rich Uygur merchant in Shanghai[11]

Abdul is a Uygur merchant from Artush who finally settled in Shanghai after the Cultural Revolution in 1977. 'Business is in our blood', he says, having started life as a modest seller of stockings and headgear in Kashgar. When he branched out he began to travel to central and eastern China via Turfan and Hami, importing the long see-through scarves which are so popular with women in Xinjiang. He first set himself up in Zhejiang province, just south of Shanghai and continued to export fabrics to western China. At first there was not much competition, but this changed in the 1980s with the arrival of other Uygur entrepreneurs from Xinjiang. As with Hashim and Salim, buying and selling the textiles of Shanghai has been the basis of his fortune. His first attempt at diversification beyond Kashgar involved selling textiles into Kazakhstan, Kyrgyzstan and Uzbekistan, starting in 1995. Business boomed and he built a market for 500 shops in Tashkent, Uzbekistan with the support of a Uygur friend from Artush. But business opportunities in Uzbekistan proved to be unstable, and the market was closed down in 2003. The official reason given was that proper authorisation for this marketplace had not been given and no documents of proof existed. The Uzbek government has a long history of hostility towards Uygur businessmen, and even before this happened, many bureaucratic obstacles had been thrown in his direction. Other Uygur merchants doing business with central Asia reported that the profits were good but that they lived in fear of police harassment. When they returned to Xinjiang he said they 'hugged the police and said that home was safe and China had laws'.

Abdul was not caught out by the collapse of the Tashkent market because by then he had also diversified into the Shanghai restaurant business, in a manner reminiscent of Hashim's father. Abdul's Uygur friend has since this failure, started again and built a second market area in Tashkent. The restaurant business began with a small eating house or *ashxane* which made and sold fresh *naan* (bread). Other *ashxane* exist specialising in, for example, making kebab. The typical starting point for these small Uygur restaurants is to become a petty vendor of fast food. Six years later he was able to build on a number of these and set up a more ambitious restaurant. In 2006 he owned six small *naan* shops and one restaurant employing between 35 and 58 Uygurs, plus a number of part-time Uygur students studying in Shanghai. He and his wife have also purchased urban property in Ürümqi. His wife also played an important role in exporting Shanghai textiles—she would attend to the business in Shanghai while Abdul received the goods in the various central Asian markets in which he had established outlets. More recently, her main function is to train Uygur labourers in the restaurant business and attend to their official documents including Health Certificates, Temporary Residence Permits and Work Permits with Tax Numbers. The Shanghai government is strict in insisting on all employers filing these three documents.

Over time, Abdul's wife has played an increasing role in the family business because literacy has become indispensable for not only conforming to official regulations but also handling the volume of transactions that their businesses generate. In 2006 Abdul was still illiterate and unschooled, and according to local gossip, until 2004 did not have a mobile phone as he could not dial the numbers. Ninety per cent of Abdul's Shanghai staff are migrants from Kashgar and Artush. They are all Uygur specialists: *naan* and kebab makers, makers of pomegranate juice, dancers and musicians. One of the most prestigious Uygur restaurants in Shanghai has four dancing girls who are prohibited from performing at any venues except the restaurant as a way of preserving their good name and reputation. Abdul's employees are typically single and in their 20s, with little or no knowledge of Mandarin. The owners of the restaurants are, therefore, also guardians who enforce strict rules about the movements of these young people. For example, when a young employee goes out to shop for, say, needles and thread, they must be accompanied by an experienced adult because without a good knowledge of the Han language they may be questioned by the local police and taken away. The Uygur are physically distinctive from the Han and Hui and given the association of some Shanghai Uygur youth with local criminals, they are at risk of being discriminated against by the authorities.

Had Abdul continued to depend on his wife alone for expanding his business, he would have had limited opportunities. But fortunately, he befriended another Uygur of roughly similar age whose family roots in Shanghai began in 1948. Javed was an engineering graduate who in 1994 gave up a good government position and migrated to Turkey. But Javed's wife did not enjoy living in Turkey, so they returned to Shanghai to find themselves unemployed. Fortunately, before going to Turkey and during his stay there, Javed had developed a small import-export business in curtains. This allowed them to survive until Javed met Abdul and realised that Abdul's illiteracy was limiting his capacity to expand the business: 'he needs my educated brain.' says Javed, 'and my connection in Shanghai as an old Shanghainese. I need his boldness and capital to invest.' Together Abdul and Javed have formed a new business venture which also includes the manager of a state-owned textile firm.

What insights does this case study reveal for our hypothesis that the mobility of the Uygur minority is directly related to Uygur entrepreneurship? For more than 30 years, the life of Abdul has been a life of migration to search out business opportunities. Well before he settled in Shanghai in the late 1970s, he was constantly moving in search of more interesting textiles. In Abdul we see the intimate, long-term connection between labour mobility and entrepreneurship. We also come to appreciate that his business acumen was no duller for lack of education or even elementary schooling. To a considerable degree he made up for his illiteracy by developing partnerships with other Uygur businessmen and advisors who supported his ventures in central Asia, enabled him to expand his restaurant business in Shanghai and who are now working with him on a large project that seeks to promote tourism along the 'old Silk Road'. In bringing these partners into his circle he directly created employment for them and their employees while his *naan* shops and restaurants in Shanghai employ an estimated 80 persons, most of whom send money back home to their parents. Perhaps his illiteracy drove him into creating wider business alliances and hence more ambitious commercial projects such as building a large market in Tashkent?

Conclusion: Uygur entrepreneurship and the state

Uygur entrepreneurship is a little understood phenomenon as is the history of Uygur trade with eastern China, the border countries and internationally. Trade patterns and investment have facilitated migration of Uygur entrepreneurs and labour. The case studies in this paper suggest that despite the assumption in much of the literature of Xinjiang that the Uygurs suffer from ongoing immiserisation, the traditions of entrepreneurship amongst the Uygurs are still very much alive. Many of the Uygur business people interviewed by us said that they had 'business in their blood'. Their perception of business opportunities has compelled them to widen their business networks to other parts of China, neighbouring countries and abroad. Migration is a typical aspect of these extensive business interests, but there are always exceptions to the rule. For example, despite his commercial successes, extensive travels and business deals in south/central Asia and Shanghai, Salim has not migrated away from his ancestral town of Artush. As we have argued, this is because if you are importing skins from south and central Asia it is best to stay put in Artush which is right next door to the markets from which you are sourcing your raw materials. Hashim's father, by contrast, moved around a great deal and was also a temporary resident in Shanghai. But he has retired back to Kashgar where his sons' wives and children also live. The sons, however, spend considerable amounts of time in Shanghai as temporary residents managing the business that their father built. Our final case study of Abdul is of a Uygur merchant who has been a permanent resident of Shanghai for many decades but was an itinerant trader before that and continues to travel widely in search of new commercial openings.

But whether the entrepreneurs of Kashgar migrate temporarily or permanently or not at all, their business dealings with the cities of south/central Asia and the eastern Chinese seaboard all generate further linkages which in turn create niche employment in those cities for Uygur migrants of all kinds: temporary, permanent and itinerant; managers and labourers; entrepreneurs and advisors/partners. This paper has focused on the Kashgari entrepreneurs of Shanghai, but many other Uygur businessmen thrive in that cosmopolitan city—one of our interviewees originated from Ili and had distinguished himself by introducing into China's hosiery industry stockings interwoven with gold threads. He had copied this from a tourist lady of Turkish origin whom he had seen in Shanghai.

The achievements of these entrepreneurs are especially impressive given the lack of state patronage to their efforts. However, without state support (which includes easier access to bank loans), Uygur entrepreneurs do not have reliable networks beyond their own community. Without the patronage of the state sector, the military and paramilitary, the wealth of these entrepreneurs is unlikely to reach the scale achieved by Xinjiang's millionaire entrepreneurs—Aikelamu Aishayoufu and Sun Guangxin, for example (Vicziany & Zhang 2004). Given this, how can the Uygur traders and restaurateurs analysed in this chapter expand their businesses? In a previous paper we suggested that it might be easier for a Uygur entrepreneur to grow his concern by setting up a business in the US rather than hope for expansion in Xinjiang (Vicziany & Zhang 2004).

In the food vendor and restaurant business a critical ingredient in success is to locate the business in a good area with reliable customers and a brisk business. To achieve this, one of the kebab restaurateurs we interviewed had set up a joint venture with a Han businessman, hoping to secure Chinese influence in setting up the business in a good location. The Han partner ran off with RMB100,000 of his capital and after an expensive court case and a decision that went against the Uygur businessman, they had to transfer an additional RMB 100,000 to the person from whom they had purchased the land. In the end the restaurant was set up with a mere RMB 23,000 in cash. When asked what went wrong in this joint venture, this Kashgari Uygur said that this 'only happened because we did not speak Chinese very well and did not understand Chinese very well'. Incidents such as these cannot be controlled by any state authority, for cheating and embezzlement are rife in post-reform China. The burden of proof is hard to meet in a cross-cultural setting where a lot of suspicion is directed at the Uygur community in general. Joint ventures with Chinese partners, in other words, can increase the risk of business rather than reduce it. On the other hand, the state can play a more generous role in the provision of business licenses. There is a persistent view amongst the Uygur entrepreneurs that the formalities associated with setting up and managing their businesses are more difficult to complete than in the case of Han business people. Governments in China need to work harder at eliminating these perceptions and addressing the problems that may exist in this area. But it would be wrong to say that governments in China were invariably unfair or unjust in matters related to Uygur business. One of the entrepreneurs we interviewed said that a couple of his restaurants were located in the path of new freeways and government buildings, but that they had been well compensated for the loss of land and business. The Shanghai government had been 'fair and just' in a manner that would never have happened in Xinjiang. Of course, it is difficult to generalise from a single case study—certainly the Beijing government in recent years has been less sympathetic to the rapid growth of some 'ethnic villages'. In March 1999, for example, a Uygur village in western Beijing was razed on the justification that it was harbouring criminals (Khun cited in Ma & Xiang 2003:166–7).

Some affirmative action by governments in China to promote minority entrepreneurship in China would not be misplaced. This is especially so because the expanding business opportunities for the Uygurs are not exclusive to them. There are competing entrepreneurs not only in China but also in the neighbouring Islamic republics and Pakistan. Sean Roberts, for example, has noted that foreign buyers from neighbouring countries have started to source their goods directly from the industrial towns of eastern China, thereby bypassing the towns of Xinjiang that used to act as trade entrepots in the past (Roberts 2004:222–3). Xinjiang might still have bargains to offer, but higher quality goods are easier to obtain in quantity from the factories of origin that are located along China's eastern seaboard. Roberts notes that the Uygur merchants who operate from the bazaars of central Asia have survived this challenge by specialising in the sale of particular products that they have pooled from diverse sources inside China (Roberts 2004:223). Yet it is only a matter of time before south and central Asian entrepreneurs discover the same idea, thereby putting the Uygur merchants under more pressure.

Promoting Uygur entrepreneurship is not merely one way of creating jobs for Uygurs and reducing poverty in Xinjiang. Major national interests can also be served by China using the cultural and social networks of the Uygurs to promote expanded cross-border trade. China has a growing energy crisis and since the late 1990s has become an importer of oil and gas. At first it was hoped that the extent of import dependency could be reduced by oil and gas extraction in Xinjiang. But new estimates suggest that the oil reserves of the Tarim basin are fewer than two billion barrels, a tiny fraction of the original figure of 482 billion (Gladney 2003:21). Despite diversifying China's energy imports to include Sudanese oil, Kazakhstan remains a major source of supply. No sooner had the oil pipeline from Kazakhstan to China been completed via the Altai Pass in December 2005, bilateral discussions began on the subject of a natural gas pipeline (*China Daily* 2006a). Although the bulk of the bilateral trade between China and Kazakhstan (worth US$6.1 billion in 2005) takes place via state-owned enterprises, the large number of Uygurs in Kazakhstan (and the other Islamic republics in the region) provides a wider economic base for other trade opportunities which are valuable if China wants to contain its potential trade deficit with its neighbours. Trade also creates employment and wealth; encouraging Uygur entrepreneurship will contribute more to the ethnic stability in Xinjiang than coercive measures that seek to achieve regional 'security'.

Notes

We are grateful to Dr Ayxe Eli (Max Planck Institute, Halle) for her work as the research assistant to this project.

1 As Mackerras (2004:table 2) shows, between the 1990 and 2000 census the Uygur population fell by a further 2.3% while the Han population increased by 3%.

2 As Gladney (2003:11) notes, the Uygur diaspora of some half a million, has about 25 international websites and organisations working for the independence of 'East Turkistan'; these are all engaged in a discussion of the conditions of Uygurs in China and how and why they would leave if they could.

3 Table 7.2 in Tsui (2003) shows that of 718 responses in two surveys of Uygurs, 62% of responses indicated dependence on relative and ethnic friends (35% and 27% respectively), 27% on government, 4.5% on non-Uygur and 5.8% on mosques.

4 The Uygur are an Islamic minority or 'nationality' that speaks Uygur, a Turkic language. They regard themselves as the ancestors of numerous famous Islamic kingdoms dating from the seventh century onwards. Originally based in the northern parts of China, over the centuries these kingdoms and socio-cultural groups moved further south establishing political and social bastions in the region around Kashgar and Hothan. The Uygur are distinctive from the Hui minority who are ethnically Chinese and converted to Islam. Today, the two Islamic minorities are also regionally distinctive with the Ugyur living predominantly in Xinjiang and the Hui in central and eastern China.

5 These families involved a total population of 25,617 of which 16,416 were rural labourers. The sample covered the 12 western provinces of Inner Mongolia, Guangxi, Sichuan, Guizhou, Yunnan, Tibet, Chongqing, Shanxi, Gansu, Qinghai, Ningxia and Xinjiang. A detailed breakdown of the characteristics of migrants from these provinces was not provided.

6 Fieldwork by Vicziany in Xinjiang in 2001, 2003, 2004 and 2005.

7 Hoy and Qiang (2003) report that other small Uygur communities can be found in the Beijing metropolis at Madian, Jintai Lu, Hepingli and Tianquiao.

8 Solinger (1999:11) notes that her book 'explores the manner in which peasant migration into the cities of China at the end of socialism distinguished it…from seemingly similar cityward movement elsewhere in the developing world'. Her study does not consider the special case of China's minorities, who have also been on the move.

9 According to Hoy and Qiang (2003:162) the registered Uygurs of Beijing in the 1990s numbered 1,736 or 0.5% of the minority population. This information appears to be based on the Population Census data for 1990 and published in 1992.

10 The other Muslim minorities of the PRC are: Dongxiang (0.4 million), Kyrgyz (0.2 million), Salar (0.09 million), Tajik (0.04 million), Uzbek (0.014 million), Baonan (0.005 million) (Gladney 2003:7).

11 The biographies of the Kashgar and Ili entrepreneurs of Shanghai are based on interviews with a dozen business people conducted on 19–25 December 2005. We also interviewed entrepreneurs and labourers from Ürümqi, Hami, Korla and Ili.

chapter five

Labour mobility and the ASEAN–China free trade area

David Treisman

Overview

The proposed Association of South East Asian Nations (ASEAN)–China free trade area will encompass at least 1.7 billion consumers and sustain trade volumes in excess of US$1.23 trillion (ASEAN-CEGEC 2001:2). An ASEAN–China free trade area will have a considerable impact on economies in the Asia-Pacific region. A timetable has been outlined for achieving the required provision of free trade in goods, service and investment by the year 2015 (ASEAN 2002:Article 3).

The Asia-Pacific's unprecedented GDP growth in the first half of the 1990s was underpinned by a change in the demand for labour across the region resulting from increases in exports and investment (Manning 2000). The GDP growth rates experienced during the first half of the 1990s are now, post-1997 Asian financial crisis, returning to the region and a desire for closer regional economic integration is beginning to resurface. As a fundamental factor of production, labour will always play a significant role in the Asia-Pacific. However, while there is growing emphasis given to internal labour migration issues in China, as other contributions to this volume attest, concerns over labour and labour mobility between China and the rest of Asia have been given insufficient attention by policy makers in their desire to move toward greater regional economic integration.

This chapter will argue that the impact of an ASEAN–China free trade area on the region's labour and labour mobility has not been adequately dealt with by policymakers. The purpose of this chapter is to provide a foundation on which to examine the inter-connectedness between China and ASEAN's exports, trade and investment and labour mobility in light of the burgeoning free trade area.

The following section provides an overview of the proposed ASEAN–China Free trade area. Subsequent sections outline the nature and extent of China and ASEAN's trade in goods, services and investment and the impact of an ASEAN–China free trade area on labour and labour mobility within the Asia-Pacific region. The final section concludes the chapter.

The ASEAN–China free trade agreement

In November 2002 the Eighth ASEAN Summit held in Phnom Penh culminated in the signing of the *Framework Agreement on Comprehensive Economic Co-operation Between the Association of South East Asian Nations and the People's Republic of China* (the Framework Agreement). The Framework Agreement was the formalisation of the shared desire of ASEAN and China for greater regional integration in the wake of the 1997 Asian financial crisis (ASEAN 2002). The Framework Agreement was intended to begin the process toward the formation of a free trade area between the ten member nations of ASEAN and China. The Framework Agreement outlined a broad arrangement for economic co-operation in order to, among other things, 'increase intra-regional trade and investment' and 'enhance the attractiveness of the Parties [China and ASEAN] to capital and talent' (ASEAN 2002:preamble). The Framework Agreement provided for a phased removal of barriers and deepening of economic linkages between ASEAN and China that is intended to be completed by 2015. The Framework Agreement also stipulated a ten-year timescale in which to form a free trade area (ASEAN 2002:Articles 2 & 3).

An ASEAN–China free trade area will have a considerable impact on the regional and world economy as it will encompass a 1.7 billion consumer base with a US$ 2 trillion GDP and total trade of US$ 1.23 trillion (ASEAN-CEGEC 2001:2). The process toward the formation of an ASEAN–China free trade area took a major step forward with the conclusion of an agreement on trade in goods signed between ASEAN and China in November 2004 at the Tenth ASEAN Summit and appears to be on track in the negotiation of agreements on services and investment (ASEAN 2004a; 2005).

Exports, investments and services and the ASEAN–China free trade area

The process toward the formation of an ASEAN–China free trade area is still developing and the economic efficiencies inherent in such an area are not as yet demonstrable. However, the scale and scope of such a free trade area will have an impact on unemployment and labour mobility within ASEAN and China. As the demand for labour is dependent upon demand for the goods and/or services produced using these labour inputs, so this demand, in turn, is dependent upon sector competitiveness between ASEAN and China (Gwartney, Stroup & Sobel

2000). ASEAN and China have several overlapping complimentary sectors of production.

Trade between ASEAN and China continues to rise, with a disproportionate dominance of Chinese trade over the newer ASEAN members; namely, Laos, Myanmar and Vietnam (all of whom share a border with China). ASEAN is China's fifth largest export-market; however, both ASEAN's and China's trade remain oriented towards the developed market economies of Japan, the United States and the European Union (ASEAN-CEGEC 2001).

The importance of extra-regional trade to both ASEAN and China cannot be overemphasised. The United States, European Union and Japan are ASEAN and China's largest export markets. These exports are dominated by similar goods and services. Thus intra-regional competitiveness is apparent and overrides intra-regional trade. Accordingly, intra-regional competition is critical and will be heavily influenced by the similarity (overlapping) of exports extra-regionally (Yue 2004).

Table 1: Overlap of exports between China and ASEAN countries

ASEAN member country	**Percentage overlap in exports with China to the US 1990–2002**
Indonesia	83.5
Thailand	76.1
Philippines	57.0
Malaysia	54.5
Singapore	44.2

Source: Yue (2004).

Table 1 demonstrates the significant overlap in exports in ASEAN and China's extra-regional competition for markets. A recent Asian Development Bank Institute paper examined the impact of competition between China and ASEAN in the key export markets of Japan and United States. The paper's empirical findings indicated that ASEAN has lost overall market share to China in the Japanese and United States markets and most notably lost market share in exports of electrics, electronics, engineering, labour-intensive and high-technology products. The technological sophistication of ASEAN exporters relative to their Chinese competitors was found to have provided general but limited protection (Weiss & Gao 2003).

Yue (2004) argues that in order to mitigate the predominance of China's extra-regional trade to that of ASEAN, ASEAN will need to increase the pace with which it introduces economic reforms and industrial restructuring in order to provide a means of improving skills and technology. However, most of ASEAN's member states remain preoccupied with political and social stability and/or lack the required resources with which to reform and restructure (Yue 2004).

Chinese imports from ASEAN are dominated by computer, machinery and electrical equipment, which constitute 38.2% of ASEAN exports to China (ASEAN-CEGEC 2001:9). ASEAN imports from China are similarly dominated by computer, machinery and electrical equipment that constitute approximately 50% of Chinese exports to ASEAN (ASEAN-CEGEC 2001:10). The composition of trade in computer, machinery and electrical equipment differ between China and ASEAN, with the majority of the Chinese exports comprising complete computer, machinery and electrical equipment for general or specialised use. ASEAN's exports of computer, machinery and electrical equipment comprised mainly of electronic components and devices, which are predominately exports from Malaysia, Philippines, Singapore and Thailand. ASEAN does maintain a comparative advantage in the production of mineral products, plastics/rubber, wood, wood articles, pulp and paper and fats and oils (ASEAN-CEGEC 2001).

The importance of computer, machinery and electrical equipment in the trade relationship between ASEAN and China is emphasised by policy makers as being indicative of intra-industry trade, based on product differentiation and economies of scale. In accordance with this argument, policy makers believe that the rise in trade-based investment between ASEAN and China has largely been made through multinational corporations and it is these multinational corporations' inter-regional strategic investment schemes that will perpetuate further trade-based investment between the regions. However, ASEAN and China are not significant sources of foreign direct investment in each others economies and compete for foreign investment globally (ASEAN 2005).

ASEAN's trade in commercial services is greater than that of China in volume. In 2000 China is estimated to have exported US$ 30.15 billion in services and imported US$ 35.86 billion in services, while ASEAN exported US$ 62.5 billion and imported US$ 69.75 billion in services (ASEAN-CEGEC 2001:13). Trade in services between ASEAN and China is expected to grow in accordance with the overall expected growth of the Chinese and ASEAN economies. The expected growth in services in the ASEAN–China free trade area has the potential to significantly impact on the regional and global economy.

ASEAN and China have a broad-based economic relationship that has been strengthened through the conclusion of the Framework Agreement and the Agreement on Trade in Goods. ASEAN and China remain competitors for foreign direct investment, services and exports in goods extra-regionally. ASEAN and China would, in the long run, gain from closer economic integration. The desire for closer integration is explicitly outlined in the Framework Agreement. In the short run the ASEAN Secretariat recognises that:

> ...the ensuing intensified competition in each region's domestic market given the similarity in industrial structures of ASEAN and China may entail short-run costs in the form of displacement of workers and rationalisation of some industries and firms. (ASEAN 2005:2)

Labour and the ASEAN–China free trade area

Labour and labour mobility within the proposed ASEAN–China Free trade area has been given little consideration in the negotiation process and neither the Framework Agreement nor the Agreement on Trade in Goods explicitly discusses the role of labour within the free trade area. Labour mobility across regions is an indicator of integration between markets. Without consideration of labour mobility between ASEAN and China, the ability of the free trade area to 'increase economic efficiency' will be hindered.

The ASEAN labour ministers recognise the need and desire for a common market for labour within their own member countries (ASEAN 2004b). The development of a common market for labour between ASEAN members is in its infancy and remains focussed on the free flow of professional services by the year 2020 (Soesastro 2003). It is difficult to quantify the actual flow of labour, as ASEAN and China's labour migration statistics are inaccurate and the recording of labour movement is inconsistent (Wickramasekera 2002; ILO 2004).

The ASEAN–China Free trade area is expected to have a considerable impact on labour as a free trade area consisting of at least 1.7 billion consumers will require a large base of household income which, in turn, will require broad-based employment. It has been argued that in the Asia-Pacific region three factors will be decisive in determining labour mobility within the region; namely, rapid economic growth, expansion of foreign direct investment and the slow-down in labour supply growth (Manning 2000). A fourth factor that can be added to this list is political imperatives.

Rapid economic growth in the Asia-Pacific has been largely driven by sustained high exports levels. Rapid economic growth in export-led economies has created an increased demand for unskilled labour (Manning 2000). China and ASEAN are economies that are export-led in their growth, the levels of which are expected to increase rapidly over a sustained time period. The ASEAN–China free trade area is expected to create additional intra-regional demand for goods and thus demand for unskilled labour is likely to persist. The Chinese response to an increase in the demand for unskilled labour has been to source additional labour from its rural areas, although since the Spring Festival in 2004 there have been labour shortages in some regions along the coast (for further details see Chapter 2). Unskilled labour tends to move around ASEAN; however, this does not occur under the guise of a common market for labour and as such, its prevalence is restricted to limited areas. ASEAN and China's policy on labour mobility across the free trade area remains ambiguous and will need to be addressed as this issue may begin to threaten exports. At this point, regardless of the economic factors, there is no mobility of labour across the free trade area as such freedom of movement is not contemplated by the respective political regimes.

Foreign direct investment (FDI) in the Asia-Pacific region, coupled with economic growth, has historically culminated in a labour demand that has been supplied through foreign labourers (Manning 2000). FDI intra- and extra-regionally is expected to increase under the ASEAN–China free trade area. The increase in FDI is expected to occur predominantly through the expansion of multinational corporations' operations across the region and thus is likely to further stimulate the demand for labour and the supply of foreign labour within the free trade area.

Labour and labour mobility has been given insufficient attention in the formation of an ASEAN–China free trade area. Economic growth through exports is expected to be maintained along with the demand for unskilled labour. Similarly, the demand for skilled labour will increase as the operations of multinationals expand through further foreign direct investment. No unified policy on regional labour mobility has been put forward. The substitutability of products from either ASEAN or China still remains in question, especially in light of the similarity in ASEAN and China's industrial structures. The similarities in the industrial bases of China and ASEAN are expected to cause short-run unemployment and rationalisation of industries. As Dorothy Solinger's chapter in this volume indicates, the resultant job losses in China from industry rationalisation in China will need to be managed sensitively given the large amounts of labour shedding from the state-owned sector that have occurred since the mid-1990s. The possible domination of the free trade area by China and the politically sensitive issue of freedom of movement also pose potential difficulties for the Framework Agreement in meeting its mandate and for the improvement of labour mobility intra-regionally.

Conclusion

An ASEAN–China free trade area will have a considerable impact on the regional and world economy. The Framework Agreement has placed greater economic integration between ASEAN and China firmly on the policy agenda.

A deadline of 2015 has been set for the removal of barriers and the deepening of economic linkages between ASEAN and China. This realisation of a free trade area between ASEAN and China by this deadline took a considerable step forward with the conclusion of the ASEAN–China Agreement on Trade in Goods.

What are the likely effects on the demand for labour through the creation of an ASEAN–China free trade area? The answer to the question is increasingly important. The demand for labour is derived from the demand for the product that the labour produces. This demand for labour is further dependent on the substitutability of the products produced and by the labour input itself.

ASEAN currently maintains a comparative advantage in several export sectors and it provides several complimentary components in the production of computer, machinery and electrical equipment in China. Similarly, ASEAN currently provides a greater volume of commercial services than China with trade-based investment within the region expected to benefit all parties concerned. The similarity in industrial structures between ASEAN member states and China is expected to create short-term unemployment and rationalisation.

The similarity in industrial structures and the high dependency of growth by ASEAN and China on exports combined with the effects of labour mobility (or immobility, as the case may be) raises doubts that the mandated purpose of the Framework Agreement, in increasing intra-regional trade, investment and enhancing the attractiveness of ASEAN and China to capital and talent, will be fulfilled.

ASEAN and China will need to address concerns over labour and labour mobility more formally in order to fulfil the mandate of the Framework Agreement. Similarly, ASEAN will need to increase the pace of its policy formulation and implementation in the creation of a common market for labour in order to prevent domination by China in the proposed free trade area.

Section II

Emerging issues for China's floating population

chapter six

Working conditions of migrant labourers

Serena Lillywhite

Overview of working conditions and labour mobility in China

This chapter provides a broad overview of the working conditions and discrimination faced by many of China's migrant workers in the export processing factories located in the Pearl River Delta. A case study of the working and living conditions in selected factories that manufacture spectacles for the global market is included. Since the mid-1990s there have been enormous changes in China's labour market. There is increased pressure for urban employment as the labour force grows faster than jobs become available. Reform of state-owned enterprises has had perhaps the most significant impact and resulted in vast numbers of workers being retrenched. Despite statistical uncertainties, evidence suggests that over 27 million workers were laid off from 1998 to 2002 (UN 2005b). Rural–urban migration has also changed the labour market landscape. Accurate labour statistics in China are difficult to obtain, due in part to workers' mobility and the lack of urban *hukou* (household registration) status for rural–urban migrants, which historically has resulted in migrant workers being excluded from official statistics (Meng, Gregory & Wang 2005; Appleton et al 2001). China's Ministry of Labour and Social Security estimates there are 130 million migrant workers (China View 2006) and the 2000 census identified that 74.9% of inter-provincial migrant workers were seeking employment in the eastern provinces (UN 2005b). However, 'by 2004, the number of rural migrants reached 140 million, representing the largest population movement in China's history' (UN 2005b:8). The exact proportion of migrant workers in the export-oriented factories is not known, although the widely held view is that it is about 80%. The United Nations Research Institute for Social Development has identified that women make up 80% of the workforce in export processing facilities (Davin 2001).

Despite China's significant progress in addressing poverty, literacy, education, employment, and public health, these developments have occurred faster in urban than rural areas, and considerable inequity remains between rural provinces. The

UNDP *China Development Report* (UN 2005b) confirmed that rural locations continue to have higher levels of illiteracy, higher mortality, higher malnutrition among children, little access to medical services, and fewer opportunities for education, employment and participation in society. In this context, it is not difficult to understand the motivation for workers, predominantly female aged between 16 and 25 years, to seek employment in China's manufacturing sector, despite growing knowledge of the long hours, wage discrimination and crowded living conditions with insufficient water and power, and poor quality food.

Much has been written about the working conditions of China's rural migrants by academics and activists from the anti-sweat shop movement.[1] There have been some noteworthy improvements, particularly in occupational health and safety and physical factory environments. Rural and urban workers encounter the same factory environments, occupational health and safety conditions and limitations in raising grievances and settling disputes. However, wages, hours, fines, and access to social security entitlements continue to be the source of greatest disparity between rural and urban workers. In addition, harsh dormitory conditions are more often endured by migrant workers as local workers have more options to live outside the factory or have access to better factory accommodation to reflect their seniority within factory management.

China is increasingly referred to as 'the world's factory', with migrant workers contributing significantly to its economic boom. Most of these workers are employed in private enterprises in China's burgeoning urban industrialised and manufacturing zones. There is growing awareness among not only civil society advocates, but also multinational enterprises and the Chinese government, that the burden of economic development is being felt most by China's migrant workers. Whilst the situation varies from city to city, and between factories, rural migrant workers moving to cities face many forms of employment discrimination and social inequality. This chapter focuses on wages, hours, fines and access to social security entitlements. Consideration will also be given to the personal hardship and abuse migrant workers encounter, resulting in social exclusion, isolation and loneliness.

Generational differences in migrant labour also need to be considered. The 'new generation Chinese migrant worker', aged 18 to 25, is characterised as more educated, with higher career expectations, demanding a higher quality of life and less tolerant of poor conditions than their parents. Yet most young migrant workers are unable to find jobs that meet their aspirations and end up facing the same discrimination as their parents (Frost 2005a). As a consequence they will change jobs frequently if conditions are bad and salaries low. The new generation of migrant workers is highly mobile, which contributes to instability in labour supply (Ho, B 2006).

Working for nothing—wage discrimination, arrears and fines

China's labour law (PRC 1994) clearly stipulates minimum wage rates (based on a living wage deemed appropriate for location), penalty and overtime rates. However, minimum wages are rarely paid, with migrant workers incurring the greatest wage discrimination: 'On average, migrant workers earn roughly 80% of the wages of local urban workers with the same skills' (UN 2005b). Not only do migrant workers receive a lower wage with the same skill set, but practices in the optical industry suggest that migrant workers may be paid less for performing the same job as a local worker.

There is growing awareness of wage irregularities and lack of compliance with the law among workers, factory managers, Department of Labour officials, trade union representatives and some multinational enterprises sourcing goods in China. Little has been achieved in addressing this fundamental labour rights issue, with migrant incomes progressively falling in real terms (Chan 2003). According to the Ministry of Labour and Social Security, 'salaries of migrant workers in the Pearl River Delta have grown by only 68 RMB (US$8.20) over the last 12 years, far behind the increase in living expenses'(CLB 2004).

Migrant workers face further remuneration hardship as wages are increasingly not being paid, being paid irregularly, and held in arrears by factory managers (either as a worker management technique or as a result of poor fiscal planning and cash flow problems). It has been estimated that 72% of migrants have suffered from varying degrees of wage defaults (Chan 2005). This issue is most serious in the export-oriented factories, with reports of unpaid wages common, sometimes up to one year in arrears. There has been little success to date in resolving the issue of declining and unpaid wages. According to Chan, 'the best authorities could do was to assist a small number of workers 'chase back' owed wages prior to the Chinese New Year holiday…Today it looks like migrant workers have found their own solution—by withdrawing labour and staying at home causing a shortage of migrant workers' (Chan 2005:5).

Labour shortages and factory conditions

In 2004, China's Ministry of Labour and Social Security reported a shortfall of two million migrant workers for the Guandong region (*Economist* 2004). As discussed more fully in the chapter in this volume by Wang Dewen, Cai Fang and Gao Wenshu, the reported labour shortages could potentially reduce China's key competitive advantage: an endless supply of cheap labour. In shortest supply are women aged 18–25 (Harney 2004) who are most sought after because they work quickly and comply with factory rules. This is having the greatest impact in the manufacturing, wholesale and retailing and hospitality sectors.

There is growing evidence that labour shortages are having a positive impact on conditions in some workplaces. Some factories are improving the food and increasing the flexibility of living arrangements in an attempt to retain workers. Chan makes an interesting observation that, 'unable to collectively bargain at the workplace, the rural population of China, without organising themselves, are engaging in a form of spontaneous collective action [by not returning to factories with poor conditions after Chinese New Year] and initiating changes in China's macro-labour market. In this sense, from the poor work conditions something positive is being generated' (Chan 2005:6).

An arbitrary system of fines and deductions exists throughout the manufacturing sector for 'misdemeanours'. Whilst this practice is common, each factory has determined its own fines. For example, in the optical industry deductions are made for absenteeism, refusal to undertake overtime, not meeting production quotas, untidy dormitories, spending too long in the toilet, arguing with other workers and management, exceeding the allocation of water for personal use, returning to the dormitory after curfew, playing cards in the dormitory and having dormitory lights on after 'lights out'.[2] This practice can significantly further reduce workers' income. In some instances fines are part of a strategy to manage workers and minimise overhead costs.

Working 9 to 5—'no way to make a living'

The issue of wages and hours are widely considered as the greatest challenge in improving labour standards. According to Ryder (2006), 'China is trying to sweatshop its way to success, through low wages and exploitation of a workforce that has no effective means of representation. The people toiling behind the hollow miracle often work 60–70 hour weeks, live in 16-bed dormitories, can earn less than USD$44 per month and face unemployment if injured at work'.

Long hours of work and excessive overtime are also a major characteristic of migrant working conditions, particularly in export processing factories. China's labour law stipulates eight hours a day and 40 hours per week. Legally, overtime is limited to a maximum of three hours each day, and should not exceed 36 hours a month. Workers are entitled to one day off in every seven (PRC 1994: Article 41). This requirement is rarely met. Most migrants work six days a week, usually 70 hours a week and up to 100 hours a week in peak production periods (Chan 2005). Multinational enterprises, and in particular international brands, often allow a limit of 60 hours per week in their codes of conduct, although this technically does not comply with national law. Research conducted by Verité[3] confirms that 'both legal limits and the guidelines outlined in corporate codes of conduct are routinely violated in Chinese supplier factories' (Verité 2004:8). Further research by Verité in 2003 in 40 export factories (predominantly garment, shoe and knitting) confirmed that 20–24 hours overtime a week is common, suggesting that overtime in excess of the Chinese legal monthly maximum is widespread for much of the year.

Underpayment of overtime and piece rate entitlements is common, with many workers themselves uncertain of their legal entitlements and how much to expect when they are paid, resulting in unequal and unfair payment for work completed. Failure to pay legal overtime rates that reflect whether the overtime was undertaken on a normal workday, a scheduled day off or on a holiday, is widespread.

Financial incentives are a key factor in migrant workers' decisions to seek employment in export processing factories. Their objective is to remit as much income as possible to their families for a concentrated period of 6–9 years, as well as to broadening their opportunities and life experiences, before returning home. This implies workers have choices in hours, which is rarely the case, particularly during peak production, when workers face arbitrary fines for not participating in overtime or meeting production quotas. 'The combination of financial pressures arising from underpayment of wages, and coercion related to factory rules or quota requirements can function like forced overtime'(Verité 2004:15), although factory managers rarely concede that overtime is compulsory when asked.[4]

Factory managers are aware of the production inefficiencies (including reduced quality) that excessive overtime can bring. But overtime is still regarded as the best option to meet production emergencies. A related practice is the employment of 'temporary' workers. This results in employers evading the legal obligations that contract workers should enjoy. It further increases the practice of long hours, excessive overtime, and lack of social security entitlements. It was recently reported that temporary workers in a Chengdu factory of a major multinational company face significant discrimination: 'The factory employs 500 workers, 300 of whom are temporary. Temporary workers earn much less than formal workers. Formal workers can earn up to 1,700–2,000 RMB per month but temporary workers earn only 400–500 RMB, which is lower than the minimum wage. The factory canteen is divided between formal and temporary workers...other discrimination includes harsher punishment (fines), the need to pay for uniforms (free for formal workers), and the lack of social insurance as stipulated by China's Labour Law' (Ho, M 2006).

Occupational health and safety

The application of China's occupational health and safety laws[5] varies considerably between factories and sectors of industry. For example, China's mining industry is notorious for its poor safety record, workplace injuries and deaths. In the manufacturing sector, injuries and illness tend to be linked to hazardous chemicals and toxic fumes; cuts, abrasions and loss of fingers; repetitive strains; eye strain and back pain; hearing loss; and the mental and physical health implications of long hours of repetitive work. It has been reported that more than 200 million workers are exposed to occupational hazards, including about 100 million migrant workers in small and medium-sized enterprises and 136 million rural labourers working in township and village enterprises, making migrant workers most vulnerable to occupational diseases (Frost 2006).

Excessive overtime significantly impacts on migrant workers' physical and psychological well-being. Fatigue, exhaustion, sadness and depression are linked to long working hours (Verité 2004). There is increased recognition that migrant workers are developing serious mental health problems, often associated with frustration over their inability to raise grievances and speak about discrimination. There is also concern about serious health effects of long-term exposure to hazardous chemicals and toxic fumes, particularly in electroplating and injection moulding processes. These may not surface for many years, with compensation unlikely. The Verité study has confirmed that workers are beginning to recognise the health implications of long shifts. Even health professionals are beginning to report the grave health effects of excessive overtime (Verité 2004).

Another concern is the increase in Hepatitis B and the risk of it and other communicable diseases spreading through factory, dormitory and canteen environments. While it is illegal in China to discriminate against workers who test positive to Hepatitis B, there are growing reports of lack of employment opportunities and retrenchment of workers with Hepatitis B. Migrant workers are particularly vulnerable.

Social security entitlement

As Ingrid Nielsen and Russell Smyth discuss in their chapter, migrant workers face further discrimination with regard to social security entitlements. Despite the legal requirements of both employers and employees to contribute to health insurance, to compensate for workplace injuries, and pension funds, to assist with retirement, compliance is sporadic. In 2005, the Bureau of Labour and Social Security Bureau reported that 'while many migrant workers have occupational insurance, only 15% have retirement insurance, and only 10% have health insurance. Even fewer have unemployment or maternity insurance' (Frost 2005b). The reasons cited include lack of trust and confidence in the system, companies' reluctance to insure migrant workers due to increased labour costs, and prohibitive insurance fees (companies are required to pay 28% and workers 11% of the total wage to cover all insurance fees). A further barrier is that workers seldom work in the same city for 15 years, as required to access pension benefits. There is widespread agreement that China's social security and welfare entitlement system needs to be significantly amended to fit China's increasingly mobile labour market. This policy restructuring must be undertaken in parallel with changes to the *hukou* (household registration) system, so migrant workers have confidence that contributing to social security is worthwhile and that they will be able to access the benefits at any time, regardless of their place of residence. In the meantime, many workers are 'opting out' of social security schemes. This results in workers being unable to access public health services in the event of an immediate accident or illness (unless critical) due to cost. Further, the lack of insurance does not provide for long-term compensation for occupational illnesses that may take years to manifest.

Social exclusion

The social impact of systematic discrimination against migrant workers and their personal experiences of living away from home receives less attention than wages and hours. There is growing recognition, however, that migrant workers endure sexual, emotional and verbal abuse in the workplace and factory dormitories. Interviews with workers conducted by Yang (2005) confirm that migrant workers want to be treated with dignity and respect.

Long hours of repetitive work far from home contribute to workers' isolation. Many reveal their loneliness and frustration at being unable to participate in social activities and urban life despite becoming the largest cohort in certain cities. Like all young people they want to see films, go shopping, spend time with friends and develop intimate and sexual relationships. But as Chapter 8 demonstrates, the leisure activities of migrants are limited compared to urban locals. The gender imbalance in almost all factories and processing zones, along with dormitory accommodation, makes it difficult for young migrant women to form intimate relationships. 'Female factory workers often face lonely boring lives as single women. They want love, a normal social life and families. They need information on reproductive health and how to deal with sexual harassment, along with knowledge and facilities for gynaecological disease prevention in factories' (Liu 2005: 8).

For the 'new generation migrant worker' the reality of social isolation does not meet their aspirations and expectations of factory employment.

Case study: Migrant working conditions in focus—China's optical manufacturing sector[6]

Setting the scene

China currently produces 90% of the world's optical frames, including those imported by a small Australian company called Mod-Style. Since 2000, Mod-Style has been owned by the Brotherhood of St Laurence (BSL), an Australian non-government organisation (NGO) with a vision of promoting social justice and a whole of society framework for a poverty-free Australia. Mod-Style imports and wholesales optical frames for Australia's independent optical retailers.

The BSL accepted ownership of Mod-Style with a clear commitment to map the supply chain in China and understand the working and living conditions of migrant workers employed in supplier factories. This required consideration of compliance with China's labour law, barriers and opportunities to improving factory conditions, and an assessment of global trends in corporate social responsibility and China's response to growing customer expectations to source goods from factories with decent working conditions. Extensive discussions were held with optical factory owners in China and their representatives in Hong Kong, the Hong Kong Optical Manufacturers Association, brand name customers who use the same suppliers in China and NGOs, academics, trade unions and industrial hygienists based in Hong Kong, China, Australia, Europe and the United States. This work is ongoing.

The BSL experience provides insight into the complexity of China's migrant labour market, working conditions and the discrimination they encounter. The research confirms that whilst migrant workers face widespread discrimination, wage inequity and long hours, caution is required in labelling all export-oriented factories sweatshops. Conditions vary based on factors such as industry sector, production processes, factory size, ownership, management practices, labour shortages, customer expectations and purchasing power.

Factories and their processes are not homogeneous; there are differences in conditions for workers, compliance with labour and environmental standards, and managerial style, as there are in Australia. For example, some factories meet their obligations and provide social security entitlements for workers, but also have a heavy security presence and an arbitrary system of fines and deductions. Other factories provide state-of-the-art facilities and architect-designed plants, yet expect workers to undertake excessive overtime without appropriate pay.

Mapping the supply chain

Investigating the working conditions has involved identifying and regularly visiting the factories. Difficulties can arise due to complex production and subcontracting networks, licensing arrangements, geographic and language challenges and the additional constraints that small enterprises face as a result of limited resources and capacity.

When the BSL commenced this work in China in 2000, it had approximately 20 suppliers. This has since been consolidated to 8–10 factories. The decision to reduce suppliers was not based on a policy of 'cut–and-run' from factories with poor conditions, but was rather a choice to identify those factories that not only met commercial requirements, but also demonstrated a willingness to discuss labour rights issues and make incremental improvements to the working and living conditions of migrant workers. The intent was to establish long-term, stable, direct relationships with fewer suppliers. This rewards selected factories through increased orders, creates opportunities for improved communication with factory managers and results in better understanding of production complexities and growing labour mobility concerns.

All supplier factories are wholly Hong Kong-owned family businesses, with the well-educated and astute second generation significantly involved in the operations, often employing a mainland Chinese factory manager. Those factories with 1,500 workers or more have clearly appropriated the benefits of foreign direct investment, adapted technology and processes from Europe and Japan and created highly competitive operations. The size of factories influences not only conditions but also the complexity of subcontracting arrangements, with smaller factories often outsourcing electroplating processes and larger factories sometimes outsourcing small orders.

Understanding the workforce

The workforce in the optical industry is representative of the export-oriented manufacturing sector in China. The vast majority of workers (70–80%) are migrant workers, with young women aged 16–25 making up 85% of the workforce in all factories visited (12 to date, four of them more than once). Within this sector, 70% of all factory jobs are considered 'low-skilled' and 30% of positions are 'technical' and managerial. Senior positions are most often held by Hong Kong Chinese, relatives of the factory owner or 'local' Chinese from Shenzhen and Guangzhou.

These workers are primarily motivated by a financial objective, have a low level of education (though possibly higher than their parents), are generally not well-informed of their labour rights and are mostly employed in repetitive jobs. Staff turnover is high, with most workers staying with a factory for one to two years (this is longer than in some other sectors). Attracting and retaining workers is an increasing priority for factory management, with the migrant labour shortages that are occurring in the toy, textile, footwear and apparel sectors also evident in the optical industry. In late 2005, factory managers reported new incentives to encourage workers to return from the 2006 Chinee New Year holiday. These have included purchasing hard-to-obtain train tickets for workers, transporting them to train and bus stations and promising higher wages:

> 'We need to improve workers' conditions to keep good workers, have a stable workforce and avoid worker shortages'.
>
> Managing Director / owner Factory D, 2005

> 'Five to 10% of workers in each department did not return after the 2005 Chinese New Year holiday'.
>
> Factory supervisor, Factory C, 2005

The factory environment

China's optical industry exhibits varying environmental standards and physical conditions. The larger factories, which undertake electroplating on site, have sophisticated equipment, ventilation and waste management. In addition, some factories have their own water treatment plants, recycling programs and chemical inventory systems. However, this cannot be said for the smaller factories which have clearly not made the same investment in facilities, equipment and processes. Overall, factories' physical environments were generally better than anticipated. Most of the factories are clean, well-lit, with heating and cooling in some areas, or production shifts to 'beat the heat':

> 'During the summer work takes place at night as it is too hot for spraying and some other techniques'.
>
> Managing Director / owner, Factory B, 2005

Fire exits are well-marked and clear, although barred windows still feature in ground floor production areas. Dust masks, ear plugs and hair caps are provided (though wearing is not enforced). Some factories have specialised hands-free machines to reduce finger injuries. The overall impression, independently confirmed by Hong Kong based NGO's, is that these optical factories provide a better working environment and facilities than usually reported in the toy, footwear, textile and apparel industries .

In other respects, however, it cannot be said that the Chinese workers have achieved 'decent work' in the sense understood by the International Labour Organisation, or reasonable living conditions. For example, dormitory accommodation is often spartan and dehumanising. In the worst cases limits are placed on water usage and time for toilet breaks. Large, clean new factories do not guarantee good working conditions and may often mask serious human rights abuses:

> 'Workers can go to the toilet twice in the morning and twice in the afternoon. They will be fined if they spend too long there'.
>
> Vice President, Factory G, 2001

Labour standards

Significant human and labour rights issues exist in these factories, particularly with regard to wages, hours and social security entitlements. As in other export-processing sectors, these remain key areas of discrimination against migrant workers. There are clear breaches of China's labour law, often accompanied by hierarchical and at times repressive managerial regimes.

While factory managers claim that minimum wages are paid, the amount of overtime being undertaken and production targets (displayed on factory notice boards) suggest that workers are doing excessive overtime to compensate for low wages and to meet management expectations.

Overtime is a complex issue. On the one hand, workers want to undertake some overtime to supplement low wages, wage inequities and non-payment of wages. However, managers need to address growing consumer concerns about overtime and compliance with the law, while still meeting their increased production quotas and shorter delivery time expectations. Within the optical industry, the practice of not paying legal minimum wages, appropriate overtime and bonus payments and of imposing arbitrary fines and deductions, forces many workers to choose a factory where they are able to work unlimited overtime in order to survive:

> 'It's becoming harder to attract and keep skilled workers as we try and reduce overtime. Many workers just choose another factory where they are able to do unlimited overtime, and so don't support our efforts to reduce hours of work and comply'.
>
> Chief Executive Officer, Factory A, 2001

'The factory enforced the labour law of maximum number of hours of overtime. Initially the workers were not happy, other times supervisors were unhappy as they do not do OT so sometimes their salary is less than the workers. We had to negotiate a bonus one-by-one with each supervisor. Now workers are happy with more free time but this is a big problem when orders come in'.

Owner's son, Factory E, 2005

Optical factory managers have reported that they cannot comply with the legal hours of work. One view is that NGOs should accept this and campaign for workers to receive adequate remuneration for hours and overtime worked. However, this does not address the issue of industrial accidents and work-related deaths caused by overwork (Liu 2002) or the impact on workers' psychological well-being. To add to the complexity, there is growing recognition amongst some factory managers of the production inefficiencies and quality implications of prolonged and excessive overtime:

'A worn out workforce is of no use to me as they cannot concentrate and pose more of a risk to quality of production than a well-rested shift-driven team'.

Manager / owner, Factory H, 2005

'Actually it (voluntary overtime) depends on the supervisor, we do not want people doing OT if they really do not want to because the quality will not be high, but it is necessary at times, this is part of the employment process'.

Operation Manager, Factory F, 2001

Contradictions are ever-present. Growing demands for fair and decent working conditions from some global optical brands are at odds with their own sourcing timeframes and ordering processes. The frequency of peak production phases in the industry confirms that migrant workers get little relief from the often compulsory overtime during these 'production emergencies'. These coincide with peak global purchasing prior to Christmas, the lead-up to the two-week Chinese New Year holiday, and just before and after the major optical trade fairs—New York in March, Italy in May, France in October and Hong Kong in November:

'If the work needs to be done, it is compulsory.'

Managing Director / owner, Factory B, 2005

Workers have limited opportunity to raise grievances or disputes without fear of reprisal. In the optical sector, as in many others, the All China Federation of Trade Unions (ACFTU) does not function as an independent trade union to protect workers' rights or campaign for industrial improvements. Even the ACFTU is not clear about its responsibility to address labour disputes and grievances.[7] Despite these barriers, workers are beginning to complain about unfair practices:

> 'Sometimes workers complain if they think they have been treated unfairly. Usually about overtime payment and payment for bonuses for working fast and exceeding quotas, this is the most common reason.'
>
> Operation Manager, Factory F, 2001

In addition to wages and hours, access to social security entitlements is a source of discrimination encountered by migrant workers in this industry. Again, practice is mixed. Some factory managers meet all requirements, others make deductions but do not forward to the appropriate authorities and many grapple to understand the legal requirements:

> 'We need to continuously meet with the local Department of Labour to seek clarification of the law, but authorities often cannot help with interpretation particularly with regards to social security and insurance and bonus payments'.
>
> Director, Factory A, 2001

Workers frequently request a nil contribution (preferring the payment as part of their wage), as they have no confidence in being able to access entitlements that are currently linked to their *hukou* status. There is scepticism that payments made to urban authorities will not be transferred to rural villages for access on retirement. Similarly, many workers are prepared to risk having no accident insurance:

> 'All our workers, most that are poorly educated and from rural provinces, have no confidence they will ever access these benefits again'.
>
> Director, Factory A, 2001
>
> 'Actually if they have been with the factory for a long time and are skilled and not careless, we will help them with accident compensation'.
>
> Vice President, Factory G, 2001
>
> 'One-off costs such as building additional dormitories to improve living conditions and accommodate workers [to reduce overtime] are not too onerous. Meeting insurance and pension contributions is our greatest concern'.
>
> Director, Factory A, 2001

Management practices

Management practices in the optical sector are representative of many export-processing factories. There is a highly hierarchical structure, often authoritarian. All workers have a designated status which is clearly depicted on their identification badge. Relatives of the owner, managers and local workers have the greatest status, followed by supervisors and technical workers, then those who have been with the factory for some time (two or more years) who are 'good' workers, followed by 'ordinary workers' (one to two years), with temporary or probationary workers holding the lowest position.

All optical factory managers seek a stable, skilled and compliant workforce. For this reason young women are preferred and considered more capable of undertaking delicate production processes:

> 'We prefer young female workers; they cause less trouble and fighting. Older workers must have experience in the optical industry to get a job'.
>
> Factory supervisor, Factory C, 2005

Despite the hierarchical management structure, there are examples of factory managers operating in a manner that does afford workers some dignity and respect. BSL research has shown that smaller optical factories may not be as modern and appealing, but often appear to have a less harsh factory culture. The manager or owner is more 'hands on' and involved in worker issues. In some cases they themselves have worked on a factory floor. For example, at one factory 17 workers refused to do overtime because they considered the overtime request unreasonable and would have resulted in the workers missing out on the day's water supply when they returned to the dormitory. In this situation the supervisor wanted the workers fined, however, the manager chose to negotiate an outcome. The drought in Southern China is causing significant concern for factory owners and workers. This factory has drilled four wells in response to water shortages. The same factory has a system of fines for workers as a management and disciplinary mechanism, yet claims to return fines to workers at year's end:

> 'All fines go into a special fund to be spent on the workers' end-of-year activity.'
>
> Managing Director / owner, Factory D, 2005

Health and safety

Health and safety in the optical sector is most evident to prevent finger and hand injuries, usually as a result of hand-tooling and acetate cutting machines. Workers are encouraged to wear safety equipment (such as masks and earplugs) but this is rarely enforced. Similarly, it is common to see machines 'unguarded' to speed up production. In this context, when workers are unwell or accidents occur, the blame is most frequently placed on the worker, and rarely attributed to fatigue from excessive overtime, or the pressure to meet targets and bonus payments:

> 'Accidents are a result of workers being careless, not safety issues.'

Managing Director / owner, Factory D, 2005

'Accidents are very few, usually cut fingers, and this is the workers' fault because they do not concentrate and try to work too quickly…there is a bonus system for meeting quotas but we encourage them to take care, that is why there is so many safety signs'.

Operation Manager, Factory F, 2001

Sick workers are seen as an inconvenience and a potential disruption to production. There are extreme examples of 'keeping workers working' and practices to deter workers from taking a day off:

'If workers are unwell or feeling tired we give them a glucose injection so they can work; if they are really sick they go to the hospital.'

Factory supervisor, Factory C, 2005

'If they are really sick and not just pretending then we will provide them with food while recovering at the dormitory. If we think they are not sick we stop their food and they must go outside to eat.'

Vice President, Factory G, 2001

Leanings and future directions

The BSL experience has confirmed that migrant workers face significant discrimination relating to wages, hours and access to social security entitlements. In this regard the optical industry reflects labour practices in China's export processing factories. However, conditions do vary from factory to factory and there are some genuine attempts by factory managers to understand workers' concerns, and to improve conditions—albeit if only to attract and retain a stable workforce.

There is growing interest from factory managers in the link between improved working conditions, compliance with China's labour law and the potential competitive advantage and business success this may bring. Conversely, as production networks become more complex, the factory becomes more remote, and 'arms-length' relationships make it harder for foreign enterprises to map supply chains and conditions. In turn, this makes it more difficult to exert influence to reduce migrant worker discrimination, to communicate directly with factory managers and to implement desired business values.

No single organisation has all the answers. The best results are achieved through innovative multi-stakeholder initiatives that foster incremental improvements and global collaboration amongst enterprises, trade unions, industry associations, NGOs and governments.

Conclusion

Changes are occurring in China's labour market. Labour shortages as rural workers increasingly choose not to migrate may in itself be a major catalyst for hastening China's progress towards policy objectives of a 'harmonious society',[8] not only a more efficient economy, but a more equitable social and economic order. This may provide a culturally appropriate platform for China to embrace corporate social responsibility.

In recent years the government has modified its policy towards the rural floating population and migrant labour. In some regions the *hukou* system is being reformed, wage arrears are being addressed through both administrative and legal measures, and there is progress in ensuring the children of migrant workers are going to school (UN 2005b). There is also growing awareness among workers of legal entitlements and willingness to seek assistance from lawyers and paralegals to seek compensation.

Increasing the work opportunities for migrants in urban areas in occupations other than low skilled processing and construction and increasing wages for these workers will help ease income inequality and discrimination. In addition,

> enforcing minimum wage payments and overtime premiums, closing loopholes related to piece rates, and adjusting minimum wages so that they more closely reflect actual living costs would all have the effect of increasing worker pay…In general workers' need to do overtime hours could decrease as their standard pay increases (Verité 2004:17).

China's policy makers will need to give greater consideration to macro economic restructuring that includes the education, training and social needs of migrant workers. This will assist in recognising their contribution to economic development, reduce social discrimination, and encourage a more even and sustainable distribution of the benefits of foreign direct investment and export processing factories in China.

Notes

1 See material by academics and field researchers such as Anita Chan (http://rspas.anu.edu/ccc/pubs/chan_a.php), Liu Kaiming, and organisations such as the Hong Kong Christian Industrial Committee (www.hkcic.og.hk), the Asia Monitor Resource Centre (www.amrc.org.hk) and China Labour Watch (www.chinalabourwatch.org).

2 Based on the author's observations in frequent visits to factories in southern China engaged in spectacle production between 2000 and 2005.

3 Verité is an independent, not-for-profit social auditing, research, and training organisation with a mission to ensure that people worldwide work under safe, fair and legal conditions.

4 Responses of managers in 12 optical factories to questions asked by the author in the period March 2001–November 2005.

5 The Law of the People's Republic of China on Occupational Disease Prevention and Control (May 2002) and the Law of the People's Republic of China on Safe Production (November 2002).

6 Versions of this case study have appeared in earlier conference papers and publications by Lillywhite: see Lillywhite (2002; 2003; 2005).

7 Views expressed by a representative of the Guangzhou Federation of Trade Unions at the CSR Asia, 'The supply chain talks back' conference, Shekou, November 2005.

8 In 2004, the Chinese government committed to building a socialist harmonious society. This is closely integrated with the ideal of 'building a Xiaokang society in an all-round way' (see UN 2005b).

chapter seven

'Better city, better life'—for whom?

Ingrid Nielsen and Russell Smyth

Introduction

China's workforce is on the move. Various estimates of the size of China's floating population have been proposed in other contributions to this volume. A conservative estimate is that 120–150 million peasants have relocated to China's cities (Pan 2002) with the number expected to increase to 300 million by 2010 (Lague 2003). While these workers have been the workhorses that have fuelled China's high growth rate, making China the world's factory, they face much discrimination stemming from the fact that they typically do not have an urban *hukou*. In a few years Shanghai will host Expo2010 which has the theme 'Better city, better life'. Chapters 6 and 8 in this volume have documented discrimination against migrants in working and living conditions. An obvious question that discrimination of this sort against migrants poses is a 'Better city, better life'—for whom? This chapter explores this issue through considering the difficulties that migrants face in getting access to social insurance. The answer provided to the 'for whom' question in this chapter is that when it comes to social insurance, perhaps the privileged few with an urban *hukou* have a better life, but not China's migrants. While China has a comprehensive social insurance scheme for individuals with an urban *hukou* consisting of pension, unemployment, medical, industrial injury and maternity insurances, the fact remains that most migrants in China's cities have little or no social insurance coverage at all.

In the last few years the central government has ostensibly started to address the lack of migrant social insurance through dismantling the urban registration system and enacting regulations that provide for migrants to receive basic social insurance coverage. A theme running through this chapter is that while the central government is paying lip service to improving migrant rights including their right to social insurance coverage, generally there is a big gap between the rhetoric and reality. The dismantling of the urban registration scheme has been slow, while the implementation of regulations designed to improve social insurance of migrants have been delegated to municipal governments who have adopted a haphazard approach to extending coverage.

In this chapter we first provide an overview of the avenues open to migrants to obtain social insurance coverage. In this section we begin by discussing the extent to which it is feasible for migrants to obtain an urban *hukou* and then proceed to consider the anomalies in regulations established to extend social insurance coverage to migrants. In later sections we focus on the situation in Shanghai. We provide an overview of the demographic and economic characteristics of migrants in Shanghai and then consider their social insurance position. In examining the social insurance position of migrants in Shanghai we draw on two case studies of firms based on fieldwork in late 2003 to illustrate differing attitudes to the payment of social insurance to migrant workers.

Migrants and access to social insurance in China

Migrant access to urban social insurance

The Residential Registration System (*hukou)*, established in 1958, was an institutional barrier designed to prevent rural–urban migration. As discussed previously in James Zhang's chapter, between 1984 and 2000, the system was progressively relaxed to allow rural labourers to leave their villages to seek non-agricultural work opportunities, although it remained difficult for them to obtain an urban *hukou*. From the 1980s migrants were able to obtain two special types of residential registration status; namely, the temporary residential permit and blue-stamp *hukou* or blue card. While the central government maintained the rural–urban divide, it allowed these special permits to be allocated at the discretion of municipal governments. The temporary residence permit could be issued to anyone who had a legitimate job in the city, while the blue card was restricted to investors, those who owned property or white-collar professionals. To obtain a blue card, one was required to pay an 'urban infrastructure construction fee' that varied from a few thousand RMB in small cities to 50,000 RMB in large cities. The blue card operated as a regular urban *hukou* with its holders enjoying most of the same rights as those with an urban *hukou* including social insurance. In the 1990s, the central government also permitted some cities to sell urban *hukou* on a market price basis. Between 1990 and 1994 three million urban *hukou* were sold to migrants in various cities across China at an average price of 8,300 RMB a piece (Chan & Zhang 1999; Liu 2005). In large cities an urban *hukou* was more expensive; for example, in Beijing in 1994 an urban *hukou* cost as much as 50,000 RMB and in Shenzhen Special Economic Zone an urban *hukou* cost 40,000–60,000 RMB (McGranahan & Tacoli 2005).

In March 2001 the Chinese government announced its intention to reform the *hukou* system on a more systematic basis and in October 2001 China started experimental reform in 20,000 small towns (Huang & Zhan 2005:8). In 2001 the State Development and Planning Committee (which, since 2003 has been known as the National Development and Reform Committee) also drafted a five-year plan with the aim of eliminating restrictions on the flow of migrant workers and establishing a unified system of employment registration and matching social security system (Huang & Zhan 2005). In November 2005 the Chinese government announced an experimental program to operate in 11 provinces that allows migrants to obtain an urban *hukou* and have the same rights including social insurance entitlements that is available to urban residents (Kahn 2005; Manthorpe 2005).

The current status of the *hukou* reforms is that they are at best piecemeal, even in those 11 provinces in which the central government is experimenting. This is because in order to obtain an urban *hukou*, a migrant first has to meet certain conditions such as owning property, having investments to a certain value or having educational qualifications to a certain level. This requirement means that for most migrants, obtaining an urban registration together with the social insurance entitlements that come with having an urban registration is a remote possibility. Whether the hurdle is specified in terms of property ownership, investments or educational attainment, varies from city to city. The value of the property, required investment or required educational attainment also varies from one location to another, depending on its perceived desirability as a place to live.

Municipal governments have used the reforms to the registration system as a means to attract better educated individuals and investment to their cities. For example, in order to obtain an urban *hukou* in Nanjing in Jiangsu, a migrant with three family members must purchase a 60-square metre apartment, while a migrant with four family members must purchase an 80-square metre apartment (NMG 2003). In Wuxi, also in Jiangsu, in order to obtain an urban registration, a migrant must purchase a 100-square metre apartment or invest 1 million RMB and have paid 100,000 RMB in taxes for two consecutive years (WMG 2003). Some cities, such as Beijing, Guangzhou and Shenzhen, will only grant urban *hukou* to migrants with technical qualifications, postgraduate degrees or other 'special talents'. The Beijing Municipal government will immediately grant an urban *hukou* to someone with a PhD, but people with a Master's degree must wait three years before being eligible for social services, while migrants with a bachelor's degree do not qualify (Manthorpe 2005).

The principal reason why obtaining an urban registration remains a pipedream for most migrant workers is that few have the capital to be classified as investors, and most cannot afford to purchase housing that is sold at market rates. This cost of purchasing housing at market prices is magnified by the rapid increase in urban real estate prices in China in recent years. According to the World Bank, housing prices worldwide are, on average, equivalent to five to seven years' household income, but in China, are 11 times household income. In a survey of 2000 people in 16 major cities including Beijing and Shanghai conducted in February 2006, four in every five respondents stated that they were worried about rising house prices (Fu 2006). The registration reforms have had the effect of encouraging migrants to settle in county-level cities where the barriers to obtaining an urban registration are not set as high (Liang & Ma 2004). But, there are relatively few employment opportunities in the smaller county-level cities, so migrants are reluctant to settle in these localities. Given these circumstances most migrants continue to stream into the large cities, but are unable to meet the hurdles for urban registration and do not qualify for the social insurance that is available to those with an urban *hukou*.

Social insurance provisions for migrants

Migrants who are unable to obtain an urban *hukou* have to rely on social insurance schemes that are specifically designed to provide coverage for migrant workers. At the national level the basis of the extension of social insurance coverage to migrant workers rests on various pieces of legislation. First, Article 72 of the Chinese Labour Law operational since 1995 deems all workers employed in towns and cities are expected to join a social insurance scheme. Second, in January 2003, the State Council Office's No. 1 Document stated 'excessive and unfair restrictions' on migrants should be abolished. Pursuant to this Document, central ministries have promulgated policies designed to improve the workplace and social insurance position of migrant workers. In January 2004, the Ministry of Health issued a document to improve health protection and control the incidence of vocational illnesses among migrant workers. In June 2004, the Ministry of Labour and Social Security mandated employers must take out work-related injury and accident insurance for migrant workers, particularly those in high-risk industries such as construction and mining (Huang & Zhan 2005).

The national regulations are intended to provide only 'guiding principles' with the actual details governing the implementation of migrant social insurance schemes left to municipal governments. Different municipal governments have interpreted the 'guiding principles' encompassed in the national regulations in different manners. The result is that there are wide disparities in coverage and enforcement between cities, reflected in municipal regulations. For example, in April 2005 Shenzhen introduced a 'social insurance card' that provides migrant workers with access to medical and industrial injury insurance (*Shenzhen Daily* 2005). In October 2004 Tianjin introduced an industrial injury insurance scheme for migrants working in industries where they were likely to incur heavy injuries such as construction. However, many migrants working outside the construction sector receive no social insurance coverage. In some occupations, such as catering, where serious injuries are less likely to occur, minor injuries such as burns still happen frequently. When injuries occur in these industries, makeshift solutions have to suffice. Li (2006) interviewed 29 migrant workers in relation to their access to social insurance in Tianjin. One of Li's (2006) typical respondents stated: 'I was burnt at work several times while selling hot food to customers. My boss gave another colleague some cash [and asked] her to go to the pharmacy to buy some simple medicine and some medical cotton and bandages for me' (Li 2006:187).

Even when municipalities have regulations in place covering migrant workers, employers do not always comply with those regulations. This means that apart from whether specific municipalities have relevant regulations, myriad factors influence whether migrants actually receive social insurance coverage in practice. The nature of the ownership structure of the enterprise influences the welfare level of migrant workers. China's state-owned enterprises (SOEs) have a long history of employing rural workers with the so-called 'peasant worker' (*yigong yinong*) system dating back to the 1950s (Lei 2005). A reform, implemented in 1991, required SOEs to treat migrant workers hired on a temporary basis similar to permanent urban workers in terms of benefits such as food subsidies, holidays, sick-leave and medical care (Seeborg, Jin & Zhu 2000). While Solinger (1995) argues that some inequities between permanent urban workers and migrants continued after the 1991 reforms, the fact remains that SOEs are more likely to treat their contract migrant workers similarly to their urban employees in terms of provision of social insurance, than non-state enterprises. Most non-state-owned enterprises do not provide social insurance coverage to migrants with the explicit objective of reducing their labour costs. Of the position in Tianjin, Li (2006:62) writes: 'in practice employers are reluctant to contribute to social insurances for ex-farmers. Many urban employers find 34% of the salaries [the contribution rate in Tianjin] for social insurance contributions unbearable'. In contrast to the state-owned sector, non-state enterprises tend to pay social insurance contributions only for their key migrant workers.

The type of migrant worker also influences whether the migrant receives social insurance (Nielsen, Zhang et al 2005). There are three major types of migrants. The first type is the 'key workers', defined as the skilled migrant workers who have been employed at an enterprise for a long time. These key workers generally receive equal pay to their urban counterparts and enjoy all social insurances except for a housing subsidy. The second kind of migrant worker is casual and unskilled. While the evidence suggests that migrants are better educated than rural residents who do not migrate (Wu & Zhou 1996; Seeborg, Jin & Zhu 2000), most migrant workers are unskilled with low levels of human capital. These individuals have the lowest social status and most have little or no social insurance. The third kind of migrant worker is those assigned by employment agencies. These workers sign labour contracts with the agencies and have little relationship with the enterprise where they work. In order to reduce labour costs, enterprises are increasingly drawing their labour from agencies, rather than signing contracts directly with migrant workers. The companies only pay a contract salary to the agencies and are not responsible for the social security of the migrant workers. Instead, it is the agencies who are in charge of providing social insurance coverage to their workers. In practice, agencies will generally only purchase commercial old-age insurance for key workers.

An important reason why employers are reluctant to pay social insurance to migrants is the high labour turnover. Municipal regulations typically provide that migrant workers should be able to cash their social insurance contributions once they decide to leave. However, employers are required to apply for termination of social insurance on behalf of their employees. This means that employers have to handle the application for the withdrawal of social insurance contributions whenever a migrant worker leaves. Because of the high turnover rate among migrant workers, employers are reluctant to deal with all the paperwork. From the migrant worker's perspective, the result is that migrants who choose to contribute may end up with nothing, which is a disincentive to contribute (Li 2005; Nielsen, Zhang et al 2005). Many migrant workers voluntarily forgo their rights to social insurance under municipal regulations because in a competitive labour market, employers prefer to hire the 'less troublesome' (Li 2005). The result is that, overall, social insurance coverage among migrant workers continues to be extremely low. For instance, one survey of migrant workers conducted by the Institute of Economics in the Chinese Academy of Social Sciences in 2004 found that only 2–3% received any unemployment insurance and that fewer than 5% received pension insurance (UN 2005b).

Demographic and economic profiles of migrants in Shanghai

According to the 2000 National Census, the four provinces or cities with provincial status with the largest migrant populations were Guangdong (21 million), Zhejiang (5.4 million), Jiangsu (5 million) and Shanghai (4.4 million). The size of Shanghai's migrant population is more significant than these figures seem to indicate, given the relatively small size of its population. Table 1 shows the ratio of migrants to those holding an urban *hukou* in Shanghai's 19 districts.

Table 1: Distribution of migrants among Shanghai's districts in 2003

District	Population in 2000 (10,000)	Population in 2003 (10,000)	Percentage increase in population	Population holding an urban *hukou* in 2003 (10,000)	Ratio of migrants to those holding an urban *hukou* (urban *hukou* holders = 100)
Total	387.11	498.79	28.85	1,341.77	37.17
Nine central districts	130.07	130.26	0.15	611.00	21.32
Ten suburban districts	257.05	368.53	43.37	718.90	51.26
Pudong	73.28	102.34	39.66	176.69	58.11
Xuhui	23.31	20.50	-12.05	88.61	23.62
Changning	16.27	17.31	6.39	61.71	28.02
Putuo	23.11	23.36	1.08	84.53	27.99
Zhabei	14.40	14.63	1.60	70.79	20.68
Hongkou	14.38	14.74	2.50	79.22	18.78
Yangpu	19.68	20.34	3.35	108.17	19.69
Hunagpu	9.43	10.01	6.15	61.87	16.22
Luwan	4.85	5.12	5.57	32.84	15.65
Jingan	4.64	4.25	-8.41	32.07	13.28
Baoshan	37.44	43.98	17.47	85.43	51.81
Minhang	48.10	73.38	52.56	75.12	97.79
Jiading	25.40	40.01	57.52	51.18	78.45
Jinshan	6.08	7.52	23.68	52.71	14.29
Songjiang	19.05	32.55	70.87	50.68	64.37
Qingpu	16.82	27.01	60.58	45.83	60.53
Nanhui	12.42	16.56	33.33	69.91	23.72
Fengxian	13.06	19.77	51.38	50.87	38.92
Chongming	5.40	5.41	0.19	63.84	8.53

Source: NBS 2004b

Overall, the ratio of migrants to those with an urban *hukou* is 37%, while in six districts (Baoshan, Jiading, Minhang, Pudong, Qingpu and Songjiang) migrants actually outnumbered those holding an urban *hukou*. Shanghai experienced rapid growth in its migrant population in the second half of the 1990s. In the 1995 One Percent Sample Survey Shanghai recorded only 1.7 million migrants. Five years later the migrant population of Shanghai more than doubled, reflecting the rapid growth of Pudong and economic expansion of the city (Liang & Ma 2004). This is reflected in the popular expression among migrants, 'east, west, south, north, centre; to find a job go to Pudong' (*dong, xi, nan, zhong, da gong, dao Pudong*).

Table 2 shows the home provinces of migrants in Shanghai. More than 50% of migrants in Shanghai come from the surrounding provinces of Anhui and Jiangsu. Other prominent 'source provinces' are Jiangxi, and Zhejiang, which are also geographically close to Shanghai and Sichuan in China's western region.

Table 2: Home provinces of migrants in Shanghai in 2000 and 2003 (%)

	2000	2003
Anhui	32.2	34.5
Jiangsu	24.0	22.4
Sichuan	7.3	7.7
Zhejiang	9.9	7.2
Jiangxi	6.0	6.2
Henan	4.1	4.7
Hubei	2.7	3.6
Fujian	2.8	2.5

Source: NBS 2004b

Table 3 shows the length of residence of migrants in Shanghai. In 1993 more than half of the total migrants stayed in Shanghai fewer than six months, while only 6.3% remained in Shanghai for more than five years.

Table 3: Length of residence of migrants in Shanghai, 1993, 1997, 2000, 2003 (%)

	< half a year	0.5–1 year	1–5 years	> 5 years
1993	50.7	20.4	22.6	6.3
1997	28.7	19.5	37.1	14.7
2000	21.0	21.6	39.3	40.2
2003	23.2	12.2	40.2	24.4

Source: NBS 2004b

Over time, the duration spent in Shanghai has become longer. In 2003 fewer than a quarter of migrants in Shanghai stayed less than six months, while almost a quarter stayed five years or more. These figures are consistent with a survey by the Bureau of Labour and Social Security in Shanghai in 2002 that found 30% of migrant workers had stayed for more than four years, 25% had stayed for more than three years and 20% of migrant workers had been in Shanghai more than two years (Zhao 2002). There is also evidence from other cities as well that migrant spells are increasing in length and a growing number of migrants view their residence in the cities as being long-term (Jacka 2005). The duration spell of migrants in Beijing mirrors that in Shanghai. The 1997 Beijing migrant census reported that 64% of respondents had been away from their hometown more than six months. By 2002 the figure had increased to 74% (Jacka 2005). Migrants are now a major source of population growth in China's largest cities, such as Beijing and Shanghai.

Table 4: Age and gender profiles of migrants in Shanghai in 2003

Age	Gender ratio (female =100)	Percentage of the city's migrant population	Male (%)	Female (%)
Total	133.99	100	100	100
0–4	122.68	4.03	3.87	4.23
5–9	136.48	4.39	4.42	4.34
10–14	128.92	3.81	3.75	3.90
15–19	94.40	9.02	7.65	10.86
20–24	107.27	15.92	14.39	17.97
25–29	123.92	16.84	16.27	17.59
30–34	141.03	18.28	18.68	17.75
35–39	170.61	12.89	14.19	11.14
40–44	196.61	5.71	6.61	4.51
45–49	208.17	3.89	4.59	2.96
50–54	177.84	2.59	2.89	2.18
55–59	164.16	1.24	1.34	1.10
60–64	142.48	0.67	0.69	0.65
65–69	114.22	0.40	0.38	0.44
70+	94.73	0.32	0.27	0.39

Source: NBS 2004b

Table 4 shows the age and gender profile of migrants in Shanghai. Consistent with the findings from the 2000 National Census, which are discussed in Liang and Ma (2004), most migrants who come to Shanghai are in the prime of their working lives. Overall 33% of migrants are in the age group 20 to 29 and 64% of migrants in the age group 20 to 40. This demographic profile means that migrants are much younger than the local population (Wang, Zuo & Ruan 2002). There is an over-representation of males in the migrant population. For all age groups, except the 15–19 and over 70 categories, there are more male migrants than female migrants, whereas in the local population there is an almost equal distribution between males and females (Wang, Zuo & Ruan 2002).

Table 5: Accommodation of migrants in Shanghai in 2000 and 2003 (%)

	2000	2003
Rental	63.9	73.5
Dormitory	20.0	18.8
Owner-occupier	4.5	4.3
Relatives and friends	5.0	1.8
Hotels and motels	1.4	0.8
Hospital	0.2	0.5
Other	5.0	0.3

Source: NBS 2004b

The accommodation of migrants in Shanghai is shown in Table 5. Most migrants live in rental accommodation or in dormitories provided by their employers. As documented in chapter 8 in this volume, most migrants in China's cities live in crowded and insanitary housing that increase the risk of illness. The survey by the Bureau of Labour and Social Security in Shanghai in 2002 cited earlier found that on average 12 migrant workers shared a room of 20 square metres (Zhao 2002).

Table 6: Educational attainment of migrants in Shanghai in 2000 and 2003 (%)

	2000	2003
Illiterate or semi-literate	5.5	3.8
Primary school	24.6	22.1
Junior secondary school	55.2	58.8
Senior secondary school	11.2	11.3
College and above	3.7	4.0

Source: NBS 2004b

Table 7: Occupation of migrants in Shanghai in 2000 and 2003 (%)

	2000	2003
Technician	3.8	5.4
Government	0.5	0.3
Service	27.4	29.1
Agriculture	7.3	3.7
Manufacturing	25.9	33.9
Construction	19.5	19.8
Other	15.6	7.8

Source: NBS 2004b

Table 8 Monthly income of migrants in 2003 (%)

300 RMB and below	4.4
301–500 RMB	19.2
501–800 RMB	45.2
801–1,000 RMB	19.2
1,001–1,500 RMB	6.6
1,501–2,000 RMB	3.0
2,001–5,000 RMB	2.1
5,001 RMB and above	0.3

Source: NBS 2004b

Table 6 shows the educational attainment of migrants in Shanghai. While there are relatively few migrants with a senior secondary school education or above, 50–60% have a junior secondary school education. This education profile is similar to that for migrants as a whole from the 2000 National Census (Liang & Ma 2004). As documented in other chapters in this volume by Serena Lillywhite and Nielsen and Smyth, there is a segmented labour market between migrants and those with an urban *hukou*.

Table 7 indicates that most migrants were employed in the manufacturing, service or construction sectors in the 'Three D' (dangerous, dirty and demeaning) jobs. Female migrants are concentrated in the manufacturing and services sectors, while a high proportion of male migrants work in the construction sector (Roberts 2001). Table 8 shows the monthly income of migrants in 2003. Overall, 23.6% of migrants earned less than 500 RMB per month, 64.4% of migrants earned between 500 RMB and 1,000 RMB per month and 9.6% earned between 1,000 RMB and 2,000 RMB per month, while just 2.4% earned more than 2,000 RMB per month. The average wage for a migrant in Shanghai in 2003 was 650 RMB. By way of comparison, the average wage in Shanghai in 2003 for those with an urban registration was 2,200 RMB.

Social insurance position of migrants in Shanghai

Employer obligations to migrant workers in Shanghai are prescribed by the *Interim Procedures on Comprehensive Insurance for External Labour Forces in Shanghai* that came into operation on 1 September 2002. The social insurance premiums for migrant workers for each firm are levied on a base which is 60% of the average previous year's monthly wage of all workers in Shanghai, multiplied by the number of migrant workers employed by the firm (Article 9). Employers of migrant workers in Shanghai are required to pay 12.5% of this base, while for outside construction teams the comparable rate is 7.5% (Article 9). The payments are made into a fund established by the Shanghai municipal government (Article 11) that is monitored by the Department of Finance and Auditor-General in Shanghai (Article 12). Migrant workers are not required to contribute to the social insurance fund. These provisions entitle migrant workers to coverage for work-related injuries, hospital treatment and pensions on retirement (Articles 13–16), but not coverage for maternity or unemployment insurance. The Labour Security Administrative Authority in Shanghai is responsible for monitoring and supervision of claims by migrant workers (Article 19). In the event of a dispute between employer and employee in relation to payment of social insurance contributions, either party can apply directly to a labour dispute arbitration committee or to a labour dispute mediation (Article 21).

An important group of migrants who are not covered by the migrant social insurance scheme in Shanghai are domestic service workers (Article 3). At the beginning of 2006 it was reported that there were 200,000 domestic service workers in Shanghai with unmet demand for another 70,000. The report stated that labour turnover among domestic service workers in Shanghai is high with about 40% of domestic helpers leaving their jobs within a year and returning to their hometowns because of the high cost of living in the city (*Shanghai Daily* 2006a). Shanghai has a separate accident insurance scheme for domestic service workers that pays if the domestic helper is killed or injured on the job, but this means that they are not entitled to pensions or other medical insurance, except for workplace injuries (*Shanghai Daily* 2006a).

In November 2005, the official figure was that 2.26 million migrants were covered by Shanghai's social insurance scheme (*Shanghai Daily* 2005c), which represents over half of the migrants in Shanghai. In reality, the actual number of migrants receiving social insurance is smaller than this figure suggests because of low compliance rates. Employer non-compliance with social insurance obligations in Shanghai in general is very high. Audited data on some 2,200 firms collected by the Bureau of Labour and Social Security and analysed by Nyland, Smyth and Zhu (2006) indicated that in 2001, 70% of firms in Shanghai were paying less than their prescribed social insurance contributions.

This figure is for social insurance contributions under the urban model for those with an urban *hukou*. If non-compliance rates for migrant social insurance were considered in isolation using data since the *Interim Procedures on Comprehensive Insurance for External Labour Forces in Shanghai* came into effect, the rate of non-compliance would be much higher than 70%. There is no comprehensive audited data of this nature available, although patchy evidence can be gained from different sources. In the Bureau of Labour and Social Security survey of migrant workers in Shanghai, fewer than 20% of respondents could get full or partial compensation for medical insurance and 24% complained of being injured at work, but their employer refused to meet medical insurance (Zhao 2002). According to one report, the Shanghai Labour Inspection Team receives 20,000 complaints annually from migrant workers, most of which focus on the employer's failure to contribute social insurance funds (*Shanghai Daily* 2005c). This number is quite startling given the pressure migrants are under not to complain, lest they be labeled 'difficult workers' by employers. A random inspection of firms employing migrants in March 2006 found that almost 3,000 companies had failed to make social insurance contributions for more than 60,000 migrant employees. The unpaid social insurance exceeded 50 million RMB (*Shanghai Daily* 2006b).

The remainder of this section uses two case studies to illustrate differing attitudes of firms in Shanghai towards paying social insurance to migrants. The case studies are based on interviews conducted by the second author as part of a research team examining the broader issues of firm compliance with social insurance in Shanghai and the extension of the city's social insurance scheme to those who previously had little or no coverage. The interviews at both firms were conducted with senior management in November 2003, just over 12 months after the introduction of the regulations on the payment of migrant social insurance by the Shanghai municipal government.

Case study 1: Nimingde Chengtuan[1]

Nimingde Chengtuan (NC) was founded in in Urumqi in Xinjiang Autonomous Region in the mid-1980s by two brothers who were very much 'migrant entrepreneurs' in the spirit of how that term is used in the chapter in this volume on Uygurs by Marika Vicziany and Guibin Zhang. The brothers made a fortune through listing on the embryonic Chinese stock market in the early 1990s that allowed them to expand their business interests initially from Urumqi to Shanghai and then overseas. NC is now a privately-owned investment conglomerate with its head office in Shanghai and global presence in a broad range of businesses, including manufacturing, agribusiness, tourism, entertainment and financial services. In 2002 it employed 15,000 people worldwide and in 2002 had sales turnover of 40 billion RMB. In China the strategy of NC is to acquire underperforming manufacturing firms, often SOEs, and restructure these firms with the aim of strategic value creation. It has a controlling interest in three publicly listed manufacturing enterprises on the Shanghai stock exchange and minority interests in several others.

At its Shanghai headquarters where all its employees either have a Shanghai urban *hukou* or are 'key migrant workers', it pays the government-prescribed urban social insurance plus additional medical and pension insurance that it uses as a human resources strategy to attract and retain good staff. In the manufacturing firms that NC acquires it pays the minimum prescribed social insurance contributions for those with an urban *hukou*. The manufacturing firms also employ a number of migrant workers on an intermittent basis. In most cases NC ignores regulations requiring employers to pay social insurance for migrant workers and simply pays nothing. The justification given in the interview was that because of the high labour turnover among migrants, the paperwork associated with the withdrawal of social insurance contributions each time a migrant moved on was too cumbersome. Moreover, it was argued that migrants often left without giving notice so it generally was impossible to find them. The exception is that NC will sometimes take out medical insurance where there are a high number of industrial injuries.

While NC did not admit to the practice, at the interview it was suggested that it was common for other firms in industries with hazardous or toxic materials to hire migrant workers on short-term contracts (12–36 months) and not renew the contracts. The motivation of the employer is to move the migrant workers on before they start to show signs of poor health. It was suggested that this practice is common in Shanghai in the lighting industry and in Guangdong in the footwear industry where symptoms of toxic poisoning can emerge in as little as six months. As the chapter by Sukhan Jackson and her colleagues illustrates, there is a lot of evidence to suggest that many migrant workers return home with serious occupational diseases such as tuberculosis. Other evidence is provided in a recent news report that states 7,800 cases of pneumoconiosis were recorded among migrant workers who had returned home in Guangxi Zhuang Autonomous Region, by the end of 2005 with about 300 new cases being newly diagnosed each year (*China Daily* 2006d). One might expect hazardous work practices to be restricted to Chinese and Taiwanese firms that are known to be exploitative. At the interview, however, it was argued that this was common not only in Chinese factories, but also among large foreign joint ventures including those with household multinationals.

Case study 2: Zhizao Gongsi

Zhizao Gongsi (ZG) was founded in the late 1970s and controls five companies in manufacturing and trading. Altogether it employs 1,000 people; of which 20% are managerial staff or white collar workers and 80% are blue collar workers. Of the approximately 800 blue collar workers, 500 to 600 are migrants without a Shanghai urban *hukou*. ZG offers migrant workers what it calls its 'migrant comprehensive package'. The migrant comprehensive package consists of (a) wages of 1,000 RMB per month, (b) free accommodation and meals in dormitories owned by ZG, (c) social insurance of 141 RMB per month and (d) a training program consisting of training once a quarter. The total value of the migrant comprehensive package is about 1,500 RMB per month. The migrant comprehensive package of 1,500 RMB per month was at the upper end of what migrants could expect to receive in Shanghai and as pointed out in the interview, generated a high level of commitment among migrant workers. For the equivalent amount most people with an urban *hukou* would not work.

Prior to the introduction of the *Interim Procedures on Comprehensive Insurance for External Labour Forces in Shanghai* in September 2002 there was no migrant insurance scheme in Shanghai. Instead, the Shanghai government collected fees from firms that employed migrant labour. The fee was levied at 70 RMB a month per worker consisting of a 50-RMB 'urban infrastructure development fee' and a 20-RMB 'administration fee'. The collection of these fees was somewhat arbitrary and not strictly enforced. The Human Resources Manager, who was interviewed, recalled that at a previous firm in which he had worked, that company had owed 700,000 RMB in fees for hiring migrant workers. However, when the Shanghai Bureau of Labour and Social Security came to collect, the firm argued that it could not pay and ended up paying only 35,000 RMB. How did the firm succeed in getting the other 665,000 RMB waived? Initially the firm delayed payment and then it struck a deal. As the firm was a major taxpayer, the Bureau did not want to offend the company.

Conclusion

The central government has taken steps to improve the rights of migrant workers including their access to social insurance through beginning the dismantling of the *hukou* system and enacting regulations that provide a basis for extending social insurance coverage to migrant workers. But there is still a long way to go. The central government states that it is committed to ensuring equality between those with an urban *hukou* and migrants in China's cities, in recognition of the role that migrants have played in fuelling China's high growth. There is, however, a big gap between the rhetoric and practice. The reality is that the dismantling of the *hukou* system has been slow, with only those migrants who are well-educated or with funds to invest in businesses or able to purchase housing that can typically secure an urban *hukou*. The national regulations stating that migrants should receive social insurance are just 'guiding principles'. Municipal governments have been left to interpret these 'guiding principles' in enacting specific legislation which means that coverage varies greatly from city to city.

The case studies of the two firms in Shanghai suggest two differing approaches to paying social insurance to migrant workers. NC was fairly typical of firms in Shanghai in late 2003 when the interviews took place—choosing to pay nothing at all. ZG was rather exceptional in the breadth of its 'migrant comprehensive package', paying benefits at the upper end of what migrants could expect to receive. It has to be remembered, though, that the interviews took place only 12 months after the migrant insurance scheme was introduced and employer awareness of their obligations to migrant workers under the scheme would not be as high as it is three years later. Representatives from the Shanghai Labour Inspection Team have stated that most firms found not to have paid social insurance contributions to migrants claimed to be unaware of their obligations and that this situation is changing with publicity campaigns promoting greater awareness (*Shanghai Daily* 2005b). Since the interviews for the case studies took place, the Shanghai municipal government has taken steps to improve monitoring and enforcement of employers' social insurance obligations to migrants. The Labour Inspection Team commenced a program of 'spot checks' in Shanghai in March 2006 (*Shanghai Daily* 2006b). There are sporadic reports that a limited number of companies have been taken to court for failure to make social insurance contributions to migrants (*Shanghai Daily* 2005b). Some companies have also been 'shamed' in the media for failure to make social insurance contributions for migrants. An example is the Shanghai Baillan Garment Company, 'a renowned women's clothing manufacturer in Jinshan' that 'had [not] paid into the social insurance fund for 60 migrant workers for more than a year'. The outstanding contributions totaled 41,538 RMB (*Shanghai Daily* 2005b). The media reports that the Labour Inspection Team is having some success. In the first ten months of 2005 5,700 cases of payment defaults were handled and 68 million RMB recovered (*Shanghai Daily* 2005b).

While improved monitoring and enforcement is helping, 'top down' solutions reflected in a regulatory response can only go part of the way to addressing the problem. The fact is that even if 68 million RMB in outstanding social insurance contributions were recovered in the first ten months of 2005, this is likely to be only the tip of the iceberg. To really make a difference there needs to be a 'bottom-up' response. The situation is unlikely to change until migrants start to vote with their feet. Wang Dewen, Cai Fang and Gao Wenshu's chapter documents that the poor social insurance and working conditions migrants face is starting to change in some provinces such as Fujian and Guangdong where an emerging migrant labour shortage problem is making it more difficult for employers to pick and choose between workers. This development is a positive first step for the improvement of migrant rights. If employers continue to pay more heed to the need for improved social protection and working conditions for migrants, the theme for Shanghai Expo2010 of a 'Better city, better Life' will certainly embrace all those living in China's cities.

Note

1 The firms in the two case studies are given pseudonyms to protect their identities.

chapter eight

The comparative basic living conditions and leisure activities of China's off-farm migrants and urban locals

Ingrid Nielsen and Russell Smyth

Introduction

It has been noted that happiness is perhaps the most direct indicator of the effects of leisure (Lu & Hu 2005). Of course it is hardly surprising that engaging in leisure activities brings happiness, since such activities are generally undertaken by choice. The effects of leisure, though, extend beyond the immediate. Indeed, the longer-term satisfaction that one derives from leisure activities is an important contributor to overall subjective wellbeing (Carruthers & Hood 2004; Haworth & Hill 1992; Hills & Argyle 1998). For this reason the literature on leisure composition and leisure effects in developed Western nations, where leisure consumption mirrors the concomitant Western values of material comfort and personal freedom, is quite extensive

Not so in China, though, where the first discussions of leisure and leisure effects did not appear in the academic literature until well into the 1990s. One reason for the lack of research into leisure in China is simply that the modern notion of leisure is relatively new in socialist China.[1] As Yin (2005) observed, the nature and degree of leisure consumption is very much related to how open a nation is to the outside world. In the Chinese context, economic reforms introduced in China in 1978 gave rapid rise to consumerism, and along with the freedom to consume came a 'freedom to have fun' (Lull 1991:131)—a *leisure consumerism*. Rapid marketisation and the introduction of the five-day work week in 1995 saw concurrent increases in living standards, time and money to spend on leisure, and exposure to Western leisure influences. The resultant advent of an individualistic pursuit of enjoyment stands in stark contrast to Maoist asceticism, where hitherto it was considered that 'pursuing a hobby may sap one's will to make progress' (Wang 1995:155).

But in response to Deng's relatively hedonistic aphorism 'to get rich is glorious', Chinese, or at least the urban populace, have begun to spend and have fun. Chai (1992) reported that disposable income in China grew at a rate of 11.7% per annum between 1978 and 1985. Between 1978 and 1990, the overall standard of living in China more than doubled. During the first decade of the reforms, per capita material consumption rose from 216 RMB in 1978 to 486 RMB in 1990, at an annual growth rate of 9.1% (Chai 1992). In terms of spending targeted specifically to leisure, Hanser (2004) reported that spending on entertainment and recreation among China's urban households rose from 8% in 1980 to 13% in 1991; and that the average daily hours of leisure enjoyed by urban Chinese rose from two to four hours across this time period. A survey undertaken in 1995 reported that urban Chinese spent on average six hours a day pursuing leisure activities (Wang 1995).

In contrast though, qualitative studies undertaken by Chan (2002), Jacka (2005) and Li (2006) reported that leisure and entertainment are generally not part of the lives of China's off-farm migrant workers. There has not, however, been any quantitative documentation of the leisure activities, or lack thereof, of migrant workers in China's cities. The current chapter complements Serena Lillywhite's chapter on the working conditions of migrants by examining what migrants do when they are not at work and the broader issue of the comparative living standards of migrants and urbanites. The comparative dimension of the chapter adds to the extant literature by considering whether registration status is an important influence over the composition and frequency of leisure activities in major urban centres of mainland China.

In this chapter, we draw on a dataset of 882 urban Chinese and 781 off-farm migrant workers to compare the types and frequency of leisure activities undertaken by these two groups. Against the backdrop of an analysis of basic living conditions, we explore the patterns of leisure consumption of these two groups, simultaneously exposed to 'novel forms of leisure' (Davis 2000:2), yet differentiated by the historic legacy of the *hukou* system, which Irwin (1999:34) observed means that the worlds of migrants and urbanites 'for all the physical proximity [remain] culturally leagues apart'. Rather than consider 'traditional' forms of leisure such as cooking, gambling, *mah-jong*, spending time with friends singing and dancing, our study focuses on participation in new forms of leisure that may be considered decidedly Western in orientation, such as going out to a nightclub or video arcade, that hitherto were not available to Chinese prior to globalisation and integration with the outside world.

The remainder of the chapter is set out as follows: the next section reviews the small literature on leisure consumption, the effects of leisure on life satisfaction and living conditions of migrants and the urban population in China. We then outline the background to the empirical study, including the research methodology and the basic demographic characteristics and living conditions of the respondents. Next, we present an analysis of the differences in income, savings and expenditure on leisure among migrants and urban locals, and conclude in the final section.

Leisure consumption, life satisfaction and living conditions among Chinese urban residents and migrant workers

As noted, studies of leisure consumption in China are quite scant because leisure has not, until recently, been characteristic of the lives of the Chinese in the socialist period. Lately, within the context of better living standards and shorter working hours, a market for leisure has grown that demands investigation into the areas of life quality enrichment and leisure management.

Quantitative studies of leisure in China are confined to a handful conducted among samples of local urban residents. Chou, Chow and Chi (2004) looked at leisure participation among older adults in Hong Kong and found that watching television and listening to the radio were the highest ranked leisure activities among those aged over 60. Guan (2003) looked at leisure participation among Chinese children and she too found that watching television was the most frequently undertaken leisure activity among this group.

In two of the few studies to model the effects of leisure among adult samples of mainland Chinese, Lu and Hu (2002; 2005) found that engaging in satisfying leisure activities had both positive short-term and long-term effects. Moreover, these positive effects extended across a wide spectrum, including mood, health, education and social integration. Mirroring results from decades of Western studies (see Andrew & Withey 1976; Beard & Ragheb 1980; Kirkcaldy & Furnham 1991), these limited Chinese data suggest that interpersonal factors, time and the economy are facilitators of, and barriers to, leisure in urban China. While no systematic quantitative study of the leisure consumption of migrant workers has been undertaken, there is some compelling narrative evidence and evidence from media reports and labour rights campaigns that indicates migrants have little time for leisure, and are often restricted from participating in certain leisure activities.

Li (2006) interviewed 29 migrants in Tianjin about their leisure activities. Twenty interviewees in Li's sample indicated that they never went out after work because they were exhausted and wanted to rest or did not want to spend money on socialising. As one migrant whom Li (2006) interviewed stated: 'Wherever you go you need to spend money. Since I came here I have only been to a park once with my friends. The park entrance fee was three RMB. It was not nearly as beautiful as the countryside. I regretted that I went there'. Jacka documented narratives of migrant women who were members of the Beijing Migrant

Women's Club—a non-governmental organisation set up in 1996 with the aim of providing migrant women with 'a place to get together and share experiences' (Jacka 2005:53). Jacka reported that despite feeling constantly homesick and lonely, migrant women in Beijing have very little time for recreation or leisure activities that might serve to alleviate their negative mood.

When migrant workers do have time for leisure, it seems that their access to certain forms of leisure is significantly curtailed. A report by Qiang (2005) in the *Nanfang Weekend* quoted one migrant worker as saying that if he has time for leisure, he chooses to go to free public venues, such as parks, because entertainment venues in the cities are not designed for migrants. Many migrant women in the Jacka (2005) study reported that even if they had the luxury of time, their movements and contacts with others were frequently restricted by their employers—particularly in the case of live-in housemaids and workers in the small sweat shops. As Serena Lillywhite documents in her chapter, migrants are often forced to work in oppressive conditions. Many millions of migrants work in the types of factories for which the English term is 'sweat shop'. A survey of migrant workers (75% of whom were female) in the Pearl River Delta in the mid-1990s found that most were working in such factories 12 hours a day (ILO 2001). But as Qiang (2005) explained, while in English the term used to describe these factories is 'sweat shop', the Chinese term is *xue han gongchang*, which translates as 'blood and sweat factory'. The Clean Clothes Campaign also reported that the long hours worked by migrant workers preclude any time for leisure (Kwan 2000). Kwan reported that 14-hour days, 7-day weeks (without overtime penalties) are not unusual for migrant workers, despite Chinese Labour Law prescribing 40 hours per week before overtime rates apply. Other reports by the US National Labor Committee tell of 15-hour days, with one day off per month.

While such blatant disregard for the wellbeing of migrant workers is beginning to emerge more frequently through news reports, many migrants still suffer relatively more silently. Jacka (2005) described how migrant women in China's cities experience profound homesickness and loneliness. A *China Daily* (2003a) report quotes Genevieve Domenach-Chich, a UNESCO project team leader, as saying that migrant women in China's cities suffer from 'psychological poverty', due to their feelings of loneliness and isolation in urban areas and because migrants are simply not welcome in many public venues. Domenach-Chich said: 'A migrant woman in her 30s told me her dream was to enter a restaurant without being considered a *mingong* (migrant worker), but as someone else, as a decent urban resident' (*China Daily* 2003a). Among the migrants Li (2006) interviewed in Tianjin some older workers who had come to Tianjin prior to the relaxation of rules on migrants being in the city were still haunted by police checking and, as a consequence, preferred to remain indoors to avoid unnecessary harassment. While participation in leisure activities might reasonably improve the quality of life of China's migrants, it is simply not a part of their daily lives.

Previous studies have documented more generally that the living conditions of migrants are often very poor. Solinger (1999) provided extensive evidence that the living conditions of migrants, often in shanty towns on the outskirts of big cities, are inferior to those of local urbanites. Guang and Zhang (2005) have recently argued that the living conditions of migrant workers in China's big cities are far inferior to those of off-farm workers. There is a lot of evidence that migrants experience poorer housing conditions than urbanites (Shen 2002; Wu 2002; 2004). Drawing on samples from Beijing and Shanghai, Wu (2002; 2004) argued that reforms to urban housing provision have completely overlooked the needs of the migrant population. In reality, migrant housing disadvantage in Beijing and Shanghai reflects socio-economic differences—migrants have lower education and income than urbanites—as well as institutional restrictions associated with the *hukou* system.

In the following sections we report upon a study that compares the basic living conditions and leisure activities of migrants and urban residents across ten mainland cities. We begin by outlining the background to the study, including characteristics of the study locales and participants; then compare the types and frequency of leisure activities undertaken by the two groups.

Background to the study and the characteristics of respondents

Respondents in the study were recruited from locations within Hunan province, Zhejiang province, Heilongjiang province and the metropolis of Tianjin. In total, 781 migrant workers and 882 urban local residents completed our questionnaires (see Table 1). In China large differences exist not only between rural and urban areas, but even within the same province. There are often sizeable differences between big, medium-sized and small cities. Thus we have chosen three cities in each province consisting of the provincial capital, (except for Zhejiang where Ningbo was selected), one prefecture level city and one county level city. In Hunan, the three cities selected were Changsha, the provincial capital; Changde a prefecture level city and Lingli, a county level city of Changde. In Zhejiang, the three cities selected were Ningbo, a major industrial port city; Jiaxing, a prefecture level city, and Tongxiang, a county level city of Jiaxing. In Heilongjiang, the three cities selected were Harbin, the provincial capital, Suihua, a prefecture level city and Qing an, a county level city in Suihua. In Tianjin the sampling was restricted to the city proper.

Table 1: Breakdown of sample by location

Province (city)	Migrant workers in sample	Local residents in sample
Hunan (Changsha)	101	102
Zhejiang (Ningbo)	78	93
Heilongjiang (Harbin)	70	100
Tianjin (Tianjin)	99	100
Hunan (Changde)	82	90
Heilongjiang (Suihua)	100	110
Zhejiang (Jiaxing)	100	116
Hunan (Lingli)	44	60
Heilongjiang (Qing an)	57	60
Zhejiang (Tongxiang)	50	51
Total	781	882

We selected Heilongjiang, Hunan, Tianjin and Zhejiang to get a mixture of cities at different levels of economic development. Hunan is a province of medium economic development and suffers from land shortage. The arable land in the province is only 0.85 *mu* per capita (equivalent to approximately 0.057 of a hectare). Heilongjiang is one of China's typical old industry bases that are now declining owing to the collapse of state-owned enterprises. Heilongjiang is rich in arable land with each person having 6 *mu* of arable land (equivalent to approximately 0.4 of a hectare). Zhejiang is one of the most prosperous provinces situated on China's coast. Tianjin is representative of the four metropolises directly under the control of the central Chinese government.[2]

Estimates put the number of migrant workers at around 120–150 million (Pan 2002), with this number expected to increase to around 300 million by 2010 (Lague 2003). About half of the migrant workers in China are inter-provincial migrants (those who are working in other provinces, rather than their own home provinces), and the rest of them are working in the cities within their home provinces. Selecting Heilongjiang, Hunan, Tianjin and Zhejiang for the study ensures that a mix of inter-provincial and intra-provincial migrants is included in the sample. Tianjin and Zhejiang, as economically advanced locales, are major recipients of migrants from other provinces. In Tianjin and the three cities sampled in Zhejiang approximately 80% of the migrants in the sample were from other provinces. In the three cities in Heilongjiang 50% of migrants sampled were from provinces outside Heilongjiang and 50% were from within Heilongjiang. In the three cities surveyed in Hunan, 95% of migrants sampled were from within Hunan.

Figure 1: Gender distributions of migrants and urban locals (% of total)

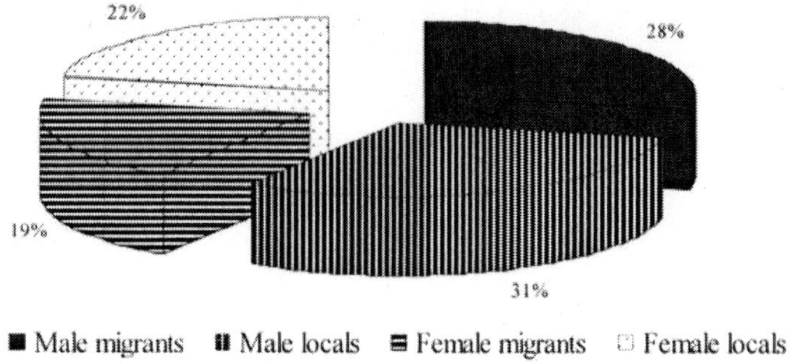

Figure 2: Age distribution of migrants

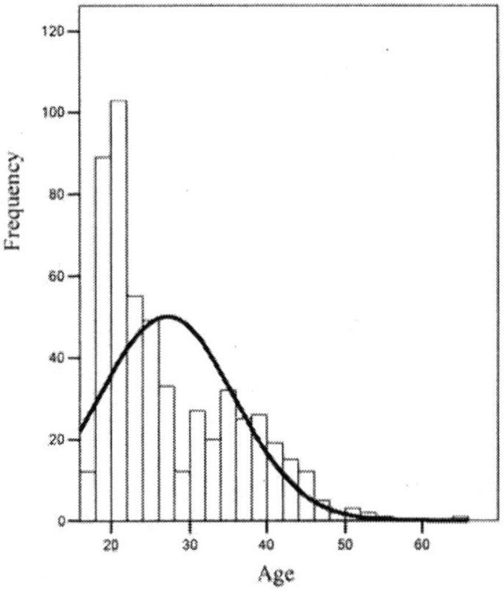

Respondents were randomly selected by local Labour Bureaus and completed a survey administered by staff trained in interviewing techniques by staff at the Beijing Ministry of Labour and Social Security. The total sample numbered 983 (59.2%) males and 680 (40.8%) females. Within gender, there were approximately even splits between residential registration (*hukou*) types. Of the males in the sample, 52.4% were local urban residents with non-agricultural *hukou,* while 47.6% were migrants with agricultural *hukou*. Of the females, 53.9% were locals and 43.2% were migrants. Within each of the two registration types, more males (60.0%) than females (40.0%) held agricultural *hukou* and more males (58.5%) than females (41.5%) held urban *hukou*; however, these group differences were not significant. Across the total sample, there was an approximately even distribution of male migrants, female migrants, male locals and female locals (see Figure 1).

Figure 2 shows the age distribution among the migrant sample. The mean age of migrants in the sample was 27.11 years (SD = 8.67 years) in a range of 16 to 65 years. The age distributions among migrants was significantly skewed (Kolmogorov-Smirnov statistic = 3.931, $p < .05$) in favour of the younger end of the distribution. That was to be expected, as several studies have reported that the majority of migrants tend to be aged under 40 (see Nielsen, Nyland et al 2006).

Figure 3: Age distribution of locals

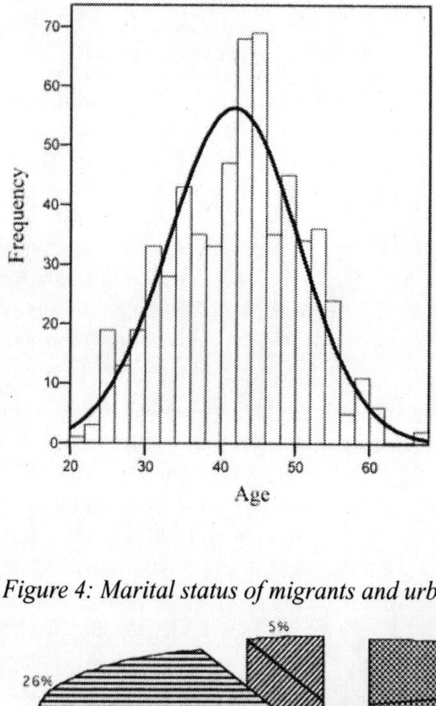

Figure 3 shows the age distribution among the sample of urban local residents. The mean age of the urban locals in the sample was 41.69 years (SD = 8.63 years) in a range of 20 to 68 years. While a sensitive Kolmogorov-Smirnov test statistic indicated a skewed distribution towards the older end of the local sample (1.588, $p < .05$), the ratio of the skewness index to its standard error was < 3.00 and the shape of the distribution approximated a normal curve overlay.

Figure 4: Marital status of migrants and urban locals (% of total)

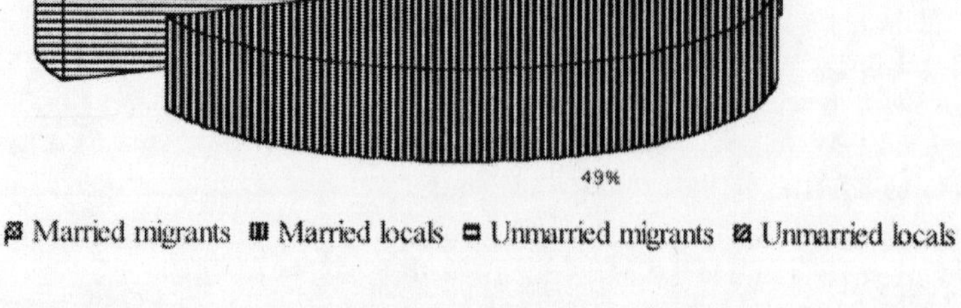

The majority of the sample (69.1%) was married. Of the unmarried respondents, 86% were migrants, while of the married respondents, 70% were local residents. The association between marital status and residential registration was, not surprisingly, highly significant (χ^2_4 (df=4) = 447.23, p <.001). The migrants in the sample were fairly evenly split between those married (43.2%) and unmarried (55.8%), yet among the locals, significantly more of the local respondents were married (88.8%) than unmarried (11.2%). Across the total sample, approximately half (49.1%) were married locals, a quarter (26%) were unmarried migrants, 20% were married migrants and the remaining 5% were unmarried locals (see Figure 4).

Table 2: Percentages across education categories for migrants, local respondents and the total sample

	percentage within migrant sample	percentage within local sample	percentage within total sample
College/university	5.5	35.4	21.4
Senior middle school	35.1	38.6	37.0
Junior middle school	53.4	23.4	37.5
Primary school	5.0	2.4	3.6
Illiterate/semi-illiterate	0.9	0.2	0.6

Table 2 shows percentage breakdowns for migrants, locals and the total sample across education categories. There was a significantly greater proportion of local residents (35.4%) *vis-à-vis* migrants (5.5%) with a college or university education, and a significantly higher proportion of migrants (54.4%) *vis-à-vis* local residents (23.4%) with a junior middle school level education (χ^2 (df=4) = 282.38, p <.001). While such educational differences between migrants and urbanites have been reported elsewhere (see Nielsen, Zhang et al 2005), they should also be interpreted within the context of further evidence that indicates that migrant workers tend to be better educated than those from rural locations that do not migrate (Hare 1999), hence differences between urban locals and non-migrating rural Chinese would be even further exacerbated.

Not surprisingly then, the vast majority of respondents (87.8%) with a college or university education were local urbanites, while the vast majority of illiterate or semi-literate (75.0%), primary school educated (66.9%) or junior middle school educated (65%) respondents were migrants. As can be seen in Figure 5, the proportion of urban residents increases steadily across the increasing levels of education.

Figure 5:Proportions of migrants and urban locals as a function of education category

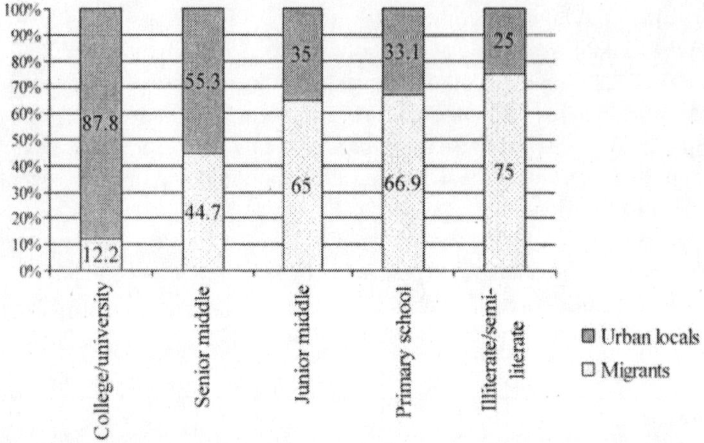

In terms of housing, the living conditions of migrants contrast markedly with the living conditions of urban locals in the sample. A large percentage of migrants in the sample (40.2%) reported living in dormitory-style housing. Such housing is typically provided to migrants by their employer and workers often share rooms with many others. Nearly half of the migrants in the sample (49.1%) reported living in accommodation provided by their enterprise, as opposed to 11.7% of urban locals. This type of housing has been documented elsewhere as being cramped, providing little or no private space (Jacka 2005). Our results are consistent with such earlier descriptions: in terms of actual usage area (in m^2), the migrants in our sample reported having on average 30.42m^2, while for locals, this area was reported as significantly larger at 58.70m^2 (t (df=1327) = 20.94, $p<.001$).

About one-quarter (24.1%) of migrants reported living in a flat and 28% said they live in a single-storey house, while among the urban locals, the vast majority (84.2%) reported living in a flat. Migrants reported having less living space than locals who also reported living in households with fewer residents, hence exacerbating further the gap in actual living area. While 84.2% of the urban local sample reported living in residences with two or more bedrooms, only 31.9% of migrants reported living in multi-bedroom residences. With this latter difference in mind, the fact that only 9.5% of locals (compared with 54.4% of migrants) said they reside with two or more other people further attests to the comparatively crowded living conditions of migrant workers.

Not surprisingly, home ownership also differed markedly between local residents and migrants. While 74.6% of the urban locals in the sample reported that they either bought or are buying their home, this was the case for only 14.5% of migrants. While such a difference is to be expected, the proportion of migrants who reported being homeowners in an urban centre is perhaps higher than expected. However, it may be that these migrants are striving to purchase an urban *hukou*, and one way of doing this would be to demonstrate that they have a stable urban residence.

Within house source, the majority of respondents (84.5%) who reported that they either own or are purchasing their home were urban locals. On the other hand, the majority of respondents living in either enterprise-provided (78.7%) or rental (73.3%) accommodation were migrants (see Figure 6).

Figure 6: Proportions of migrants and urban locals in each accommodation type

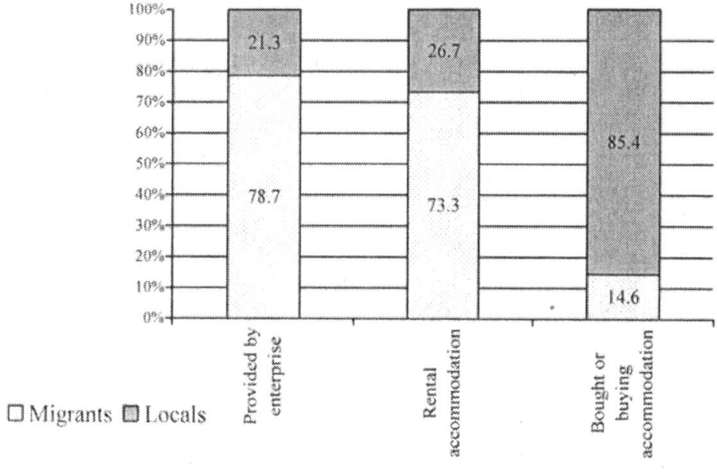

Income, savings and expenditure among migrants and urban locals and participation in leisure activities

Figures (in RMB) for mean monthly income, savings and basic expenditure of migrants and locals are depicted in Figure 7.

Local residents reported significantly higher monthly incomes than migrants ($\underline{t}$ (df=1630) = 10.051, $\underline{p}$ <.001). This result is to be expected, as urban residents typically have different occupational profiles to migrant workers (Roberts 2001;

Nielsen, Smyth & Zhang 2006)—the latter often working in the lower paid and so-called 'Three-D' jobs, or jobs that are 'dirty, dangerous and demeaning'.

Figure 7: Monthly income, savings and expenditure of migrants and urban locals

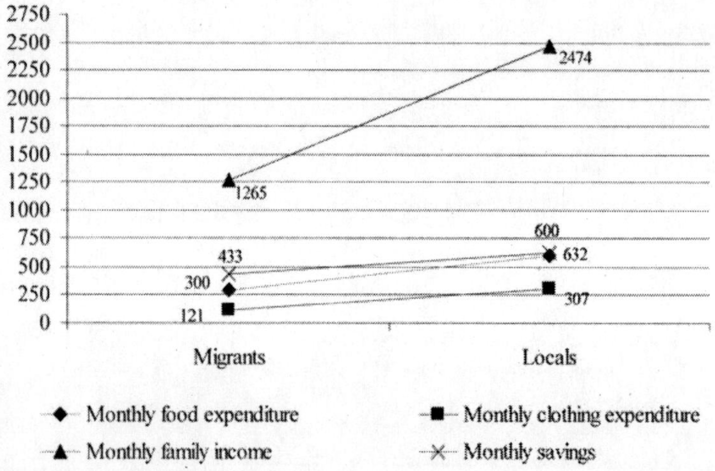

Despite having higher incomes than migrants, urbanites reported saving only 24.3% of their income, while migrants saved 34.3%. As it is common for migrant workers to send money back to remaining family in their home villages, this difference in saving proportions is to be expected. Knight and Song (2005) reported that in 1995 the average migrant remittance to their rural household was 21% of their urban income for the year. The case studies contained in Vicziany and Zhang's contribution to this volume also provide an interesting perspective, suggesting that it is common for the Uygur 'migrant entrepreneurs' to remit savings back to their hometowns in Xinjiang.

In terms of actual RMB, while local residents reported spending more per month on food ($\underline{t}$ (df=1589) = 12.615, $\underline{p}$ <.001) and clothing ($\underline{t}$ (df=1446) = 7.606, $\underline{p}$ <.001) than did migrants, the two groups spent about the same proportion of their monthly incomes on food and clothing (33.3% for migrants cf 37.9% for urbanites). Given similar proportions of spending on these two basic living items, yet proportionately less saving among urban locals, urbanites, then, spent proportionately more of their incomes than migrants on things other than basic living expenses. While spending is likely to be higher, proportionately, among urbanites on both housing and consumer durables, our results indicate that a further explanation for this difference in spending patterns lies in greater expenditure on leisure consumption.

Firstly, in terms, of engagement in leisure activities across the board, migrants reported undertaking few leisure activities. Indeed the vast majority of migrants (78.3%) reported that they had undertaken none of the following basic leisure activities in the past three months: attending a library, going to a bookstore, going to the cinema, going to a nightclub, going to a video arcade or going to the park (see Figure 8).

Figure 8: Percentage of migrants undertaking each leisure activity some time during the past three months as a function of frequency

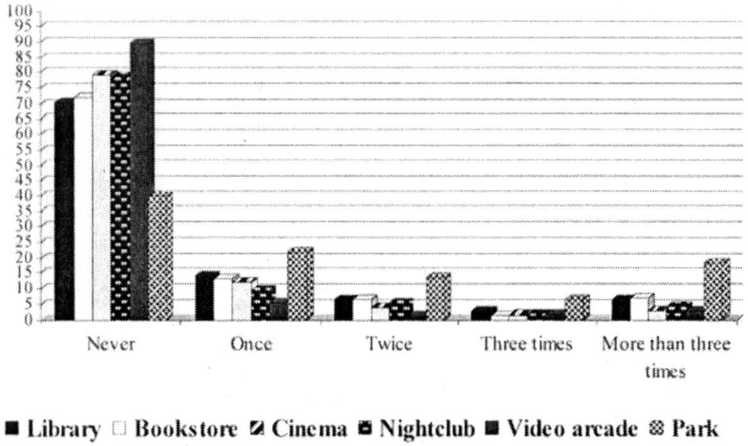

Of those migrants who did undertake some leisure activity, the most popular were going to the park or the library—activities that attract no charge. Rarely did migrants report attending venues for which they had to pay, such as nightclubs, video arcades or the cinema. One reason for migrants' non-attendance at such venues may be the charge, or it simply may be that migrants feel unwelcome at such public venues, as has been documented elsewhere (see Chan 2002; Jacka 2005).

The leisure profile of urban locals was rather different to that of migrant workers. While 68% of urban locals reported undertaking no leisure activities in the past three months, when urban locals did partake in leisure, it tended to be more frequently than did migrants, as well as of a different nature. In particular, local residents reported visiting paying venues, such as the cinema or a nightclub much more frequently than did migrants. And locals who went to the park, went more frequently than did migrants (see Figure 9).

Figure 9: Percentage of urban locals undertaking each leisure activity some time during the past three months as a function of frequency

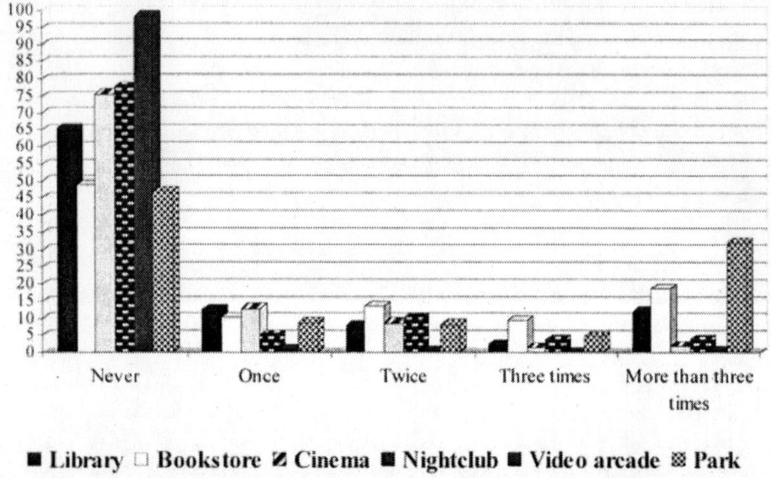

These results paint two very different pictures of leisure consumption in urban China. On the one hand, urban locals tend to undertake more leisure activities that attract charges than do migrants, perhaps helping to account for their tendency to spend a greater proportion of their incomes than migrants. Urban locals also tend to partake in a wider range of leisure activities than migrants. With the exception of going to the video arcade, locals in the sample reported far greater frequencies of multiple trips to leisure venues. That the urban local sample reported infrequent use of video arcades can probably be explained by the age profile of the sample. Migrants' leisure, on the other hand, was concentrated largely around the single activity of going to the local park.

Concluding remarks

Since the advent of market reforms in China, living standards in urban areas have steadily increased. Not surprisingly, many urban residents now welcome further reform to the economy (Nielsen, Nyland et al 2005). Accompanying these reforms has been the introduction of novel forms of leisure that China's new urban consumers have embraced with interest and vigour. As China surges further into the global economy and her residents make the transition from simply seeing and experiencing a new range of entertainment options to actually *expecting* them, the growth in leisure demand is likely to increase significantly.

Perhaps not surprisingly though, it would seem that the millions of off-farm migrants residing in urban centres in China have been slower to embrace the contemporary entertainment *milieu*. This wariness may have several foundations. First, while some migrants migrate for the experience of migration, most migrants migrate to the cities primarily to work and to provide for their families back in their hometown. If the focus for most migrants is on earning, then it would logically follow that migrants would tend to spend relatively little on entertainment. Second, the typically exhausting nature of migrants' work may simply render them unable to find either the time or the energy for leisure. This might be further reflected by the fact that when migrants do partake in leisure, it is almost exclusively a trip to the park. Such trips might simply be an escape from their overcrowded living conditions and frequently harsh workplaces to sit and relax. Third, the frequently reported negative attitudes that urban locals have towards migrants (see Nielsen, Nyland et al 2006) may discourage migrants from attending public entertainment venues. Fourth, it may by that the leisure activities that migrants would ideally wish to engage in are simply not available in the cities or that migrants partake of more traditional forms of leisure such as playing cards, visiting friends or simply walking the streets (a common sight in cities such as Beijing and Shanghai) that were not examined in this study.

On this latter point, the challenge before urban planners is to identify the range of leisure pursuits that are desired by established urban residents and off-farm migrants in China's urban centres. Identification of such leisure preferences will be a step towards providing potentially ideal leisure lifestyles, where preferences can be matched to availability. The creation of a demographically tailored pool of leisure choices in urban China is then likely to further fuel the engines of her burgeoning economy, for if you build it they will come.

Notes

1 The concept of leisure was known in China before the founding of the People's Republic. According to Maoist literature, workers in the pre-revolutionary era were burdened by a large, parasitic leisure-class.

2 The four cities with provincial status are Beijing, Chongqing, Shanghai and Tianjin.

chapter nine

Labour migration and tuberculosis in rural China: a case study of Henan province

Sukhan Jackson, Adrian C Sleigh, Wang Guo-Jie and Lui Xi-Li

Introduction

The post 1979 economic reforms have brought remarkable economic growth to China with an average annual economic growth of nearly 9% in the past 10 years (NBS 2004a:55). However, the health aspect of China's development is not so impressive. China remains one of the 22 high tuberculosis-burdened countries that together account for 80% of the world's tuberculosis cases. Indeed, tuberculosis has re-emerged since the mid-1980s as a global health emergency and major cause of death. In 2000 nearly 2 million people throughout the world died of tuberculosis. There are 4.5 million Chinese tuberculosis patients, the second highest number in the world after India (WHO 2005). Amongst China's 27 infectious diseases listed in the case report system for 2003, pulmonary tuberculosis had the second highest incidence rate (52.36/100,000) after viral hepatitis (NBS 2004a:868). Some 1.45 million new cases of tuberculosis are estimated for each year (CTCC 2004). In China about 150,000 people die every year, the highest number among all causes of death from infectious diseases. Despite efforts by health authorities, tuberculosis control seems to be relatively ineffective as shown by the incidence rate trends in Table 1:

Table 1: Tuberculosis incidence rates per 100,000 population in China, 1999–2003

1999	2000	2001	2002	2003
39.03	41.68	44.06	44.00	52.36

Source: personal communication from Henan Province's tuberculosis Institute, 2005.

Concurrently in the past decade, China's fast-tracked export-oriented industrialisation, regional economic disparities, and widening rural–urban income gap are the main driving forces for the phenomenal out-migration of farmers to the cities and other rural areas. Since liberalisation of the labour market in the early 1990s, a ceaseless tide of unregulated labour mobility is taking place throughout China. The 2000 Fifth National Census recorded internal migration at 121 million, with 88.4 million rural workers accounting for 73% of the total (Zhang 2004). At least 7–10 million new migrants are estimated to leave the farm each year.

As Serena Lillywhite documents in her contribution to this volume, migrant workers are often housed in crowded dormitories and they work excessively long hours with very few rest days. Overcrowded housing increases the exposure of susceptible people to infectious air-borne diseases such as tuberculosis. The association between overcrowded housing and tuberculosis incidence has long been recognised (see Clark, Riben & Nowgesic 2002). If migrant workers get tuberculosis, they usually return to their villages to seek diagnosis and treatment (Cao, Su & Yang 2000).

In the context of China's massive internal migration, we ask: 'Is out-migration for work a significant risk factor of tuberculosis incidence?' We explore this issue for Henan where migration for work has also been steadily increasing (Table 2). By 2003, a total of 3.07 million rural Henan residents were estimated working outside their villages, elsewhere in Henan or in other provinces (NBS 2003b).

Table 2: Number of rural migrants, Henan, 2001–03

2001	2002	2003
2,358,000	2,515,000	3,068,000

Source: personal communication, Henan Province Tuberculosis Institute, 2006.

Background to off-farm migration in PRC

A developing country that engages in rapid industrialisation and achieves high economic growth also undergoes transitional changes in demography and disease pattern. The demographic change often includes off-farm migration for paid employment in other rural areas or in cities. At the same time an epidemiological transition of disease pattern also takes place with a switch from infectious diseases to chronic diseases, as a result of a decline in infant and child mortalities and longer life expectancy (Jack 1999). In some cases such a transition is not complete and certain infections persist or reappear, frequently among the poor, while chronic non-communicable diseases also increase. The process of China's economic development is characterised by such an incomplete transition with massive population mobility and changing disease patterns.

At present, China's rural-urban migration for work is phenomenal with over 100 million workers on the move. This is predominantly non-*hukou* migration, a term describing the non-permanent employment of farm labourers in unattractive jobs shunned by local residents. Non-*hukou* migrants are the hundred-odd million of self-initiated rural migrants who do not have government approval to reside permanently in their destinations.

Hukou or household registration began in the cities in 1951 and was extended to the countryside in 1955 (Chan & Zhang 1998). Shortly after the State Council's directive in 1955 to set up a permanent system of household (*hukou*) registration, food rationing had to be implemented in the cities to ease the food shortages caused by the policy of deliberately paying low prices to farmers as a support measure for China's planned industrialisation. Only urban registered households were issued with coupons for buying rationed goods at affordable prices; and this discrimination against temporary residents became an additional barrier to labour mobility. The rationing of life's necessities in cities lasted for about 30 years. As a result of economic reforms which effectively raised agricultural output and productivity, rationing coupons were abolished in the early 1990s at the same time the labour market was liberalised.

In the years immediately after the 1979 agriculture reforms migration for work was supply-driven. The improved productivity under the new household responsibility system had resulted in a surplus supply of rural labour that must be employed off the land. Government policy at that time was to promote speedy establishment of township industrial enterprises to absorb the surplus labour. These 'redundant' farmers would temporarily migrate to the newly industrialising townships for paid employment but return to their villages after working outside for a few years.

Beginning in 1992, migration for work has been demand-driven and the number of rural–urban migrants has been increasing. Since 1992, the focus of China's economic development is mostly on the eastern seaboard and the southeast region which are opening up to foreign investment and foreign ownership, and offering generous exemptions to the current employment regulations. Labour intensive industries are flourishing in these regions, attracting multitudes of skilled and lower skilled rural workers especially from the poor interior provinces. In 1992–2000, the transient workforce increased from the already large 70 million to 121 million (Chan 1999; Zhang 2004).

Today, there is still no free choice in permanent residence because the government continues to impose a migration (transfer) quota to control the number of people qualified to change permanently their household registration.

Thus, when rural migrant workers become too sick to work, they are sent home to their villages where their households are registered.

To explore the hypothesis that work migration carried substantial risk of tuberculosis incidence, we obtained primary data from a sample of tuberculosis patients in rural Henan in 2002–04. A nationwide random sample survey for tuberculosis epidemiology in 2000 showed that tuberculosis prevalence in Henan (population 96.7 million) was 497 cases per 100,000 and prevalence of sputum-positive cases was 132 per 100,000. We collected direct evidence from 160 adult tuberculosis cases and compared their migration experience with 320 tuberculosis-free neighbourhood controls. As far as we know, we were the first to use community case-controls for tuberculosis research in China.

Methods

Our local knowledge enabled us to choose four counties that represented the socio-geographic zones typical of rural Henan from the more economically developed Gongyi to less developed counties like Linying and Zhenping. We restricted study entry to new tuberculosis cases in the economically productive age group (25–60 years) and with local household registration (*hukou*) which defined the tuberculosis cases as true residents of the respective counties. Re-treatment and non-pulmonary tuberculosis cases were excluded. We were unable to predetermine the gender and specific ages of the cases to be studied because we collected information on all eligible cases (adults with new pulmonary tuberculosis) as they occurred in sequence, until reaching our target of about 40 cases in each county. The advantage of this approach was that we captured the emerging trend of case characteristics in rural Henan. All our cases conformed to the international case definition for pulmonary tuberculosis (WHO 2005).

For each case, we had two controls of the same gender and the same five-year age group who had never had tuberculosis. The controls were chosen from neighbouring homes on the left and right of the cases. We also collected information on variables such as marital status, education, smoking before tuberculosis diagnosis, outside work history, nature and condition of employment, tuberculosis treatment costs, annual household income, and household assets.

Tuberculosis cases and their controls were interviewed in their homes between one and three months after patients registered as new tuberculosis cases. We held follow-up interviews on the tuberculosis cases after ten to 12 months in order to assess the longer-term socioeconomic consequences. We had 144 follow-ups as 11 patients had died and five were missing.

Results and discussion

All four counties contained large populations of more than 700,000 people; of which 80% were rural. These study counties detected and reported an incidence of active pulmonary tuberculosis at between 26/100,000 and 75/100,000 and smear-positive pulmonary tuberculosis at between 9/100,000 and 36/100,000 (see Table 3).

Table 3: Four study counties: selected statistics, 2002–2003

	Gongyi	Linying	Zhenping	Yuzhou
Population	790,000	710,000	950,000	1,190,000
Farmers as % of population	82	83	88	87
Average net income of rural residents (RMB)	3,725	2,749	2,468	3,007
Per capita GDP (RMB)	15,602	8,212	8,888	8,958
Birth rate (/1,000)	9.5	9.0	9.0	8.0
Death rate (/1,000)	5.2	4.0	7.0	5.0
Male:female ratio	103:100	117:100	131:100	137:100
Reported incidence of active pulmonary tuberculosis ($/10^5$)	26	42	47	75
Reported incidence of smear-positive pulmonary tuberculosis ($/10^5$)	9	15	18	36

US$1 = 8 RMB

Sources: County statistical yearbooks; data on tuberculosis incidence from Henan Province Tuberculosis Institute.

Demographics of tuberculosis cases

Our sample of 160 cases comprised 123 males (77%) and 37 females. We found the gender distribution in our sample was similar to that of tuberculosis in China in the 25–60 age group, where three-quarters of tuberculosis patients are found. Of the patients, 15% had no spouse (unmarried, widowed and divorced), 72% were heads of household, 47% had out-migrated for work and 71% had a smoking history (see Appendix 1). Only 7% were illiterate, 34% had primary school education, 47% reached junior high school, and 13% had senior or above-senior education. There was no substantial difference in the education level between the cases and their controls (47% of controls had junior high school education).

We note that the number of male migrants exceeded females by two and a half times in Henan in 2002 (NBS 2003b), which was similar to that found in the 1999 national rural sample survey of migrants conducted by the National Bureau of Statistics when males also dominated at the ratio of 202:100. This feature of males exceeding females is an interesting contrast to more than a decade ago when a Chinese Academy of Social Sciences (CASS) survey in 1986 found a larger proportion of female in-migrants to the cities in the ratio of 80 males to 100 females (Rowland 1992). Although the CASS survey had better coverage than previous datasets, the exclusion of unsanctioned rural–urban migration in the survey might understate the true picture (Rowland 1992). A favourable factor for China's economic development is that rural migrants are educated. Even in 1999 the national survey found nearly 60% were educated to junior high school (*chuzhong*) and nearly 19% had primary school education with younger migrants having better education than the old (Chan 1999).

Work migration of tuberculosis cases and controls

In all four study counties, the proportion of cases reporting work migration was higher than for the controls (Table 4). Nearly half the tuberculosis cases (47% or 75/160) had out-migrated for work compared to fewer than a third of controls (29% or 94/320), a substantial and significant difference ($p<0.001$). Our logistic regression analysis showed that rural workers with outside work history were significantly associated with tuberculosis ($p<0.05$, OR2.096, 95%CI 1.319–3.331).

Table 4: History of out-migration for work among 160 tuberculosis cases and 320 controls, Henan

	Previous migration for work			
	Tuberculosis cases		Controls	
	Number/total	%	Number/total	%
Gongyi	16/41	39.0	28/82	34.1
Linying	19/40	47.5	29/80	36.3
Zhenping	20/40	50.0	32/80	40.0
Yuzhou	20/39	51.3	5/78	6.4
Total	75/160	46.9	94/320	29.4

Multivariate regression and odds-ratio analyses of tuberculosis cases and their controls

For the case-control analysis we first identified potential confounding variables by performing matched univariate analyses for each available variable and noting any significant association ($p<0.05$) with tuberculosis status. We then used all those potentially significant variables in a final multivariate model using matched logistic regression provided they had a substantial (≥10%) influence on the estimate of the outside work effect.

Variables in the final model included outside work history, smoking, relative wealth within the village and marital status. Results showed that tuberculosis cases in rural Henan were substantially more likely to have been exposed to outside work (OR2.2, 95%CI 1.3–3.6). Smoking was also found to have a significant effect on incidence of tuberculosis. Using zero smoking as the reference, we calculated the odds ratio to be 4.3 for people smoking 1–20 cigarettes a day and 6.5 when they smoke more than 20 cigarettes a day. For the cases, smoking status referred to their habits at the time of the onset of tuberculosis symptoms and for the controls, it referred to the time of the interview. We will discuss the influence of household economic status later.

Migrant work and living conditions of 51 tuberculosis cases who worked outside in last three years

We obtained some details of work conditions from 51 tuberculosis cases (32%) who reported outside work in the last 3 years. Nearly half of these 51 tuberculosis sufferers (23 or 45%) had worked in other provinces, 14 (28%) in other counties inside Henan, and 14 (28%) outside their villages in the same county. Over half of the 51 cases (53%) had indoor jobs while the rest worked outdoors; the largest group (25%) worked in factories, followed by construction (21%). A total of 12% had worked in the manufacture of export goods and 4% in foreign joint ventures.

As Serena Lillywhite notes in Chapter 6 and as discussed elsewhere (see Murphy 2002), rural out-migrants are generally vulnerable to labour exploitation. Among these 51 tuberculosis cases, 80% did not rest on Sundays; 73% had worked for 9–12 hours a day; 8% for 13–18 hours; and only 20% worked the eight-hour day normal for most Chinese employees. Crowded sleeping arrangements were typical. Half of them (49%) slept in dormitories with other people. The majority shared with more than six persons and lived in rooms measuring 16–25 m^2, and in one case 60 people shared the dormitory. Females (cases and controls) were less represented in hard physical labour.

We also found substantial differences in work conditions when we compared the 51 tuberculosis cases with 57 controls who had similar work histories over the same time period. Non-conditional logistic regression was used to model the influence of work and other factors. Gender, age, smoking and socioeconomic status were not found to be significant causes of tuberculosis in this restricted sub-set of 51 cases and 57 controls. More research into these issues is needed for off-farm migrant workers in China.

Our final multivariate model of significant work conditions had four variables: unpleasant workplace, more than eight work-hours a day, no rest day each week, and crowded dormitories. All the four variables were significantly associated with tuberculosis ($P<0.05$) with odds ratios exceeding 3.5. Crowded living quarters would increase the exposure to infectious tuberculosis disease for the susceptible poor migrants, and may increase the probability of transmission.

Household economic status (HES) of tuberculosis cases

The three indicators used to measure household economic status were (a) average annual household income (b) household assets and (c) relative wealth within the village (Table 5). Annual household income indicates the household's economic status in the short term but does not show accumulation of wealth. A more useful indicator of accumulation capacity is household assets which is perhaps a more reliable measure of HES than annual household income. Relative wealth within the village is broader than the other two indicators, but also involves making a value judgement. Our study confirms that good HES can protect people from tuberculosis disease and that household poverty is an important risk of tuberculosis in rural China. The HES of the cases was lower than that of the controls (Table 5).

a. Average annual household income of the 160 tuberculosis cases was 4,994 RMB compared with 5,604 RMB for the 320 controls, the difference was not significant ($t=1.3$, $p=0.17$). Using the official absolute poverty line of 625 RMB/person/year and the average household size in Henan's countryside being four, we estimated household absolute poverty to be 2,563 RMB/year. We found 29.4% of the cases (47/160) to be in household absolute poverty compared to 22.5% of the controls.
b. Household assets. Average value of household assets of tuberculosis cases was 21,812 RMB, significantly fewer than 24,489 RMB of the controls ($t=2.55$, $p=0.01$). Nearly one-third (31%) of the cases were in the lowest quartile (≤16,699 RMB) compared to one-fifth (20%) of the controls.
c. Relative wealth within village. Nearly half (46%) of cases ranked themselves in the lowest third for the village compared to one-fifth (20%) of the controls.

Table 5: Household economic status of 160 cases (before tuberculosis) and 320 controls

	Case %	Controls %	Adjusted OR* (95%CI)
Annual household income (RMB)**			
<2,563 (poverty line)	29.4	22.5	Reference
2,564–5,125	42.5	42.8	0.67 (0.39–1.14)
≥5,126	28.1	34.7	0.54 (0.26–1.12)
Household assets (RMB)***			
0–16,699 (lowest quarter)	31.3	20.0	Reference
16,700–21,076	26.9	25.9	0.74 (0.41–1.32)
21,077–28,779	21.3	26.6	0.52 (0.28–0.94)
≥28,780	20.6	27.5	0.48 (0.25–0.92)
Relative wealth within village			
Lower third	46.3	19.7	Reference
Middle and upper thirds	53.8	80.3	0.2 (0.1–0.4)

*matched analysis

**Household poverty line (estimated to be 2563 RMB/household/year based on average four persons per household and Chinese official poverty line of 625 RMB/person/year).

***Household assets were calculated from average market prices in study counties; lowest quarter 0-16,699; second quarter ≥16,700-<21,077; third quarter ≥21,077-<28,780; highest quarter ≥28,780.

US$1 = 8 RMB

Regression and odds ratio analyses of household economic status (HES)

Conditional logistic regression model was used to analyze the odds ratio of HES. Univariate conditional logistic regression analysis results showed that all three household economic indicators were associated with tuberculosis; the better the household economic status, the less risk of tuberculosis.

We obtained results from analyses of a multivariate conditional logistic regression model and adjusted the OR (with 95% CI) of several variables (education, number of rooms in house, smoking history, marital status, previous out-migration for work) with each of the three HES variables. After adjustments, two HES variables—household assets and 'relative wealth within village' were still significantly correlated with tuberculosis incidence; only the adjusted OR of annual household income was not significantly different.

Economic costs of tuberculosis disease

The average cost of tuberculosis disease of the 144 patients was 7,367 RMB. Average direct cost of treatment was 1,948 RMB (Table 6 items 1–5). Direct costs included medical costs and non-medical costs. Medical costs were the expenses in county tuberculosis clinics, in private clinics and general hospitals including laboratory tests, clinical examinations, tuberculosis and non tuberculosis medicines. Direct non-medical costs were transport and food consumed during travel to seek treatment.

When symptoms appeared, patients usually consulted the doctors in private clinics or general hospitals; our results show such expenditure in private clinics and hospitals averaged 567 RMB.[1] When suspected of tuberculosis, patients were transferred to the county tuberculosis clinics where the average cost was calculated to be 1,180 RMB. We consider indirect costs to include the opportunity costs of loss of productive time of patients and carers; the income loss for individual patients averaged 4,559 RMB (Table 6).

The average total cost of tuberculosis was high in our study, at 7,367 RMB. This was a heavy burden on the family with an average annual household income of 4,994 RMB. Even if income losses of patients and companions (items 8 and 9 in Table 6) were excluded, the average total cost was 2,772 RMB, accounting for 55.5% of annual household income. Some analysts estimate that a cost-burden greater than 10% of household income is likely to be catastrophic for the family (Russell 2004). Most households in our study had little capacity to pay for treatment. We found that two-thirds (66%) borrowed from relatives or friends, 8.3% from banks, 45% sold assets such as wheat, pigs, cattle, and so on. Undoubtedly, tuberculosis disease often leads to deeper impoverishment of the patient's household.

The Chinese government, in 1991–1999, adopted the international 'Directly Observed Therapy Short-course' (DOTS) strategy from the World Health Organisation. After 2002 the DOTS programme was expanded in Henan; and tuberculosis patients were given free treatment in the county tuberculosis clinics for six months under a loan from the World Bank/UK DFID and Japanese aid. But it is important to understand the high treatment cost illustrated in Table 6 persisted despite the free treatment. Our results show that the average total cost of treatment in county tuberculosis clinics was estimated at 1,256 RMB (Table 6 items 1 and 3). Tuberculosis patients still incurred treatment costs because Chinese doctors usually extended tuberculosis treatment beyond the free six months; so patients had to pay out-of-pocket for the extended treatment period. Like elsewhere in China, health providers in our study counties had a tendency to over-service with unnecessary examinations and tests, and overprescribe drugs outside the listed free items. Such opportunistic behaviour may be explained by the difficult financial situation of the poorer local governments to match the provincial government funding for tuberculosis (obtained as a World Bank loan), as stipulated by the central government and the Ministry of Health. Since some of the local governments were slow to release the funds, their tuberculosis clinics had to find ways and means to cover operating costs, salaries and other costs.

Table 6: Treatment costs of 144 tuberculosis cases within 10–12 months in four study counties*

	Av cost RMB	% total av
Cost items in county tuberculsosi clinics		
- drugs HRZE**	445.00	
- other tuberculsois drugs	86.10	
- other prescribed drugs	476.30	
- sputum tests	18.90	
- x-rays	96.50	
- blood tests	55.20	
- urine tests	2.20	
1. Average total cost in county tuberculosis clinics	1,180.10	16.0
2. Cost in general hospitals or private clinics	567.30	7.7
3. Cost in tuberculosis clinics above county level	75.50	1.0
4. Travel for tests/drugs: patients and companions	92.90	1.3
5. Food during travel: patients and companions	32.60	0.4
6. Self-medication (Chinese medicine)	117.30	
7. Nutritious food	706.00	
8. Loss of income for patients	4,559.40	
9. Loss of income for companions	36.00	
Total average cost of illness for 144 cases	7,366.90	100

*After 10-12 months 11 people had died and five went missing. US$1 = 8 RMB
** The four standard drugs for tuberculosis.

Conclusions

Our study has provided evidence that tuberculosis disease was linked to out-migration for work ($p<0.05$), with an exposure odds ratio greater than two after adjusting for other variables including smoking. We measured the household economic status (HES) of our tuberculosis cases and found they had lower

HES than their matched neighbourhood controls. Although the association of tuberculosis with poverty has been noted for China, direct evidence has been lacking. Here, we have collected direct evidence from individual tuberculosis cases and their households.

We also obtained first-hand information on the inferior working conditions of migrant workers, reflecting some of the negative outcomes of globalisation and the growth of export industries. We cannot conclude from this study alone why migrant workers are more likely to get active tuberculosis. However, our multivariate regression and odds-ratio analyses showed that four workplace conditions were significantly associated with tuberculosis: crowded dormitories, long working-shifts, no rest day each week and unpleasant workplaces. Our study of 160 cases and 320 controls found a strong link between poverty, off-farm migration and tuberculosis.

There has been much publicity especially in the media about the plight of migrant workers (Yardley 2004) but the focus is on unpaid wages, discrimination and legal rights, with scarce attention paid to labour exploitation and crowded living quarters. The government must impose stricter workplace regulations to prevent exploitative working hours and sub-standard dormitories. The home counties of the rural migrants are now bearing the ill-health costs and so do the individual tuberculosis sufferers. Adequate public health funding is urgently needed in the rural areas as part of China's poverty eradication programme. Economic aspects of tuberculosis in China are explored further in Jackson et al (2006a; 2006b). What is critically needed is effective financial support for poverty-stricken tuberculosis sufferers who are falling deeper into the poverty trap because of income losses and the associated economic burden of the disease.

Notes

Research funded by UNDP/World Bank/WHO Special Programme for Research and Training in Tropical Diseases (TDR) A10166.

1. Some tuberculosis sufferers preferred to visit the general hospitals or private clinics for injections or drips because they believed injections were better than oral TB medicine. Additionally, when side-effects appeared in the course of treatment, patients would see private doctors in nearby health stations or hospitals.

Appendix 1: Characterisitcs of 160 tuberculosis cases and 320 controls

Characteristics	Cases (160)		Controls (320)	
	N	%	N	%
Cases and controls in county				
- Gongyi	41	25.6	82	25.6
- Lingyin	40	25.0	80	25.0
- Zhenping	40	25.0	80	25.0
- Yuzhou	39	24.4	39	24.4
Male	123	76.9	246	76.9
Female	37	23.1	74	23.1
Age				
25–29	19	11.9	38	11.9
30–34	22	13.8	43	13.4
35–39	19	11.9	38	11.9
40–44	13	8.1	28	8.8
45–49	26	16.3	51	15.9
50–54	31	19.4	61	19.1
55–60	30	18.8	61	19.1
Married	136	85.0	301	94.1
Not married	24	15.0	19	5.9
Head of household	115	71.9	242	75.6
Not head of household	45	28.1	78	24.4
Outside work history	75	46.9	94	29.4
No outside work history	85	53.1	226	70.6
Education				
- Nil	11	6.9	17	5.3
- Primary	54	33.8	99	30.9
- Junior secondary	75	46.9	151	47.2
- Senior secondary and above	20	12.5	53	16.6
Smoker before tuberculosis	113	70.6	175	54.7
Non-smoker before tuberculosis	47	29.4	145	45.3

Section III

Comparative perspectives

chapter ten

Workers and migrants: India and China circa 2005

Amiya Kumar Bagchi

Introduction

Every human being is unique. Each is then classified as somebody's daughter/son and somebody claims to be her father/mother. Membership in the family is then extended to membership in a particular kind of family; the particular kind is decided on the basis of place of residence, clan, linguistic or ethnic ascription, and in the Indian case, caste. He/she continues to be classified or reclassified in these and many other ways throughout life. And of course, gender becomes intertwined with all these different sorting procedures.

Humans are also migratory by nature. That is why practically all the regions of the globe were found to be inhabited when globetrotters and voyagers began exploring regions hitherto unknown to them.

Migration has led to further complexities in classifying people and in the treatment of one group by another. Ancient migrants from Palestine, and people claiming a familial or religious affinity with them have continued to regard themselves as Jews whether they are settled in Astrakhan, Cochin or Montevideo. Jews were often welcomed in Arab domains as traders and finance ministers long before the horrible complexities of the Palestinian-Israeli divide. Indian potentates often welcomed migratory *sahukars* as sources of credit before British laws turned them into exploiting ogres in the imagination of the peasants among whom they worked.

I am prefacing my chapter with these platitudes because we often become immured in the discourse of our own times and our own disciplines. Human beings were working as peasants, artisans, surgeons or washerwomen long before the concept of a labour market came up. Migrants have not been regarded as threats in all societies at all times. Australia, for example, is predominantly peopled by migrants and descendants of migrants, and from the time governments were set up in the constituent territories of Australia, they provided a host of incentives for potential migrants and settlers.

For several millennia people have worked as hunter-gatherers, farmers, shepherds, craftsmen, nurturers of children or musicians, shamans and artists. They have migrated permanently or seasonally in search of new pastures or habitations. They have opened up new lands to plant corn, rice or beans and founded villages and cities. Except in a few European countries and their overseas settlements and in pockets of China, India or West Asia and North Africa, until the 19th century they have not engaged in these activities predominantly as hostages of a labour market or as migratory labour power. Labour markets have to be created and nurtured and so has migratory labour as an essential component of those markets. The tales of genesis, nurturing and disciplining that market and that component are as complicated as the history of modern times—however short or long we want to make the time span of that modernity.

Labour markets and migrant labour in contemporary India

There was a wage labour market in India before British colonialism. There was also an extensive, landless, proletariat degraded into conditions of untouchability and agrestic servitude. The British withdrew legal recognition of slavery, but did little to touch praedial or domestic servitude either in India or in other British dependencies (Lovejoy & Hogendorn 1993; Bagchi 2005b). That is one of the reasons why vestiges of the *hali* system in southern Gujarat and the *kamiya* system in Jharkhand survive (Breman 1996). British policies of little investment in India, and massive extraction of surplus led to the creation of a large class of destitute peasants and artisans whose only recourse was to work as wage labourers on any terms. Not content with disciplining workers primarily through the threat of starvation, until the 1910s, the British gave an enormous amount of non-market coercive power both to the landlords in whose territories the peasants worked, and to the owners of plantations and mines to which the destitute labour force flocked. In fact, many mine-owners combined the power of landlords and capitalists (Rothermund & Wadhwa 1978; Bagchi 1989:ch 1). There are many other areas in which there is a marked continuity between colonial times and the post-independence labour markets. For example, much has been made of the distinction between workers in the informal and the formal sectors since the introduction of that terminology in the international discourse by Hart (1973). In India, a distinction with the same connotation was made between workers in the unorganised and organised sectors long before independence. But it was known that workers toiled in the formal sector without any rights of job protection (not that workers formally on the rolls of such enterprises had much protection either) and that the formal and informal economies in industry, mines and banking were intimately connected, although there might be continual jostling for more room within that intimate relation (Bagchi 2002b; 2002a).

After independence in India, economic and industrial growth picked up, but so did the growth rate of population and the labour force. After reaching a peak in 1955–65, industrial growth suffered a deceleration to the end of the 1970s. While the Green Revolution quickened agricultural growth, it was not enough to remove the huge backlog of underemployment and seasonal unemployment in the rural areas. The traditional patterns of bondage were often loosened through state policies, and more importantly, through the spread of ideas of individual agency, casual bondage came up as a 'voluntary' choice of people who faced severe constraints in the markets for credit, produce and labour. The threat of unemployment and loss of subsistence is a powerful enforcer of discipline, and in many cases, a generator of new types of bondage.

Casual bondage versus floating labour is one symptom of segmentation. But there are many other markers of segmentation. In every country with functioning labour markets, gender, class, education and regional origin are markers of segmentation. In the Indian case, caste adds a marker of a type that can be found in very few other countries. As compared with China, in the Indian case, being an *Adivasi* (tribal person) also becomes an important distinguishing mark. Although China also has ethnic minorities, they form a much smaller proportion of the population than do *Adivasis* in India (about 12% of the total Indian population). Whether these markers show up in differences in wages, in conditions of work and living conditions in general, depends on the political regime, the degree of tightness in the labour market and in the long run, the speed with which investment and upgradation of major indices of human development takes place. The degree of tightness in the labour market cannot always be gauged by taking the employers' statements at face value. An employer is quite likely to complain about labour shortage, if he has to pay slightly more for the same amount of labour of the same type even if the cost of living for labourers is going up. This happened with European employers of Indian labour in the beginning of the last century, and extensive investigations revealed no shortage of the kind of labour the European firms employed (Bagchi 1972). Complaints about shortages of relatively unskilled workers in the fast-growing coastal regions of China seem to have a similar origin.

Indian rates of economic growth, capital accumulation or advances in building up human capabilities after independence were never enough to eliminate the huge backlog of underemployment of rural labourers, improve the productivity of skilled labourers and produce a tightness in the market for even nominally educated people (except perhaps at the highest levels for particular kinds of skills). But the effects of the Green Revolution in raising rural incomes, and a quickening of public sector investment were felt during the 1980s with an increase of more than three million employed in the 'organised' sector of the economy.

With regard to long-term migration from one state of the Indian Union to the others, the census data showed a steady decline in the proportion of immigrants to the resident population between the censuses of 1961 and 1991, in rural and urban areas (Kundu & Gupta 2000), even as there emerged large differences in population and workforce growth between different states. This lack of long-term mobility has, however, been combined with large-scale seasonal and specific task-related migration from the poorer or less educated states to more prosperous and better-educated ones. There has also been large-scale immigration from Bangladesh and Nepal into India, giving rise to serious political problems. We shall turn to the findings of some studies of such migration.

Meanwhile, let us look at the expectations of neo-liberal economists and the actual impact effect of 'economic reforms' on employment. These economists wanted a change in the economic strategy of the government, claiming, among other things, that the earlier regime of regulation hampered the growth of labour-intensive small-scale industries, by giving undue privileges to workers in the organised sector, thus putting a ratchet under the cost of labour in those industries. The ripple effect generated by this also inhibited employment in the unorganised sector of industry, and did not provide sufficient encouragement for labour-intensive exports. It was claimed further that lifting of the heavy hand of government would release private sector energy and would lead to a rise in rates of investment and economic growth. Also it was assumed that the lifting of official regulations would generate a high rate of growth of employment in the organised private sector. From 1991, India formally became attuned to the beat of the Washington consensus. Employment in the organised private sector rose by less than a million between 1991–92 and 1997–98, and then stagnated. Meanwhile, employment in the organised public sector actually declined so that such employment was static at around 27 million between 1991–92 and 2001–02 (RBI 2004). According to the 55th round of the National Sample Survey (NSS), for urban and rural areas together, the workforce participation rate was 397 per thousand, which would yield a workforce of more than 400 million in 2002–3 (the 2001 census yielded a population figure of 1,027 million).

Thus with fewer than 1% of the Indian work force enjoying anything like 'decent work' as defined by the International Labour Organisation (ILO), the labour market is awash with casual work and precarious self-employment. Between 1983 and 1999–2000, there was a steady increase in the proportion of casually employed male workers in rural and urban areas, and a fall in the proportion of males with regular employment. There was a rise in the proportion of regular employees among rural females (*Sarvekshana* 2002). But it should be noted that regular employment as such does not provide job security or any kind of social insurance. Much of the increase in regular employment among urban females is accounted for by domestic service. The usually low rates of unemployment as measured by the NSS are small comfort in a situation in which employment is often not enough to lift a person above the narrowly (and incorrectly) measured poverty level. Moreover, the usual measures of unemployment are based on what is called 'usual status employment'. But a person who is employed by the usual status criterion may be unemployed on the day of the survey or even for part of the week or the year preceding the survey. The NSS authorities use the difference as an indicator of the degree of underemployment. The measurement of true underemployment would, however, require a different conceptual framework and throw up much larger numbers. Underemployment is measured by the NSSO (National Sample Survey Organisation) in several different ways: one is the difference between the number of persons per 1,000 who were supposed to be usually employed and the number who had worked during the preceding seven days, taking into account all the hours worked by those who had worked any of those seven days. Another is the difference between the same number of usually employed and those who were considered to have been employed in the preceding week. The NSS 55th Round (1999–2000) report pointed out that 'the unemployed person–day rates…were higher than the rates obtained for persons, thereby indicating a high degree of unemployment. This is mainly due to the absence of regular employment for many workers' (*Sarvekshana* 2002:17). In the same Round (1999–2000), apart from questions about daily employment status, the weekly employment status and the usual status of unemployment and employment, the usually employed were also asked 'whether they worked more or less regularly throughout the year' (*Sarvekshana* 2002:26). By this criterion, women faced a greater insecurity of employment than men in rural and urban areas in 1999–2000 (*Sarvekshana* 2002: statement 27). Even among those who were supposed to have been employed according to their usual status, 10.5% of the males and 13.3% of the females in rural areas, and 6.5% of the males and 8.9% of the females in urban areas, did not work regularly. The degree of underemployment was, as expected, highest among casual workers. For instance, 'as high as 23 and 20% of female casual labourers engaged in public works did not work regularly throughout the year in urban and rural areas respectively' (*Sarvekshana* 2002:26). In addition, a substantial proportion of usually working persons of 15 years and above—ranging from 5.8% among rural females to 10.5% among urban males—were looking for additional work; a substantial fraction in the same group also wanted to change their jobs, mainly because their work was not sufficiently remunerative

(*Sarvekshana* 2002:tables 28 & 29). All these numbers together would amount to a very high degree of underemployment.

The central government Planning Commission took official cognisance of the seriousness of the unemployment situation and appointed two study groups, both under the chairmanship of SP Gupta, a member of the commission. The first was to study the development of small-scale industries with an eye to the generation of employment and the other was to suggest measures for attaining a target of generating an additional ten million jobs a year (PC 2001; 2002). The study groups estimated that, in spite of a slowdown of labour force growth from 2.43% between 1983 and 1993–94 to 1.31% between 1993–94 and 1999–2000, the incidence of unemployment was higher in the latter year, because the employment growth rate had fallen to 1.07%.

The reports concluded that even if the target growth rate of 8% a year were attained during the Tenth Five Year Plan period (a figure that is above the rate of growth attained by the Indian economy so far), the rate of unemployment would double by the end of the plan period, i.e., 2006–07. Since organised sector employment had turned negative, and the much-hyped service sector also had low employment elasticity, the study groups hit upon small-scale industries as the provider of the needed employment growth.

However, practically all the measures suggested by the study group to stimulate the small-scale industries are those already reversed by neo-liberal reforms. Reservation of particular industries for the small-scale sector had been abolished over a broad range of manufactures, privileged procurement by the government had gone the same way, and the compulsory direction of credit to the priority sector, including agriculture and small-scale industry had been whittled down. Unlike China, liberalisation of trade and domestic investment in India was accompanied by financial liberalisation. One major directive to public sector banks was to bring down their non-performing assets. Since political expediency dictated that big defaulters of bank loans could not be hauled up or penalised, the axe fell on small borrowers, cultivators and small-scale industrialists and on the employees of banks whose retrenchment was meant to bring down the salary bill. Foreign banks were virtually exempted from directed lending to the priority sector. The result was predictable, the proportions of bank credit extended to agriculture, small-scale industry and small borrowers has come down drastically since 1990 (Shetty 2005).[1] The proportion of institutional credit relative to the value of agricultural output has also fallen, as has agricultural growth compared with the pre-reform decades (Bagchi 2005c). I suspect that the same thing has happened to the relationship between bank credit and the value of small-scale sector output. Thus Indian agriculture and large swathes of the manufacturing industry have become constrained in both demand and credit during the era of financial liberalisation. An increasingly large section of the Indian population has faced financial exclusion, which has affected their prospects of self-employment and of becoming employers of wage labourers.

It is well known that the output elasticity of agriculture and industry has come down in the reform period. But this phenomenon must also be linked to other features of the reform period. One is the slow growth, if not the actual decline of public investment in agriculture (WB 2005a), which in its turn is related both to the central government's attempt to contain the deficit and its attempt to pass on most of the financial stringency demanded by the exercise to the constituent State governments. The latter, however, are largely responsible for public investment in agriculture[2].

A second systemic feature of the neo-liberal regime that has dampened output and employment growth in the labour-intensive sectors is the linking of agriculture and small-scale industry with the market in shares and derivatives. While forward trading in agricultural commodities may serve as a device to hedge risk, creating derivatives out of them can only serve speculators and big traders and exposes the farmers to a new variety of risk over which they have as little control as they do over the weather.

A similar kind of risk invaded small-scale industry when urban co-operative banks were permitted to accept equities and bonds as collateral and were allowed to trade in them. One result was the failure of a large number of urban co-operative banks, in Gujarat, Maharashtra and Andhra Pradesh—often with links to ruling party politicians—soon after this kind of licence was extended to them. The Reserve Bank of India tightened the regulations after that, but the trend towards the merging of banking and stockbroker functions continues to be encouraged by the Indian finance ministry.[3]

As I have pointed out earlier, in a country with a high degree of concentration of landholdings and rampant use of non-market coercive power, it is difficult for many members of the proletariat to escape bondage. When their access to public sources of employment, education, health care and credit is further restricted by neo-liberal reforms, the shackles of bondage tighten and that applies to workers in some of the most prosperous states. A study of two villages in Haryana, Rawal and Mukherjee (2005) found that most of the land was held by only a few families and the majority of households were landless. The latter were mostly indebted to their landlords, borrowed money at rates ranging from 24% to 36% (and some loans were taken at even higher rates) and many of them had to live like serfs on the fields with their families. The conditions of these workers were hardly different from those of traditionally bonded labourers, since their freedom to choose jobs or living space was so greatly restricted. Haryana is a state dominated by upper caste and upper class men with scant regard for human life (Haryana has about the lowest ratio of women to men in India), and foreign direct investment does not necessarily improve worker power. This was tragically demonstrated on 24 July 2005, when hundreds of workers peacefully protesting against the arbitrary actions of the management of Honda motorcycles and scooters India were brutally beaten up by a posse of policemen (*Hindustan Times* 2005). Ultimately, after strong public pressure was applied, an agreement was reached under which the workers were allowed to form a union, but they had to promise no strikes for a year even if the company violated labour laws. It was quite obvious that the Haryana government sided almost entirely with Honda Motors in this dispute.

India has traditional forms of bondage, inherited from father and grandfather to children and grandchildren, and there are parts of India where it is still a struggle to eradicate these. But debt bondage has come back in oppressive forms, and whole families now are moved as bonded labourers to work in brick-kilns and cane fields, with little hope of getting free of their bondage to labour contractors.

The intensive study of a relatively rich and fast-growing state, Gujarat, by Breman (1996) and his collaborators (for example, Shah, Rutten & Streefkerk 2002) has yielded a horrifying picture of the living conditions of migrant workers, and workers in general. Behind that condition lies not only an ideology of communalism as a method of labour control (Breman 2002; CCT 2002; Varadarajan 2002; Varshney 2002), but also the structural imbalances of Gujarat's fast growth during the last two decades (Bagchi, Das & Chattopadhyay 2005). While the tertiary and secondary sectors have shown fast growth of output, agricultural output has not shown any upward trend during the last two decades or more. Moreover, organised sector industry has been highly concentrated and capital-intensive, so that there has been no growth of factory sector employment during the 1990s. At the same time, rich sugar cane farmers have used bonded migrant labourers in a search for the lowest-cost organisation of production. Vast numbers of workers, especially in the areas in which *Adivasis* are concentrated, have very little work in the fields or in non-farm work. Some of these jobless men, along with the hundreds of unemployed workers of closed cotton mills provided the storm troopers for the horrific anti-Muslim riots in Gujarat in 2002 (Devy 2002). Paradoxically, the state of Gujarat was ranked first in respect to 'economic freedom' by the Rajiv Gandhi Foundation, demonstrating what neo-liberal economists really mean by freedom—namely, license for the few at the cost of bondage for the majority.

India has also witnessed a large, and perhaps increasing, interstate flow of highly educated professionals in management, computer science and medicine. In some cases, shortages of such professionals have also surfaced because of the international mobility of such groups. In highly segmented labour markets such as those of India and China, regional and even national shortages of skilled labourers can emerge even though there may be an abundance of unskilled labourers or labourers deskilled by structural change in most parts of the country. The neo-liberal regime, with its stress on low inflation and flexible labour markets, also tends to depress global demand for workers and this in turn makes migrant labourers from developing countries unwelcome in most developed countries, except when the latter face acute shortages of skilled labourers or labourers of a kind badly remunerated, or for work considered to be too arduous by the citizens of those countries. Such international barriers against labour mobility aggravate the need for internal labour mobility and pose many challenges to the policy-makers in China and India, the two most populous countries of the world.

The neo-liberal regime is an international phenomenon and is a project sedulously promoted by G7 countries, with the US in the leading role. One of the characteristics of this regime is the removal of all restraints on the movement of capital, while permitting the international movement of labourers under tightly regulated conditions. If there is some migration still from one country to another, it is either because of desperate political conditions in the country from which migration takes place or because the host country needs the labour. Alarmist notions notwithstanding, some of the most populous developing countries are also countries of net immigration in the long run. In 1995, for instance, it was estimated that India, Pakistan and Iran had immigrants numbering 8.66 million, 7.27 million and 3.59 million respectively, a substantial percentage of them refugees (Hugo 2004:table 5.1).

Indians, of course, migrate overseas in large numbers. But their largest outflow, for the last 25 years or so has been directed to West Asia, rather than to the developed capitalist countries. The total number of Indian migrants to the US, up to the end of the 1990s was roughly a million, whereas the number of migrants to West Asia from Kerala alone has been estimated at 1.6 million (Zachariah, Mathew & Rajan 2003:62–5). The two streams of migrants have very different characteristics. While the migrants to the Gulf countries are mostly unskilled or semi-skilled workers, technicians, nurses with a sprinkling of engineers, management specialists and doctors, the migrants to North America tend to be highly educated professionals. According to US 1990 census data, the immigrants from 'Other Asia', which includes South Asia and Africa, had a larger proportion of persons with college education than immigrants from all other regions, including Europe (Zhou 2004:table 5.1). In the G7 countries, the conditions for obtaining visas that guarantee the status of permanent residence have been made more stringent. The provision of software services *in situ* has often involved what has been called body-shopping, with the providers visiting the clients on temporary visas and then moving back to their home countries. The growth of this kind of temporary migration to the US and Western Europe is one reason why in recent years the inward flow of remittances by workers in these countries has overtaken such inflows from the Persian Gulf countries (GI 2005:para 6.10). The international migration and capital flow regime of the developed capitalist economies is serving as a device for creaming off the best stocks of human capital from the poorest countries of the world, while condemning the ordinary workers in all poor countries to low-wage work at best and unemployment at worst. It is at the same time threatening the livelihood of those workers in the developed capitalist countries who are losing their jobs in a depressed global economy affected by the short-termism of a deregulated financial system.

The re-birth of the labour market in post-Mao China

From the time communes were organised in China, there was no labour market in China. The state decided who would work where and which enterprise would recruit what kind of worker. There was massive underemployment in agriculture. Even in urban areas, there was looming unemployment. In the Cultural Revolution period, an attempt was made to solve some part of the urban unemployment problem by sending millions to the countryside. Part of the problem was turned into an opportunity for building rural infrastructure by mobilising workers on a huge scale (Riskin 1987:ch 5; Hirway & Terhal 1994:74–90). While employment in state-owned enterprises followed the life-time employment pattern, wages were severely repressed and real earnings of urban and SOE workers actually declined in the period between the 1950s and 1970s (Walder 1984; Riskin 1987:ch 11).

Labour markets in rural areas began developing with the introduction of the household responsibility system for farming and the formal disbanding of the commune system of direct control of all aspects of economic activity. The development of labour markets in rural areas occurred in step with the gradual freeing of produce markets, raising of producer prices and an increase in the growth of consumer incomes. China began to reap the benefits of the higher levels of investment during the preceding 15 years or so. The rate of growth of aggregate consumption in China in the 1980s was double that of India, and since China had a lower rate of population growth, the difference in growth of per capita consumption was even more striking (Table 1). These differences persisted in the 1990s, when India started on the path of economic and financial liberalisation.

Table 1: Average annual growth (%) of household final consumption, aggregate and per capita

	Aggregate consumption		Consumption per capita	
	1980–90	1990–2003	1980–90	1990–2003
China	8.8	8.5	7.2	7.4
India	4.2	4.9	2.0	3.1

Source: WB (2005b).

But in China too, the creation of labour markets and the extension of incentive and contract systems together with price reforms were accompanied by severe contradictions. Price reforms in SOEs and the introduction of dual-track pricing, the granting of greater autonomy to provincial and county governments led to inflation from 1985; a price scissors eroded the gains made by cultivators. These contradictions and the contradictory demands for rapid privatisation and greater equality in power and asset distribution were among the factors that lay behind the social movements and the severe repression exercised by the state to contain it. But while the state repressed opposition to reform, the moves towards marketising output, capital and labour continued (Wang, H 2005). The relaxation of the *hukou* system accelerated the mobility of rural labourers within and between provinces, but often had an adverse impact on urban workers with scarce skills; their standard of living and social protection measures also eroded. With a determined drive for exports and continued high rates of investment, rates of growth reached even higher levels in the 1990s than in the 1980s. But the output elasticity of most industrial labour remained low, and in the case of collective enterprises turned negative over the period, 1988–95 (Khan & Riskin 2001:table 6.4). There is a suspicion that the latter result may be influenced by the rapid conversion of many collective enterprises into private firms by using various devices.

Khan and Riskin (2001) found increasing disparity in wage incomes as a major factor rendering income distribution unequal between different regions, and between urban and rural areas. One reason may have been the persistence of the *hukou* system that blocked new entrants into jobs in the growing urban agglomerations. The local governments demanded fees for allowing immigrants to legally register in their jurisdiction. The subsequent dismantling of the registration system, the huge retrenchment carried out by the SOEs and the flooding of the coastal regions with new immigrants had the effect of reducing wage dispersion and arresting the growth of real wages, but generating demand for labour in export-oriented and domestic market-oriented manufacturing. The successful redirection of some investment into inland provinces also strengthened this tendency. But the experience of burgeoning labour demand itself increased labour mobility, and given the withdrawal of social protection of labourers, their insecurity and susceptibility to exploitation also rose often in violation of laws governing the treatment of workers. It is widely asserted that one-tenth of China's population is on the move and if we add the mobility within provinces, the proportion would be even higher (Wang, H 2005:78). The data on the living quarters of rural workers also indicate a huge increase in mobility in rural China in recent times (Riskin 2007:table 6). At the same time, this mobility has increased wages and the workers' share in national income, and both inter-provincial and inter-sectoral disparity in wage incomes has declined. This has occurred against the background of a decline in employment in town and village enterprises and a vast increase in employment in private enterprises between 1995 and 2002 (Khan & Riskin 2005; Riskin 2007).

According to the findings of Khan and Riskin (2005), migrants' incomes lie between full-status urban residents' incomes and average rural incomes. Fifty eight per cent of the migrants earn incomes from self-employment. Compared with this, only 5.6% of full-status urban residents were in self-employment. About 60% of the latter were employed in government and related institutions and SOEs, whereas only 6.7% of the latter were in urban SOEs (Khan & Riskin 2005:tables 14 & 15). The subsidy component of both urban and rural incomes has virtually disappeared in China.

All these results would seem to spring from a neo-liberal enterprise for freeing the market. But the state-guided neo-liberalism in China has other characteristics that do not sit well with the theory of those who, despite all evidence to the contrary, insist on treating labour markets as just a variety of commodity markets. When economic reforms, including the dismissal of several millions of SOE employees and the Asian crisis produced a crisis of urban poverty and interregional disparity, the Chinese policy-makers adopted a number of steps to counter some of the tendencies. They included a restructured poverty reduction strategy; adoption of the Great Western Development Strategy in February 2000, which led to a large increase in infrastructure investment in this region; liberalisation of the *hukou* system, facilitating a large volume of *de facto* movement of labour out of rural areas; and the adoption of a program for the protection of the urban poor. The disequalising effect of the system of urban subsidies has also been substantially reduced. Migration has somewhat eased the problem of employment growth in rural areas, but urban unemployment remains serious, despite partial alleviation of some of its worst consequences by the new system of protection (Khan & Riskin 2005).

Relief in rural China has taken many forms. According to the report of the third session of the Tenth National People's Congress (NPC), held in March 2005, the Chinese government has moved to reduce or abolish most of the taxes on agriculture and check illegal and 'unreasonable' levies on agriculture. 'Other on-going changes would seek to enhance grain distribution, improve rural education, strengthen county and township-level finances, address land management anomalies and provide support to town and township management' (*China Quarterly* 2005:467).

Later in the year, in the course of analysing the conditions required for the fulfillment of the aim of creating a 'harmonious socialist society', a *Xinhua* commentary dated 23 October, 2005 noted that:

> Fourteen provinces had already implemented the basic life subsistence guarantee system for laid-off SOE workers, and integrated into it the national unemployment insurance system. In addition, since the end of 2004 the number of provinces that had set up the insurance system for low-income rural households had risen from eight to 11. Further measures would be introduced in order to improve retirement pension, and unemployment, work injury and basic medical insurance systems for urban workers; and more effective social security provisions would be put in place for rural migrants working in cities.
>
> In order to improve the quality of the labour force, efforts should be made to strengthen compulsory education, especially in the countryside. Government initiatives would include exemption of rural students from tuition and other fees, the provision of free or subsidised textbooks, accommodation and living expenses for students from poor backgrounds. Investment in education should also be increased. Parallel measures were also needed to enhance healthcare (*China Quarterly* 2006:221).

The Chinese government is obviously faced with many difficult choices, a number of which are almost foreclosed by developments that have already defined the trajectory of the Chinese economy. Can the rural–urban gap be reduced by the initiatives mentioned above and by the government policy of pushing investment into the western provinces away from the coast? Can it spare resources for rural development, when it is faced with the task of providing proper housing and facilities for education and healthcare in the cities exploding with influx from rural areas? To take one example, Shenzhen was built as a city meant to house 8900,000 in the 1980s and 'no more than 4.8 million during the Tenth Five-year Plan (2001–05)…its total population had already reached almost 12 million. Of these, registered migrants numbered an astonishing 10.25 million…' (*China Quarterly* 2006:221–2). Whether the Chinese government can retreat from its extreme export-oriented economic policy and can redirect a major share of investments towards stimulating consumption of the people who have been left behind by the economic miracle is being keenly watched.

There are many other emerging aspects of the Chinese labour market that need to be studied carefully, especially if we want to draw analogies with the Indian labour market. Literacy rates have been higher in China than in India at least since the 1970s. But since China's economic prowess was first displayed in the area of labour-intensive manufacturing and since economic reforms seemed to impact adversely on the growth of women's literacy, it was sometimes surmised that China would remain confined to low-technology- and knowledge-intensive products. This wishful thinking among some observers comparing the performance of two countries as if they were watching a race at Ascot, was also strengthened by China's apparent backwardness in tertiary education compared with India. However, China has come up rapidly in secondary and tertiary education and devotes far more human resources to both levels of education than India. More impressively still, China is producing science and engineering graduates in such profusion that US hegemony in this area may be threatened by China and the European Union (Freeman 2005).

While these developments will sustain China's effort to move into areas demanding frontier technology, they may also exacerbate the inequality of income distribution, because the access to education has become more unequal under the socialist market economy of China than under the Maoist regime.

While new investments in housing and infrastructure may ameliorate the conditions of the migrants in the highly competitive atmosphere of the new Chinese economy, unemployment and poverty will continue to dog the heels of migrants as well as the so-called retirees and failed job-seekers.

Comparisons of China and India

Several major differences between Chinese and Indian developments have to be kept in mind when we discuss the reasons for the contrasts between Indian and Chinese performance in higher-productivity employment, rates of investment and differences in sectoral emphasis. First, as Carl Riskin and others pointed out, the abolition of landlordism released a vast amount of rentier income for productive investment and redirected the use of resources. Second, the Maoist era not only saw the construction of rural infrastructure on a vast scale, but also extensive training of rural workers in improved technology through the policies of transferring down, which saw the large-scale migration of trained urban workers into communes. Third, when labour markets were created by paring down state allocation of labour, and enterprises were instructed to compete in the production of goods, barriers of caste, community, trader or moneylender power or, up to a point, class differences did not stand in their way. Labour mobility increased phenomenally, in both the vertical and the regional or horizontal direction. We have noted that China and India have faced severe problems in finding employment for their large and ever-increasing workforces. It is also clear that equilibrium in the labour market in the face of open unemployment and large-scale underemployment is a chimerical notion. Labour markets are inherently characterised by differentiation of workers across many dimensions. Moreover, structural change produces and reproduces segmentation in ever new ways, so that there has never been any real content to the Lewisian notion of unlimited supplies of labour in a market of genuinely free workers, men or women. As I had put it in a previous publication:

> ...capitalism all the time tends to reproduce duality between advancing and declining sectors, and privileged and underprivileged workers, by continually and unpredictably changing the structure of production, and making the workers with no other assets compete among themselves for jobs and better deals...This is where Marx's macroeconomic theory of the capitalist reproduction of the reserve army of labour combines with his theory of capitalist competition to provide us with an analytical framework for discussing segmentation and dualism at many levels in terms of sectors, race, caste, gender and locality (Bagchi 2002a: 233).

These comments would apply also to the socialist market economy of China as the leaders embrace more and more of the neo-liberal package of reforms. But we have to remember that despite the enormous volume of FDI flowing into China, it has not embraced financial liberalisation in the way India has done (Sen 2005). Secondly, China has not allowed its rate of investment to go down because of opening to the outside world (Table 2).

Table 2: Gross capital formation and gross domestic saving as a percentage of GDP in 1990 and 2003

	Gross capital formation		Gross domestic saving	
	1990	2003	1990	2003
China	35	44	38	47
India	24	24	23	22

Source: WB (2005b).

Thirdly, the Chinese leaders in the provinces and the centre have been concerned to maintain consumption growth of the population and have invested massively in the housing of workers. So while the conditions of living of many migrant workers are still deplorable, there are attempts to tackle some of the worst problems faced by them. The Common Minimum Programme (CMP) adopted by the central Indian government in May 2004 promises a guarantee of employment for the whole population for at least part of the year, and a universal coverage of the public distribution that would go a long way to raise the nutrition and productivity of workers. But the CMP has been pared down under the direction of the finance ministry and the neo-liberal members of the Planning Commission (though several members of the Planning Commission oppose the neo-liberal doctrine).

Notes

1 Also see publications of the EPW Research Foundation in the *Economic and Political Weekly.*

2 For an analysis of the way neo-liberal reforms have played havoc with state government finances, see Bagchi (2004).

3 For a short analysis of the increased vulnerability to which most Indians are exposed as a result of financial liberalisation, see Bagchi (2005a).

chapter eleven

Globalisation and labour's losses: insights from the study of China, France and Mexico

Dorothy J Solinger

The concept of 'globalisation'—with its whirls of productive factors (capital, tradables, funds and stocks) circling the planet—conjures up images of abstract financial and material flows and motion. And just as surely, there is a correlative human element, similarly in the throes of mobility, tossed about by the pressures and lures of money changing hands. The very notion of rapid and relatively unobstructed movement, as in the constant propulsion of both property and people, suggests freedom, a liberty to be on the loose.

But just what kind of licence is this? As assets are switched about, with investors shifting their holdings and assets from one site to the next, why is it so often the case that people are not also able to transpose one work post into another? Must it just be the owners and purveyors of lucre who are able to relocate their gear without at once losing it, while labourers—those who once manipulated and manufactured the forms of that loot—must be forced to relinquish their places, not easily to gain a new one later? Freedom and liberty are goods, but goods, it appears are granted just to the possessors of the principal and the portfolio. As these values soar for the proprietor, their antithesis—security—slips away and collapses for the subordinate. In the process, the conversion of capital is often matched by the transfiguration of the salaried, stable producer into a displaced, disenfranchised, roaming rustler, at best a transient factory hand or a menial service-provider, at worst, an out-of-work wanderer. This is the usual tale.

And where is the state in this upheaval? I maintain that it has mutated from a sovereign into a broker, subject at once to the vagaries of the world market, as conveyed by its own corporate class and as determined by the codes decreed by the supranational confederations, clubs, consortia of which it is a member, on the one side, and by the occasional outrage visited upon it by the subservient portion of its own populace, on the other. The stakes are certainly not evenly balanced. But the outcome is not as clear as was once imagined. For even as the state has frequently seemed powerless against the pushes from the international economy, or coerced into arbitration and negotiation by its capitalists in competitive efforts to outdo rivals abroad, still, disorders delivered by those typically thought of as its own underdogs need not always be entirely without punch.

In what follows, I lay out such a story. It concerns the choice for enhanced participation in the world economy made by three quite disparate countries—China, Mexico and France—all at about the same historical juncture, the year 1980. These states vary considerably in their models of political economy, in their levels of development and in their regime type, as well as in their motives for joining: France is an advanced industrial capitalist democracy, Mexico was a middle-income, 'semi-authoritarian' state when its critical moves were made, and China a post-totalitarian/authoritarian state, with a socialist-marketising, still developing economy (Linz 1975; Linz & Stepan 1996:40–4). Not only are their domestic institutions fundamentally non-comparable, but as a set they include one multi-party state, one monopoly-party one (until 2000) and a single party state. Besides, the nature of their domestic groups' connections with, and access to, central power structures varies widely.

The many diparities among these three countries may compensate for the fact that there are only three countries in the study. And yet these states do share a few traits that justify grouping them together for purposes of analysis. For one thing, in each of them, persistent memories of a distant revolution, executed at least in part on behalf of the underclasses, had taken on mythic proportions over time—of commitments, promises and supposed (but never fully realised) obligations on the part of the regime, along with concomitant expectations and a sense of entitlement among the workers. At the same time, more recent episodes of mass protest in each (all in the late 1960s) conjured up in the minds of the political elite frightening visions of chaos and disorder, fears still instilling anxieties in these leaders years later about adopting policies that could provoke confrontation with the working class. In each, the spectre of the enraged proletarian mob disposed politicians to improve wage levels and/or workers' welfare situations at times when the grievances of labour were especially raw.

Back to my story. It continues with an outline of the interplay between state and worker that ensued in these places, once these governments connected more deeply with markets abroad. At the outset and through a considerable interlude, it would appear that the state, allied with its international partners and its domestic business, held the upper hand against the workers, as one would suspect. But the reading at this writing leaves the longer term upshot in abeyance.

While the term 'globalisation' encompasses manifold contents and meanings, a reasonable proxy for its effects can be found in the rules of supranational organisations whose manifestations and memberships mushroomed worldwide in the late twentieth century and beyond. For groupings such as the World Trade Organization (the WTO), the North American Free Trade Association (NAFTA) and the European Union (the EU) have, through the force of their frameworks, subjected states to a litany of regulations that in many ways mimic the workings of the untrammeled free market.

For instance, the rules decreed by NAFTA and the WTO demand the reduction of tariffs. The fall in tariffs facilitated the inflow of cheaper and/or higher quality foreign products into China and Mexico, and thereby intensified competition for the domestic firms in these countries. Along a different route but with a similar outcome, the European Community's early 1990s order that states that wished to join the EU bring their domestic budget deficits under 3% of gross domestic product and that they keep inflation and debt levels low in line with 'convergence criteria', all led to firm failures and a consequent cut in jobs. In China's agreement of accession to the WTO it pledged, moreover, to create an 'improved investment climate' for foreign firms, which promoted native firm buyouts, again promoting the elimination of local jobs (Gruber 2000:146–8; Cameron 2001:13–15; O'Neill 1999; Lardy 2002:22). As they worked to fulfil the commitments of these bodies, France, Mexico and China each saw abrupt floods of discharges from their factories by deciding to, preparing to and then acceding to—or, in the case of France, more fully merging its fortunes with—supranational economic organisations.

It was not only direct obedience to the rules themselves that dictated the anti-labour behavior of these states. The decision of Mexico's leaders after the country's severe debt crisis of 1982 to join the forerunner of the WTO, the General Agreement on Trade and Tariffs (GATT) (which Mexico did in 1986) was preceded by voluntary actions that aligned the government's policies with those of the GATT. For France, the choice of Mitterrand and his advisors to line up their economy with France's partners in the European Monetary System in 1983 required an immediate acquiescence to strictures set down in a 1979 intergovernmental agreement to form this system, a precursor to the EU of 1992. Here, France's choice to abide by these rules was less the result of inescapable external pressure than it was a belief among those close to the President that France's best hope for international economic strength, power and economic success was through the channel of European integration (Kitschelt et al 1998:6). And for China, the submission to the rules of first the GATT and then of the WTO in advance of being invited to join—but in the hope of and preparation for that membership—is yet one more case in point.

One might picture the three as standing at differing points along a continuum of compulsion: for Mexico, compliance appeared essential to the ongoing economic functioning of the country; in France, following a pattern out of sync with its trading partners would have meant continuing economic descent, while conformity seemed to promise heightened clout and vigor; and for China's elite, membership spelt the solution to the nation's century-plus drive for international inclusion and prominence. For each of these countries, observance of the rules of the bodies they joined imposed substantial alteration in the prior *modus operandi* of economic behaviour and strategy. For each government had for decades before run economies that were relatively closed, at least somewhat protectionist and decisively pro-employment and pro-labour, at least in the cities.

Besides Mexico's macroeconomic choices, granted, there were other causes for the late-century loss of jobs there: One of these was demographic: the numbers of people in the labour force spurted upward from 32.3 million just before NAFTA was concluded to 40.2 million in 2002 (Audley et al 2004:14); another element, technological progress, led to layoffs or reduced job creation during the 1990s (Stallings & Peres 2000:197). These factors operating together produced a substantial drop in the numbers of manufacturing jobs relative to prospective workers in the years 1988 to 1992, as compared with the period 1970 to 1981. In the earlier years, the average annual growth rate of jobs had been 3.6%, a rate 13 times higher than that in the later years. Also, while employment grew at a rate of 4.9% per year between 1970 and 1981, that rate was more than cut in half during the period 1988 to 1996, when it fell to only 2% (Peters 1996:80; Peters 2000:162). Another way of putting this decline is to say that there was a fall in the percentage of workers employed in manufacturing between 1980 and 1989 from 46% down to just 37%. Jobs in the state sector also dropped between 1988 and 1993 from 23.3% of all jobs down to a mere 10.8% (de Oliverira & Garcia 1997:213–4).

The period directly leading up to Mexico's entry into the trade agreement, 1990 to 1992, saw just 28% of the population that entered the economically active population finding work in a formal sector job (Peters 1996:79). This was also a period when 100,000 jobs were lost, as some 10% of the country's small and medium businesses went under with President Salinas' aggressive reduction in tariffs, even before NAFTA required that that be done (Morici 1993:52; Pastor & Wise 1997:432). Meanwhile, between 1988 and 1992, while one million new jobs were needed per year, a mere 583,000 were created (Castaneda 1993:65). By 1994, the first year of NAFTA's operation, Mexico was home to 2.3 million unemployed in a labour force of 35 million, with another seven to eight million estimated to inhabit the underground economy (Meyer 1998:144). These two groups, added together, amounted to 26% of the labour force.

Following Mexico's accession to NAFTA in early 1994, the picture clearly became even more grim, though in 1995 that can be blamed entirely on the peso crisis that erupted at the end of 1994. According to one count, the numbers of jobs in manufacturing declined continuously for 70 months between 1990 and 1996 (Heath 1998:54). In 1995 alone, as many as 800,000 posts disappeared (de Oliverira & Garcia 1997:212; Camp 1996:219). And where open unemployment had been cited as standing at 2.6% in 1988, it had risen to 3.7% by 1994, and then more than doubled to 7.6% in 1995 (Peters 2000:162). By 2003, after nearly a decade of NAFTA's operation, a report from the Carnegie Endowment for International Peace drew up a balance sheet, according to which the 1.3 million jobs that had been created in non-maquiladora-manufacturing at the peak in 2000 (amounting to 100,000 fewer than at the time when NAFTA came into being), neatly balanced against the 1.3 million jobs that had been lost in agriculture (Audley et al 2004:18).

For France, the general consensus among a wide array of analysts is that affirming and intensifying its commitment to Community requirements was the most fundamental root of France's exploding unemployment in the 1980s and 1990s. Other factors also played a role, such as: structural change that resulted in a disjuncture between the skills on supply and the nature of demand; 'Eurosclerosis', a term charging that Western European labour markets had dug their own ruts by overly generous wages and benefits; and the deepening internationalisation of Western European economies, entailing competition and profit-seeking by mobile capital) (Symes 1995:18; Ellman 1987:58; Scharpf 2000:108). In a study of 12 nations in Western Europe during the 1980s and 1990s, France experienced 'by far the sharpest drop in industrial employment' (Hemerijck & Schludi 2000:168). There the unemployment figure had already surpassed 12% by 1994, and it remained as high as 12.5% at the end of 1996, amounting to over three million workers, and sticking at around 12% for some time thereafter (Cameron 2001:16; Schmidt 1996:187).

Throughout Western Europe, high unemployment was an outcome of the oil and exchange rate shocks of the 1970s and, with time, also the price of the demand restraint imposed throughout the Community after 1980 in a battle to keep inflation down (Ellman 1987:55; Jackman 1998:60, 67; Bastian 1998:91; Smith 2000; Symes 1995:10). A leading analyst of Western European unemployment notes that joblessness within the European Union in the 1990s cannot not be understood apart from the rules of the European Monetary Union itself, which clearly served to aggravate it immensely (Cameron 2001:11–12; Gruber 2000:174, 177–8). With special reference to France itself, this scholar has also written that, 'France's international economic and political context and policy choice was set by the exchange rate policy in Europe...above all

French macroeconomic policy was constrained by its European Community membership' (Cameron 1995:119, 134; Boltho 1996:102). That job loss was linked to Community rules seems to be supported by its much more pronounced occurrence within the Community nations than it was in other major industrialised nations elsewhere in Western Europe beginning from the late 1970s (Jackman 1998:60).

Left to its own devices France would probably have continued to shelter surplus labour rather than push for layoffs. Even during a crisis in the steel industry in the second half of the 1970s, for the most part, layoffs were avoided by resort to early retirements and transfers (Daley 1992:146–80). It was Mitterrand and his Socialist Party's famous 'U-turn' toward the policies being executed in the rest of the Community in 1983 that led to the massive cutbacks of workers in the tens of thousands—in steel, automobiles, ship-building and textiles, ushering in the first notable burst of discharges in the country (Smith 1995:4). During the years just leading up to and spanning that reversal, the numbers let go went from about two million in 1982, or 7.3% of the workforce, to a total of 13.4% on a seasonally adjusted basis during the year 1984 (Machin & Wright 1985:28). Throughout the rest of the decade the rate continued to hover around 10%, mitigated a bit by early retirements. By 1997, the total losses over the years since 1970 had amounted to a stunning 41.6% of the original labour force (Scharpf 2000:108).

Meanwhile, in China, leaders voluntarily chose to ingest capitalist modes of reasoning about economics and the values that were internationally *au courant*. In that climate, the country's linkage with the global market unfolded, over a span of some 20 years. As this took place, two related processes ran parallel: a slowly escalating crusade to transform customary notions about employment, accompanied by gradually more and more explicit and intentional moves to bring about the dismissal of millions of workers from their posts; and an intensifying campaign to become a member first of the General Agreement on Trade and Tariffs (GATT) and, after 1995, the World Trade Organization (WTO), entailing a total revamping of the Chinese foreign trade sector (Naughton 1995; Lardy 2002). The two processes were interconnected, and both were informed by economic norms that were by then orthodox globally.

As in the other two places, the official choice to discharge labour was not the only reason for a massive loss of jobs beginning in the mid-1990s; there too the employment problem had several roots. Decades of emphasis on full urban employment (or a practicable approximation thereof) had led to vast numbers of surplus labour. As early as the late 1980s, but continuing to be the case as of the year 2000, government proclamations set the excess labour in the cities at about one third of that on the job (Bonnin 2000:154; Howard 1991:102; Imai

2002:30; Giles, Park & Cai 2003:2). Other difficulties arose when China began to modernise in earnest in and after the 1980s, as industry became progressively more capital-intense, and as labour-saving technology started to replace workers (Bhalla & Qiu 2004:104). At the same time, the mismatch between the low-skill, undereducated workforce that a range of Maoist policies had fostered and the state-of-the-art aspirations of the regime eventuated in an inexorable process of structural unemployment (Rawski 2002:7). With these forces working to crowd out human labour, in the second half of the 1980s, a 1% increase in the growth rate of GDP could yield 1.51 million jobs, but between 1991 and 1995 the yield was just half of that (Dai & Li 2000:12). In the 1980s the rate of employment growth was as high as 9% annually, but by the second half of the 1990s, during the Ninth Plan period, it had fallen to an average of just 0.9% annually (Hu 2001:10).

Even as demand-side factors were reducing the numbers on the job, official efforts—by pilot programs, pronouncements, temporary rulings, regulations and laws—to remake the labour regime channeled and speeded up the influence of these factors. The first experiments surrounding the labour system took place almost immediately after the Party's official switch to a focus on rapid modernisation in late 1978. With the initiation of industrial reforms early in the decade—with their message urging money-making and high productivity, and with their granting of new financial and decisional powers to localities, firms and managers, workers' security became ever less certain (Sheehan 1998:195; Meng 2000:82, 83, 113). Little by little, management within the plants took advantage of their newly-acquired powers and their heightened autonomy sometimes to transfer workers, and occasionally to let them go, a licence that was further enhanced when enterprise directors were allowed after 1986 to lease the firms that they had been running (Sheehan 1998:207–08; Howard 1991:102; Lee 1999a:55; Solinger 1991:175, 182–3). By the last half of the decade more and more layoffs were taking place (Walder 1987:22, 40; 1992:473, 478–9).

Meanwhile, both internal and external competition, added to the rising prices for industrial inputs that resulted from price reform, undermined the business of the state sector, and losses climbed upward there, mounting rapidly after 1990. One calculation shows a startling increase from just six billion RMB in losses in 1987 to 83 billion RMB a decade later (Lardy 2002:19; Cheng & Lo 2002:413).

Matching the intensifying drama of heightening enterprise losses went a progressive incline in the numbers of labourers suddenly thrown out of work. Making sense of Chinese unemployment statistics is notoriously difficult (Solinger 2001). But even the officially-admitted numbers 'laid off' and those newly 'unemployed' from the mid-1990s onward is arresting: An official 'White

Paper' acknowledged that between 1998 and 2001 over 25.5 million persons had been let go from state enterprises (State Council 2002:11). Between the end of 1992 and the end of 1998, state and urban collective[1] firms combined let go some 37 million workers, while the old state firms alone cut one third of their workforce in that period, the result of specific official pressure placed upon the firms (Naughton 1999:52; Lardy 2002:23). The best evidence for this pressure is a quota system devised around 1997 to force factories to dispose of set percentages of their workforces. Upper-level authorities distributed quotas specifying the number to be laid off to the enterprises under their jurisdiction, and used the fulfilment thereof as one basis for evaluating directors' work (Tian & Yuan 1997:11).

One observer's estimate that 46.59 million state and urban collective firms' workers had lost their posts as of 2001 rose to a staggering figure of 60 million by late 2004 (Hu 2001:9).[2] Additionally, a study conducted by China's official trade union at the end of the 1990s found that 48.7% of the 'reemployed' laid-off people it counted had become self-employed, while even of the other 51.3% who had been re-hired, well over half (59%) were engaged in informal work that was only temporary (Xue 2000:8). In all, the downgrading and displacement in the labour markets of these three countries was clearly colossal.

Unions and protest

And how did the displaced react? One would not have expected much sustained reaction under any of these regimes. None of the three nations could boast a union system or a true labour movement worthy of the name. After the Communist victory in 1949, China's workers were most of the time muzzled by the constraints of the Communist Party, only breaking free of that bond at a few crucial junctures, in each case to be disciplined and punished severely in the aftermath. The working class, moreover, had no channel of access to state officials nor the right to make use of any formal type of redress outside the aegis of the watchful official trade union, the All-China Federation of Trade Unions, which was itself accountable and submissive only to—and hamstrung by—the Communist Party (Cai 2004).[3]

The power of the urban labour force was also lessened by a distinction between employees of larger and medium sized state-owned firms on the one hand and smaller, collectively operated ones, on the other. A strong case has been made that workers in the state enterprises—regardless of their lacking clout—were treated sufficiently well and entertained a sufficiently shared set of goals with management that, unless aroused by large, nationwide political movements, they generally tended to work peacefully, and to put trust in their superiors and their unions (Sheehan 1998:201; Walder 1986). Strikes were permitted under earlier versions of the state constitution during and just after the 1966 to 1976 Cultural Revolution, but were banned thereafter.[4]

In France, the organisation of labour occurred through a multitude of competing, sometimes warring, unions whose mutual distrust inhibited concerted action. And in any event, workers in all the unions were generally allegiant to the creed of the 1906 Charter of Amiens, which stressed a radical rejection of the parliamentarism of so-called 'bourgeois politics' (Bell & Criddle 1998:14). This inclination disposed them to stay clear of government, as they yearned for a state ruled in accord with purely socialist values. Unions' own anaemic condition was compounded by their not being legally allowed in the firms until after a massive social upheaval in 1968, while collective bargaining in the enterprise was not required by law until as late as 1982 (Kesselman 1989:166).

Unions did go on strike with some regularity, but the episodes tended to be brief and dramatic rather than sustained, well organised or purposive (Smith 2000). The most radical of the unions—the Confederation Generale du Travail (CGT)—was also the most powerful among them, but its tight, unbending linkage with the Communist Party (which, in the post-war period, held power only briefly in coalition governments, once just after the Second World War and once from 1981 to 1984) pretty much nullified its political significance. Here too the labour force had more and less privileged sectors, in accord with the ownership of their firms and the thrust of state industrial policy at any point (Howell 1992:ch 2).

In Mexico too, despite the elevated position of the Confederation de Trabajadores Mexicanos (Confederation of Mexican Workers, the CTM) as a special sector within the ruling party, the Institutional Revolutionary Party (or the PRI), it is difficult to sustain an argument that it possessed power in its own right. Its affiliates could count on decent treatment and special advantages not so much because the PRI or the CTM represented their interests as because the PRI and the CTM leaderships were mutually linked in a pact bent on preserving their own power and on sustaining social order. Patronage that operated on a personal level could squeeze out benefits for well-connected individuals, but usually not for workers as a supplicating collectivity. And the CTM's ability to serve the PRI's purposes—for votes at elections and peace in the plants—hinged on resources the party disbursed to CTM bosses, which they in turn utilised to manipulate the workers.

Although the 1917 constitution authorised strikes, and though labour actions did occur, workers were kept on a tight leash by strict state regulations on union formation, union activities and strikes (Middlebrook 1995:ch 2). Only occasionally, as in 1968, an unusual surge of strike activity might prompt some reform (Haggard & Kaufman 1992:284). The duality of the labour market here was actualised in the dominant position of the CTM, along with two other large federations that the regime sometimes played off against it (Burgess 1999:121; Murillo 2000), and of the state-owned enterprises. Workers with these affiliations did substantially better than others.

Thus, in each of these countries, though an upper crust of the workforce managed to command a modicum of satisfactory treatment and benefits, this was in each case a function of largesse the state disbursed, for reasons of its own. In none of the three could the more privileged among the labour force thank some mediating body for agitating on its behalf, nor were they in the habit of turning hopefully to any such organ in times of stress or deprivation. Nonetheless, because of an age-old and well-ingrained ethos in each case, a code that became perhaps even more sacrosanct after disturbing events of the late 1960s in each case, at least the workers in the more favoured sectors and/or ranks grew to expect and depend upon good handling at the hands of the state. Many of these dispositions have persisted into the present.

Unquestionably China's workers became enormously more restive and demonstrative as the years of economic reform and marketisation went forward, as compared with their relative state of quiescence for most of the time during the preceding decades. In part, this heightened level of activism came from newfound liberty workers experienced in the wake of job loss: freedom, that is, from constant managerial oversight and from enterprise schedules. Besides, with their dismissal, it became pointless to worry that activism could endanger their position or their perquisites (Lee 1999b:28; Chen 2000:62; Blecher 2001:3–4). The surge in the numbers of protest meant that, nationwide, workers in one place or another who had lost their jobs or their welfare benefits were on the streets nearly daily.

Beginning in the early 1990s, even the Chinese government acknowledged a sudden upswing in demonstrations, with the official *China Daily* announcing an increase by 50% in 1994 over the previous year; one researcher reported that the government had admitted that 1998's 3.6 million workers who demonstrated amounted to three times the number of such protesters just three years earlier (Cao 1994; Liu 1997:1; Chen 2000:41). The Ministry of Public Security recorded that the numbers of incidents 'began a rise like a violent wind' from 1997, the year of the Fifteenth Party Congress which pressed for factory firing (MPS 2001:18). By the end of the decade, 100,000 labour protests had taken place, according to the Center for Human Rights and Democracy, based in Hong Kong (Jiang 2001:72).

As strikes escalated in number, the official trade union became even weaker than it had been before marketisation began: where in the past it served as a model 'transmission belt' association, relaying workers' sentiments upwards to the leadership and then delivering official orders back down the line, once the state plan lost its hold on the economy and firms in the hundreds and thousands began to careen into the red and to fold completely, state leaders grew fearful of worker rage and aggrievement and the havoc they might wreak, and therefore frequently egged the union on to find ways to placate them (Chen 2003).

The historical peak of French protest seems to have passed with the mid-1970s, after which, labour's clout declined progressively, especially after an alliance between the communists and the socialists fell apart (Boyer 1984:22–23; Ross 1984:155–65; Kesselman 1996:144–45). Following the U-turn of President Mitterrand after 1982, workers and unions were briefly reactive at first, but then became silent for most of the rest of the decade (Wilson 1985:275–6; Smith 2000:128–30; Schmidt 1999; Moss 1988:74–6). There was an outbreak of work stoppages in a number of firms in the public sector in 1988. But these were organised by independent groups outside the sphere of the unions, so, while demonstrating the continuing obstreperousness of the labour force when challenged with the elimination of its work posts, were no statement at all about the power of the unions (Smith 2000:130).

The major exception to the general timorousness of the French trade unions was a 1995 six-week shutdown of the public sector, launched in response to Prime Minister Juppe's proposals to prune the welfare system, his effort to diminish the public budgetary deficit in accord with the EU's orders. The movement evinced a persisting vibrancy among the unions—as well as their sometime (if rarely achieved) potential to arouse the rest of France. More strikes in the spring of 2003—directed against a renewed attempt of the government to revamp its pension system—aroused the unions on a national scale in the public and private sectors, as well as triggering wildcat outbursts in several localities.

In Mexico, the government was never shy about resorting to the use of the military when the top leaders believed this to be necessary (Teichman 1995:60–1, 67, 199; Kaufman 1986:198). These techniques were sharpened in quelling the resistance mounted to Carlos Salinas's bid for the Presidency in 1988, and assisted the state mightily in its determination to prevent labour discontent from interfering with its program of privatisation, economic liberalisation and retrenchment in the 1980s (Collier 1992:137; Teichman 1995:212; Middlebrook 1995:295, 300–1). The kingpins in the collaboration between the PRI and the CTM were the *charros*, hand-picked, corrupt labour bosses who ran roughshod over the workforce in the name of fulfilling regime intentions and policies

(Collier 1992:34–5; Teichman 1995:49, 56, 61–2). These individuals were to ensure that workers' demands were kept manageable; their behaviour quiescent, in periods of economic stress, so as to hold off inflation; and their votes actively pro-PRI at election times (Middlebrook 1995:153–54; Roxborough 1989:102). Though of somewhat waning effectiveness by the 1990s, *charrismo* persisted (Teichman 1995:202). Force, violence, bribery and a conditional refuge for the loyal and the compliant sustained the broad outlines of the Mexican labour regime and economic strategy historically and into the present.

Workers advantaged by this system developed a sense of rewards and expectations and depended on party bosses to supply the goods they counted upon. The legacy of favorable treatment they had experienced for dozens of years shored up their loyalty, and, at least initially, disposed them to stick with the PRI even as it reversed its connection with the workers after the early 1980s (Collier 1992:110). And the CTM itself was not entirely safe from harm. Its ultimate vulnerability lay in the PRI's ability to play this confederation off against two rival ones—the CROC and the CROM[5]—when the Party leadership was displeased with some stand or other that the CTM took temporarily, or angry over its short-term failure to march in lockstep with every policy the PRI proposed (Collier 1992:83; Roxborough 1989:104–5; Middlebrook 1989:294). Accordingly, the CTM, in the final analysis heavily dependent upon staying in the good graces of the PRI (Collier 1992:35; Middlebrook 1995:35; Camp 1996:142; Haggard & Kaufman 1995:287), exercised a critical role in assisting the PRI to suppress attempts at forming independent unions, entities that would have championed and fought for rights and benefits for groups beyond the selected elite (Sklair 1989:58, 61–2).[6] Thus, with the economic crises of the 1980s, labour unions had little choice but to accept what the government threw at them: falling real wages and insecure of employment (Meyer 1998:144).

The ongoing authoritarian power of the union bosses to intimidate the workforce in the state sector, and the unchanged chain binding bosses in the public firms to the state, provides important clues not just to the success of corporatist tactics in Mexico but also to the relatively scarce and remarkably impotent nature of labour protest in the country in the era of cutbacks after 1980 (Meyer 1998:144). The typical pattern was for the unflinching surveillance of the state—operating through brutal bossism in the union—to nip any protest in the bud to the extent possible (Middlebrook 1995:219, 265).

Consequently, while strikes in Mexico were never plentiful, their numbers dropped by 80% in the decade following the accession to power of President de la Madrid—who initiated the austerity of the 1980s (Carr 1987:222)[7]—as the regime became increasingly indiscriminate in its impulse to subvert and quash decisively worker opposition from any quarter at all. It was willing even to turn its back temporarily on its long-time ally, the CTM, rather than deal with the union's demands (Collier 1992:106–7, 139; Middlebrook 1995:260; 1989:293–4). And unlike in China, where protest leaders alone have been apprehended in demonstrations, even where violence and disruption takes place, in similar instances in Mexico ordinary followers as well stand in danger of forfeiting their jobs should they offend the leadership (Middlebrook 1995:69).

The impact: government welfare efforts

The next big question concerns these states' response to the disruptions. Of the three, it was China, where protests were the most numerous, widespread and continuous, that saw the most vigorous reaction from the central government. I have identified four features of the relationship between labour and its state in these countries that shed light on what became of state-supplied welfare after economic restructuring occurred, two pertaining to the state and two to society (here in the form of the workforce). These factors structured the changes, though the extent to which they operated varies among the countries. The first of these traits is centralisation of power, which in all three cases permitted the top leadership to shift its support base with relative ease and autonomy, free of any influence from otherwise-inclined contending parties or groups or from constitutionally-empowered levels of government, and thereby to abandon labour and its history of state-supported welfare, when the regime so chose.

Second, a long-standing wariness of potential civil turbulence and insurrection inclined the leadership in each place to placation, whenever possible. For, once the nation embarked upon economic liberalisation and grew steadily more deeply involved in the world economy, especially in China and France, a profound unease among officialdom over the prospect of unrest and 'social instability' undergirded a search for financial solutions and an effort at implementing them where they could be maximally effective from the perspective of the political elite. Indeed, at every step of the journey, imagined shadows of marching, perhaps marauding, workers danced before the eyes of the decision makers in China in particular, and they thus repeatedly and explicitly linked every speech they delivered on the subject of welfare and each new regulation with the imperative of preserving harmony, control and 'stability'.

Third, turning to the side of society and workers, there is a shared inability—or (in Mexico's case—because of the umbilicate nature of the leading party's bond to the unions) unwillingness—of unions to arrest the process of decline in the arena of welfare or in any significant way to confront the regime by putting forward demands on the part of their putative constituency. This inaction, however, was variable in the three cases, with Mexico and China much more similar to each other than either was to France. And fourth was the presence of a dual labour market, which, when combined with leaders' fears, meant that short-changing the old workforce for all three regimes was paired with a strong state commitment to strive to retain the loyalty, and to achieve the quiescence of, an elite portion of labour. The tiered labour market in all three countries allowed politicians to succour certain segments of the working class. Those workers who had enjoyed the highest level of protection (and so sustained the greatest expectations, carried over from the past) were, the regime suspected, not just the most prone to, but also most capable of, inciting disorder (Kernen & Rocca 2000: 23; Duckett 2003:12). These features of impotent unions and regime-crafted segmentation among the workers allowed the political leadership to fine-tune its benefits entirely according to its own lights—in the hope of preserving order while shoring up its own legitimacy.[8]

In the course of China's marketisation, a sharp juncture in the path of policy occurred at the 1992 Fourteenth Party Congress, when the Party significantly deepened its ongoing program of marketisation by redefining the nation's once socialist, planned economy as being a 'socialist market' one. A year later would see the birth of specific policies to restructure state enterprises, culminating at the subsequent Party Congress in 1997 in an official directive to 'reduce the labour force to enhance efficiency'. By the mid-1990s this state mission had been gathering force for well over a decade. But it was not until 1997 that these reforms finally came to affect large numbers of workers in the state-owned plants (Meng 2000:121–2).

There followed numerous examples that bolster the point about the regime's vigilance about instability. Just after the Party Congress called for cutting back the workforce, central-level authorities demanded that localities devise a 'responsibility system' to pacify potential 'social chaos' expected to issue from what was termed the 'daily increasing army of the unemployed' (*Shijie ribao* 1997:A12). In May of 2000, an official research group published a piece in an internal journal entitled, 'Establishing a social protection system is the key to our country's social stability' (SPC 2000:8–14). Another illustration is a volume on employment and social security published in 2000, which openly acknowledged that, 'Growing out of our concern for social stability, we have made very great government expenditures in social security' (Gong 2000:215).

Thus, because of the pronounced upsurge in urban poverty, inequality and joblessness that the post–1997 firings fostered, the political elite felt forced by a rising tide of progressively more frequent and ever-larger protests to unveil three brand-new programs to make up an embryonic welfare safety net (Duckett 2003). For decades, urban state workers had received work-unit-based insurance and cradle-to-grave welfare benefits.[9] But the new Chinese programs were unprecedented in the PRC and had to be forged from scratch in the era of reform. Both in the interest of peace and order in the cities, and to allow the firms to have a greater chance of surviving on their own in the marketplace, the state has attempted for over two decades—though to date far from successfully—to establish a contributory social security system that is independent from the enterprises (State Council 2002:20; Tang 2002b:18). Programs designed to fill the breach that resulted from smashing the former system—programs such as UI (Unemployment Insurance), basic living allowances for the laid-off and a minimum livelihood guarantee for the newly impoverished—though instituted as early as the mid-1980s and the early 1990s, were barely utilised before the late 1990s, when they were finally seriously and widely applied, in tandem with the upward spiral of job loss (Wong, Heady & Woo 1995:14).

The first of the new welfare programs to appear was the one for the unemployed. After four years of internal Party debate, the initial major step was taken on the road to putting to rest the strategic, socialist notion that each [urban] worker was to be granted a life-time tenured job (White 1993:138–43, 159). In 1986 the first Regulations on Unemployment Insurance appeared, designed to assist a new category of 'contract labourers' when their terms were up, so long as they met the necessary conditions. In that same year a Regulation on Discharging Employees was announced as well. But none of these decrees had much if any impact at that time (Lim & Sziraczki 1993:51–2).

By 1993, to deal with the rising numbers of workers losing their jobs, revised provisions came out, specifying that benefits go only to state enterprise workers (Li 1992:27). Five years later, so-called 'laid-off workers'—a novel, exploding category for socialist China—soon became eligible for a sum higher than UI (meant for workers once employed at firms that had been dissolved), entitled the 'basic living allowance' [*jiben shenghuofei* or *jiben shenghuo baozhang*] (Hu 2000:16–17).[10]

The payoffs were part of a program designed and widely promoted in the second half of the 1990s in response to constantly rising numbers of layoffs, in the wake of an official credit squeeze, an accompanying nationwide recession and, by 1997, an explicit governmental program to cut back the workforce. Labelled the 'Re-employment Project', this was a bureaucratically manipulated effort conceived as a temporary palliative to sustain workers furloughed by fortunate, mostly still functioning state firms (FBIS 1994:69; Chengzhen 1997; Ru, Lu & Dan 1998:86; SWB 1998:G/3). The project was to computerise information on local labour markets, provide job introduction organs offering free training, and build new marketplaces where dismissed factory workers could begin a business through preferential policies on taxes and fees. The Project also called on each firm that had furloughed any of its workers to create a 're-employment service centre', to which its laid-off workers were to be entrusted for a period up to three years (Yang 1999:19). The centre was charged with contributing to the pension, medical and social security funds on behalf of each discharged worker entrusted to it (Yang 1999:30–1). An unknown, but almost certainly relatively small, proportion of firms actually carried through on these obligations.

A third welfare program was born in response to a sudden upsurge in the numbers of the urban poor after the mid-1990s,[11] at the same time that masses of state manufacturing workers began to suffer dismissal from their posts; indeed, there is a clear correlation between these two phenomena (Cook 2000:5).[12] As the numbers of people subsisting in straitened circumstances rose with the progression of the marketisation, it became clear that a broad-based, inclusive system had to be designed for them. The idea behind the plan was twofold: to sever the bond between firms and their indigent staff and ex-staff, since often the very poorest people were attached to enterprises doing too poorly to help them; and to extend the scope of the eligible population. In 1994, the new system, named the 'minimum livelihood guarantee' [*zuidi shenghuo baozhang*, colloquially, the *dibao*], began experimentally (Wong 1998:124), and by September 1997, after spreading nationally, was formalised, with orders that localities must lodge this item in their budgets to be managed as a special account (Song 2001: 149–50). In September 1999 the State Council's 'Regulations for safeguarding urban residents' subsistence guarantees' transformed the program into law (Tang 2002a).

In spite of the minimalism that often marked the execution of all three of these welfare measures, and the motive of maintaining order that stood behind them, from the late 1990s there were many indications of the leadership's firm commitment to implementing them. Among those signs were a move to continue subsidising loss-making firms by having state banks distribute credit to them (Yang & Cai 2003:410; Chow & Xu 2001:26); a new National Social Security Fund inaugurated in 2000, which was to offer support to indebted provinces (Frazier 2004:103); the passage of a Labour Law in 1994 which, though rarely respected, at least symbolised the state's concern for proper treatment of the workforce (Gallagher 1997:13); and periodic increases in the payouts to workers whose positions had been cancelled.[13]

Another way of pointing to the determination of the state to calm hard-up workers was through its constant infusion of funds for them. According to a governmental White Paper on Employment and Social Security from spring 2002, in 2001 the central treasury allocated 98.2 billion RMB for social security payments, a figure 5.18 times that expended just three years before. During the same period, the treasury injected a total of 86.1 billion RMB in subsidies into pension insurance (State Council 2002:21, 24). Then-Premier Wen Jiabao announced in early 2004 that the central government had contributed 4.7 billion RMB of subsidies the previous year just for the purpose of job creation, while spending 70 billion for laid-off workers' and poor people's allowances, 20% more than it had paid in the previous year. Of that amount, the monies for the urban indigent doubled in the year, from 4.6 billion in 2002 to 9.2 billion in 2003 (Wen 2004; Tang 2003:243–5).

In France, the demonstrations of 1995 forced the state to call off entirely a few of its chief welfare reduction proposals and to decelerate its program of cutbacks (Kesselman 1996:158–60; Levy 2000:336–7; Rodrik 1997:1, 41–3). Later, in response to strikes in 2003 that produced some concessions (if minor ones) (Tagliabue 2003a; 2003b; Sciolino 2003), the larger message was that the French government would go only so far in offending its marginalised and benefit-deprived citizens. State leaders chose instead to sustain an ongoing budget deficit, to the point of inviting censure from the European Union. Happily for France, however, the European Court of Justice capitulated in mid-2004 with a compromise on its handling of this infraction (Bernstein 2003:A1, A12; Parker & Benoit 2004:1; Parker 2004:2; *Financial Times* 2004).

In Mexico, where unions still stood in the thrall to the state, and where, thus, labour actions were the most muted and small scale among the three countries, the payback for worker discontent was certainly the most meagre. While there had been no place for independent unions during the harshest, most authoritarian stage of the rule of the PRI (Teichman 1995:60; Middlebrook 1989:299; Samstad 2002:4), with the partial breakdown of PRI power in the 1990s, such groups did emerge openly and freely—though usually not so successfully (Carr 1987:222; Rochlin 1997:31; Collier 1992:110).[14] In mid-1996, federal officials met with dissident members of a teachers' union following a sizable national strike (Rochlin 1997:30), and in late 1997 a number of major unions broke from the official labour Congress,[15] combining with several independent ones to form the National Workers' Union.[16] There was more allying of this sort once Vicente Fox came to power in 2000 (de la Garza 2002:15–16, 25–8, 30–2; Thompson 2001).

But overall, Mexican protest—especially since 1980—has been discreet, restrained in amount and duration, and contained in scale. Its effectiveness has been limited to negligible. Insofar as there were any achievements at all—such as a 1987 Economic Solidarity Pact, in which income taxes were cut and inflation arrested, only the affiliates of the CTM received benefits, while workers as a group continued to suffer from the government's wage policy and its overall program of retrenchment (Middlebrook 1995:264–5, 295–7). Other outcomes issuing from protest mainly amounted just to delays of unfavourable policies, with the CTM's greatest accomplishment being its prevention of the Salinas administration's rewriting of the federal labour code. Yet even in this instance, the government managed to implement labour policy as if the law had indeed been altered (Middlebrook 1995:297–9).

Conclusion

So we are ready to return now to the query that opened this paper: what happens to workers when their states become more globally involved? I cannot claim to have answered this macro question in a general fashion. What I have done instead is to narrow the spotlight considerably, and to strive for specificity rather than be sweeping. I proposed a model of what has happened in three states, in all of which the leaders selected moves melding their economies with others abroad, three states where labour is reputed to be feeble and central power mighty. The outlook seemed gloomy.

But I found that after the governments in question became linked to leagues whose rules encouraged the discharge of workers, in a sense the story had just begun. Even in these places where power would seem to dictate a futile languishing of laid-off persons, we have seen that their protest, if possible, can better their lot. So my depiction—though surely not sanguine—turned out to be less dismal than anticipated. If other workers can stand and fight, one would hope their states too could find modes of accommodation.

Notes

1 These enterprises usually comprised of pre-1949 private firms merged in the 1950s and run at the level of the 'neighbourhood', under the urban district or ward.

2 Also, Hu gave me information during a private conversation, 23 September 2004, New York.

3 Pei (1997) shows how it has been possible for citizens to sue the state, but here again the victories for citizens are rarely implemented.

4 The Constitutions of 1975 and 1979 allowed for strikes, but this provision was erased in the constitution of 1982.

5 These initials stand for the Revolutionary Confederation of Workers and Peasants (CROC) and the Mexican Regional Labor Confederation (CROM).

6 On the other hand, those sectors that were most crucial to the overall economy, and which, accordingly, received the strongest state pressure for compliance, were also the ones displaying the boldest resistance to the state (Teichman 1995:49).

7 Michelle Dion (2002:20) has made the interesting finding that in the late 1980s and 1990s, though strikes decreased in number, strike petitions rose. This seems to suggest that aggrieved unions were willing to register a protest but dared not move to the streets.

8 The concern at the top with regime credibility and legitimacy appeared in a speech by Premier Zhu Rongji, in which he said that, 'This year no matter how, we can't again see new delays. We must definitely pay out the arrears of the past several months within this year and do it as fast as possible, in order to obtain the people's confidence' (Zhu 2000:6).

9 Welfare was granted at varying levels of service, with workers in the larger, favoured, state-owned firms in key industrial sectors faring best (Walder 1992).

10 Hu (2000) notes that in 1999 the ratio of the average living allowance for laid-off workers was 18.5% of that of employed workers, while the UI received by the registered unemployed population only amounted to 14.1% of employed workers' wages that year.

11 In 1995, 41% of urban households saw an income decline; the same year, the National Bureau of Statistics defined a family living in poverty as one with an income under 5,000 RMB per annum (Wong 1998:124). At this time per capita income was 6,392 RMB per year, which meant that the average household of just over three members must have had an average of nearly 20,000 RMB per year in 1998 (Chow & Xu 2001:1).

12 Aside from job loss, factors pushing people into penury also had to do with the market transition: state grain subsdies ceased in 1992, thereby sending up food prices; housing costs rose with the program to privatise apartments; and the charges for both public education and medical care climbed sharply and precipitously as their previous status as near gratuities was altered with the institution of sizable fees for service. There was also at this point a growing trend of indebted firms failing to pay wages or pensions, whether on time or else at all. The new urban poor population is concentrated among these people: those who worked in state firms that are losing

money, have ceased production, or went bankrupt; retired people's families where the support coefficient is high; those who became poor when they fell ill, owing to the high costs of medical care; and those whose term of receiving UI has ended (Song 2001:137–8).

13 This was done as it had been in 1999, almost on the eve of the 50th anniversary of the establishment of the People's Republic, very likely to stave off public demonstrations by the disadvantaged (Wu 1999).

14 Collier (1992) notes that some independent unions joined with left-wing parties and the Democratic Current to oppose an Economic Solidarity Pact in late 1987 that was to impose wage and price freezes.

15 This is a national body established in 1966 to bring together and speak for the entire organised labour movement (Middlebrook 1989:291).

16 The formal, Spanish name is the Union Nacional de Trabajadores, or UNT.

chapter twelve

The changing dynamics of labour migration in China and Mexico

Kenneth Roberts

Introduction

Migration is a dynamic demographic process; it responds to economic, socio-cultural, demographic and political conditions at migrants' places of origin and destination. Moreover, because migration creates networks in the migrant's places of origin and in migrant communities, it transforms the economic and social landscape of both areas. Zelinsky (1971) posited the existence of a 'mobility transition', with the rate of out migration tracing an inverted U-shape through time: in the short-to-medium-run, agricultural development in rural areas might increase migration by providing resources to potential migrants (Martin 1993), while in the long run a demographic transition and the convergence of wage rates might cause migration to fall (Hatton & Williamson 1998).

These long-term changes are usually accompanied by reconfigurations of several aspects of the migration system. As the volume of migration increases, it can become more or less selective of particular attributes such as age, education, or gender. Areas of origin and destination can become more concentrated or more diffuse. Migrants can specialise in particular occupations or find jobs throughout the economy. They can engage in circular migration, maintaining a base in their area of origin, or move permanently to the destination. The trajectory of any particular migration system over time will be uniquely determined for each circumstance, making generalisations difficult, but this difficulty should not dissuade us from the attempt, for understanding of the nature of the system and its likely evolution over time is important for the formation of appropriate policies.

Nowhere is the task of understanding the dynamics of a migration system more urgent than in contemporary China, which is experiencing the largest migration in human history and which faces hard choices regarding labour markets, urbanisation, and rural poverty and human rights that are impacted by migration policy. This chapter explores the potential dynamics of Chinese labour migration, drawing from experience with the dynamics of international labour migration systems, especially Mexican labour migration to the United States. If the plausibility of this analogy is accepted, it can be useful for focusing our attention on potential changes in the profile of Chinese labour migration, for not only has there been a great deal of theoretical attention paid to international migration generally, but the long duration of labour migration from Mexico to the US—over four decades in its current, most intense phase—makes it 'the largest sustained flow of migrant workers in the contemporary world' (Massey et al 1994:705), and has generated an enormous multidisciplinary literature upon which to draw.

This chapter will identify major changes in the profile of Mexico–US migration, show how they were related to changes in factors affecting the origin, the destination, and the migration process, and contrast those to parallel factors in China that may affect the migration system there. I will not argue that the same factors are operating in China nor that similar results will emerge, but rather that the penetration of capitalist relations, interacting with uniquely Chinese institutions and conditions, will create parallel, though perhaps different, outcomes. Examination of these factors and their outcomes in one context will create 'markers' that can be anticipated in another. The last section of the chapter will use these markers to generate hypotheses concerning potential changes in the profile of Chinese labour migration.

The nature of Chinese labour migration

The major type of migration happening in China today is temporary labour migration, a system of migration in which workers leave their homes for a period of time to work as low-skilled wage labourers. A temporary labour migration system exists when economic opportunities in the place of origin are limited while opportunities in the destination are only temporary, either because of the nature of the job or because of official restrictions on permanent stay. Both of these conditions are present in contemporary China: surplus labour exists on a massive scale in rural areas as a result of labour having been bottled up on the communes until the economic reforms of the early 1980s, and permanent settlement is forbidden for all but a few rural dwellers by the *hukou* system of household registration. Chinese cities have required migrants to obtain a bewildering array of documents to be legally resident, have restricted the jobs in which they could work, have charged high fees for the education of their children, and have provided only minimal accommodation on the fringes of cities or at their worksites. These constraints are reinforced by a long-standing prejudice of urbanites toward peasant workers (*mingong*), a prejudice as strong and effective as ethnicity in other countries. The combination of temporary migration, a large gap in living standards between sending and receiving areas, and restrictions against settlement makes internal migrants in China 'like immigrant labor in other settings…eager to earn money at any price, grateful for the chance to live in the city, vulnerable to threats of deportation, subject to enormous competition, and powerless because of the state's unwillingness to offer them rights, welfare, or security' (Solinger 1993:98).

By definition, all migrations require the crossing of some boundary, whether county, provincial, or international. That the boundary crossed in this case is within a single (though large and diverse) country rather than international is less important than the insight contemporary labour migrations involve 'a move between two worlds, even if it is within a single region or country' (Sassen 1999:135). The comparison of Chinese labour migration to international migration has been increasingly endorsed by other leading scholars of Chinese migration (Cai 2001; Davin 1999; Fan 2004; Mallee 2000; Xiang 2005).

Of all the contemporary examples of international migration, I have argued that the case most relevant for comparison with China is that of undocumented migration from Mexico to the US (Roberts 1997). The Mexico–US case is particularly relevant because of three factors in addition to those common to international labour migration generally. The first is the relative proximity of sending and receiving areas with wide disparities in earnings, which permits regular visits home and the maintenance of strong village-based networks. The second is that both countries devised a land policy based on an agrarian revolution that gave farmers a plot that could not be sold or mortgaged, but had to be cultivated or forfeited. This system of land tenure, combined with surplus labour and limited access by small farmers to the inputs required for commercial production, changed the function of the land from that of an economic unit to a base for a variety of household activities, including farming, raising children, agricultural sideline activities, local wage labour and (because of proximity) circular migration. The last is the imposition of free trade in agriculture upon this inefficient peasant farming, in Mexico by the North American Free Trade Association (NAFTA) and in China by the World Trade Organization (WTO).

Changes in factors affecting origin, destination and the migration process

Mexican migration to the US is now more than a century old, with the most intense period beginning about four decades ago. Scholarly examination of the process began shortly after, and more recently a series of articles have identified continuities and changes in the process over time. This section will summarise their conclusions and identify factors at the origin, the destination, and those affecting the migration process that have influenced the evolution of the Mexico-US migration system. These will be contrasted to parallel factors in China that may affect the migration system there.

The migration system linking Mexico and the US took root in the 1960s at the end of a guestworker program and accelerated rapidly during the 1970s. Massey, Durand and Malone (2002:66) call the period from 1965 to 1986 'the era of undocumented migration', over which 'the profile of a Mexican migrant remained remarkably constant'. During this period, according to Cornelius (1992:156), 'Mexican migration to the United States consisted mainly of a circular flow of mostly undocumented, mostly young adult males who left their immediate relatives behind in a rural Mexican community to work in seasonal US agriculture for several months (normally up to six months), and then returned to their community of origin'. Massey, Durand and Malone add that most migrants had low levels of educational attainment, came from a few states concentrated in the central area of Mexico and worked in only a few states in the US, especially California and Texas.

But that system underwent significant change: 'in a few short years it was transformed from a seasonal, undocumented, and regionally specific flow in which rural males predominated into an urbanised and substantially female population of permanent settlers who were increasingly dispersed throughout the United States' (Durand, Massey & Parrado 1999). Cornelius identified four changes that occurred in the profile of the migration stream: (1) increasing education and skills among migrants, (2) increasing diversification of sending areas (and, as shown in subsequent research, receiving areas), (3) an increasing proportion of women and children, and (4) increasing settlement in the destination. He hypothesised that these changes could be explained by the economic crisis in Mexico that affected all areas of the country and brought in new sending areas, by a shift in the composition of demand for migrant labour in the US to year-round jobs requiring more skilled labour, by passage of legislation that legalised many migrants, and by the maturation of migration networks. These changes can be categorised into factors affecting the origin, destination, and migration process. The following sections will discuss similarities and differences in these factors between the Mexico–US and Chinese systems of labour migration.

Factors affecting the origin

The first stage of Mexican migration to the United States began when the proportion of the population dependent on agriculture was still high, as it is in China today. Total fertility rates in Mexico stayed above six until the mid-1970s, producing in 1980 a pyramid-shaped age structure typical of developing countries, and ensuring rapid growth of the labour supply for the next two decades. But unlike China with its relatively equal landholdings, agricultural development in Mexico had created a bi-polar farm structure consisting of large capitalist farms with mechanised production of commercial crops and small subsistence units that provided only a portion of household subsistence. Many of these small farms were on *ejidal* land which, as in China today, was owned communally but farmed individually. By the early 1990s, of the 27% of the Mexican labour force still working in agriculture, half of their labour was spent in the cultivation of low-profit corn and beans, so that the sector generated only 9% of GDP but contained two-thirds of Mexico's poor (Latapí et al 1998). The elimination of input subsidies and price guarantees being imposed by NAFTA and the dismantling of the *ejido* system have exacerbated the decline in income and agricultural employment.

In studying the consequences of agricultural development in Mexico, it is clear that its effect was to increase migration, not slow it. Intense migration to the US began in several states of central Mexico where commercial production and agricultural change was raising production costs and reducing labour requirements (Roberts 1982). A major review of migration theories applied to the Mexico–US case found that 'the highest probabilities of out-migration are observed in rural communities undergoing rapid economic growth and development…*The economic transformation of the countryside creates rather than prevents international migration*' (Massey & Espinosa 1997:968, italics theirs).

The factors that have produced large numbers of migrants in China are very different from those that existed in Mexico during the early years of migration. Farms in China are small, with the average household cultivating only one-sixth of a hectare of land, and so far there is little consolidation of farm plots into larger units that would facilitate mechanisation. Total fertility rates fell rapidly through the last decades of the century, producing a vertical age structure for 2000 that is quite different from Mexico's at a similar stage in its migration history. Instead, China's surplus rural labour is a legacy of the pre-reform period, when rural labour was contained on the communes.

In 1978, before the impact of the economic reforms, Chinese agriculture employed 74% of the labour force; by 2000, the proportion had fallen to 46%, but the number of workers had grown even as the proportion fell. Because of a large decline in labour requirements, 152 million of the 328 million agricultural workers were estimated by the Ministry of Agriculture to be redundant (Aubert & Li 2002). During the late 1980s and early 1990s many found jobs in rural enterprises, but employment there declined and migration became the principal source of off-farm labour. Working for wages was clearly better than farming: a 1995 survey found that daily income from farming was 9.4 RMB, while it was 12.7 RMB from working in TVEs and 17.4 RMB from migration (Knight & Song 2003). Farming was made even less desirable by high taxes and fees imposed by cash-strapped local governments, leading to protests and rural violence in several provinces. Yet despite all of these problems, most Chinese living in rural areas still do not want to give up their farm because of the security it offers, giving them a place go when sick or unemployed (Nielsen, Smyth & Zhang 2006).

Given the constraint of retaining land rights, the key to further reductions in agricultural labour in China would be the development of rural markets for labour, machinery and especially land use that would permit farmers to keep their land and work elsewhere. This happened not only in Mexico, where it led to consolidation and large scale farming, but also in Taiwan, where there emerged instead part-time farming on small plots, facilitated by mechanisation, government subsidies, and a dispersed industrial base providing employment in rural areas.

Rural factor markets for labour and agricultural equipment are undeveloped in China: little agricultural labour is hired, and many migrants return once or twice a year to work on their own farms. This has constrained migration, with one fourth of the households in one survey who wanted to migrate unable to do so because they could not spare the labour from farming (Knight & Song 2005). Land rental is still rare, but growing: while only 3% of land was rented in 1995, a 1999 survey of by the Ministry of Agriculture found 14% of the land in six provinces was rented, two-thirds requiring no payment but only the obligation to meet the grain quota (Kung 2002).

If China follows the path of Mexico, social and cultural change in rural areas may have as profound an effect on migration as economic change. For young people in rural areas of both countries, migration offers the potential for escape from the drudgery of farm work and the constraints of village life. A Mexican survey conducted in 1989 found that 'the younger generation of workers in high-emigration communities is not disposed to taking hometown agricultural jobs, even at higher than the prevailing local wage, and even if such jobs could be available year-round' (Cornelius & Martin 1993:503). Similarly, farming is perceived to be a dead end for young Chinese workers entering the labour force: a survey of young migrant workers in three cities of coastal China found that 72% would choose to stay in the city even if their earnings in agriculture were equivalent to what they earned in the city (Wang 2003).

Factors affecting the origin areas—demography, agrarian structure, agricultural technology, rural development and cultural change—worked together in Mexico to decrease the amount of labour used in agriculture. There are several important differences in these rural factors in China that could work in an opposite direction, such as agrarian structure, or at least not be as severe, such as demography. But what seems certain is that labour requirements in agriculture will fall: in just the years between 1979 and 1988 labour requirements dropped 31% (Rawski & Mead 1998), but they are still very high compared with those of more developed neighbours. It is clear that China has just begun the process of substituting crops and technology and developing rural factor markets that will give farmers flexibility in their allocation of labour to agriculture, and that the potential for the release of rural labour is immense.

Factors affecting the destination

The second set of factors that affected the Mexico–US migration process were economic, social and political ones in the destination. During the first decades of intense labour migration, the US economy became increasingly dependent upon migrant labour in areas such as agriculture, construction, food processing and low-skill services. Migrants were perceived to be taking jobs from residents, to be using social services paid for by residents' taxes, and to be a burden on local communities. In 1986 the Immigration Reform and Control Act was passed, forged as a compromise between the interests of employers, organised labour, migrant interest groups and those who felt the country had 'lost control of its borders'. Its passage heralded 'the new era of Mexican migration to the US', the era that has lasted until the present. (Durand, Massey & Parrado 1999).

In China, the economic impact of migration on urban residents seems to be less of an issue than it has been in the US. Most Chinese migrants, such as those working in construction, other types of manual labour, petty retailing, and services are not in direct competition with urban residents for jobs. A recent book on the labour market in China concludes, 'migrant and non-migrant workers are highly imperfect substitutes or even complements: migrants do the jobs that non-migrants shun' (Knight & Song 2005:113). For the most part, the current dialogue on economic issues reflects positively on migrants, who are seen as major contributors to economic modernisation at the national level and to the material lives of urbanites at the local level.

But the social position of migrants in urban China is as difficult as that of Mexican migrants in the US: Jacka (2006:241) finds 'this local urban versus outsider rural divide constitutes a form of ethnicity and is as significant as the divide between the local population of developed nations such as the United States and Australia, and their ethnic immigrant populations'. As in the US, the balancing of economic and social concerns reflected in policy and enforcement is the major factor affecting migrants in the destination.

Chinese attitudes and policies toward migrants

While limited migration has been permitted in China since 1984, it was not until recovery from the economic downturn of 1989–90 that the growing numbers of migrants became a major issue. By then, the Chinese press:

> generally portrays a homogeneous and rather threatening image of rural migrants as large masses flowing into Chinese cities. A more simplified narrative structure of such press accounts was that overwhelming poverty pushed migrants from the countryside, forcing them to 'pour blindly' into the cities, which disturbed social stability and thus called for the urban authorities to take strong measures (control or expulsion) to restore social order (Florence 2004:48).

The 1990s was a period when rural migrant labour was considered to be *mangliu*, or a 'blind flow', and the reception given migrants by urbanites was generally hostile, reflecting perceptions about their contribution to a variety of problems accompanying the economic transition (Davin 2000).

Within this context, the state tried to gain control of migrants in the city with an interlinked web of work and residence permits, but they were costly and confusing to migrants, and the vast majority did not possess them all (Zhao, S 2000). In Beijing, five different certificates were issued by five different agencies:

> in ordinary times nobody regarded them as violating legal provisions, but with the advent of special occasions, such as important celebrations, those migrants without a complete set of the five certificates would be regarded as 'law or regulation breakers' and would be harshly treated and expelled (Li 2003:135).

But these draconian measures were increasingly at odds with the interests of other agencies of the government, and there existed competition and intergovernmental conflict over the collection of fees and taxes. Rather than work together to weave a tighter regulatory net, those charged with regulating migrants were often at cross purposes. The Ministry of Agriculture, local governments and labour export companies were all beneficiaries and promoters of migration in high out-migration rural areas. Landlords, who are mostly peasants receiving high rents for substandard dwellings on their property, were unwilling to check the birth control certificates of migrant women as required by family planning authorities. Social scientists in academia and government research agencies played a major role in changing urbanites' perceptions of migrants, arguing that migration was not 'blind' but organised (Zhao, S 2000), that migration controls hindered the development of an efficient labour market (Cai & Wang 2003), and that these controls prevented China from utilising its comparative advantage in labour (Zhao, Y 2000). Another important achievement of academic research was 'the establishment of a migrant-centered narrative which focuses on migrants' experiences and problems' in the media (Xiang & Shen 2005).

The contrast between the economic contributions of migrants and their treatment has led to policy changes at the national level. At the end of the 1990s and for the next several years, regulations were modified to make it easier to migrate to towns and small cities, to allow children to inherit *hukou* status from their father, to give investors and those who buy housing permanent residence, and even to reform major categories of *hukou* status (Wang, F-L 2005). In 2002 the State Council said that migration of rural surplus labour into urban areas is not a social problem but a normal consequence of economic development; that migrants are in the working class (*gongren jieji*) and not peasants (*nongmin*); and that policies should be fair, with formal contracts, no delayed wages, no arbitrary fees and safe working conditions (Huang & Pieke 2003). In 2004 Premier Wen Jiabao stopped on a trip in Sichuan to meet a pig farmer, the wife of a migrant construction worker owed more than a year's pay, and promised that he would be paid. The interview was covered by more than 60 reporters, causing local governments in migrant receiving areas to require companies to establish wage funds before beginning construction (Kuhn 2004). The National Labor Medal was awarded to a migrant worker for the first time in 2004 (*Xinhua News* 2004), and according to the 'Spring Breeze' action of 2005, only ID cards are required for migrants to work in a city (Liu & Cai 2005).

While legal obstacles to migrants working in cities are being removed, housing and children's education remain major barriers to integration and settlement. Buying a house is prohibitive for all but the richest migrant entrepreneurs, so that most migrants live in poor quality rented rooms on the fringes of cities (Wu 2004). Chinese migrants are even more disadvantaged than their Mexican counterparts regarding the education of their children, for Mexican children born in the US are entitled to citizenship and guaranteed an education even if born in Mexico. In China, cities were not required to educate the children of persons not registered there until 1998, and since that date they have charged prohibitively high fees for the children of migrants. Many of the estimated seven million migrant children attend migrant schools, which are cheaper but of poor quality (Kwong 2004).

Factors affecting the migration process

The last set of factors that affected the dynamics of Mexican migration were changes in the migration process linking origin and destination. These changes included better information about employment opportunities and life in the US, easier and cheaper contact between persons in Mexico and the US due to improvements in transport and communications, and most importantly, the maturation of migration networks. Migration networks reduce the costs and risks of migration, providing network members with 'social capital' that reinforces migration from particular sending areas and concentrates it in particular destinations in a process of cumulative causation (Massey et al 1994).

The importance of networks for Chinese migrants has been emphasised by a number of scholars (Cai 2001; Ma & Xiang 1998; Zhao 2001). Eight inter-provincial flows between origin and destination exceeding one million migrants were identified in the 2000 census (Liang 2007). Informal networks between these areas have been institutionalised in formal linkages, such as migrant centers representing county and provincial governments in major destinations.

Nevertheless, compared with Mexico, the formation of migrant networks is just beginning, and there are many parts of rural China from which few people migrate to work elsewhere (Ma 2004). More than one-third of the 4,000 households in a 1995 survey in eight provinces wanted to increase their migration, but had not done so because of lack of contacts (36%) and information (25%). Of those who did not want to continue migrating, 17% said it was too insecure and 9% listed the costs and hardships of travel. Most had not even considered migration as an option, suggesting a lack of information was the single biggest constraint (Knight & Song 2003). As networks mature, these constraints will ease significantly.

Potential changes in the profile of Chinese migration

If migration in China were to respond to changes in the factors identified above in a fashion similar to that linking the US and Mexico, we would expect to see the following changes in the profile of Chinese migration over the next two decades: more migration to the coastal cities (because of the intensification of migration from current sending areas), and the spread of migration to new areas, greater occupational diversification within destination areas leading to higher education and skills of migrants, more women and families in the migrant stream, and more settlement. Each of these potential changes in the profile of Chinese migration will be briefly explored.

The magnitude and regional specificity of migration flows

There is little dispute that the magnitude of Chinese migration is large and growing, with the most rapid upsurge beginning in the early to mid-1990s and increasing since then (Goodkind & West 2002). The 2000 census showed that 79 million migrants had crossed county boundaries and 42 million provincial boundaries (Liang & Ma 2004), and our examination of factors affecting the origin, destination and migration process points overwhelmingly to increased migration in China over the next two decades.

More and more migration is interprovincial rather than local. Comparison of the 1990 and 2000 censuses shows an increase in interprovincial migration from 32% to 54% of the total, much of it directed toward the dynamic coastal regions of the Pearl River Delta in Guangdong province and the Shanghai–Jiangsu–Zhejiang region of the lower Yangtze River (Liang 2007). Much of this migration is from the four major sending provinces of Anhui, Hunan, Sichuan (including Chongqing) and Jiangxi, which together have 280 million people and thus the potential to send even more migrants. Fan (2005:21) finds 'increased migration selectivity to only a few destinations and/or from only a few origins' during the 1990s, and calls this phenomenon "spatial focusing"'.

This same spatial focusing existed during the early stage of Mexico–US migration: the majority of migrants came from just a few states in the central part of the county and went mainly to Texas and California. But as the rural situation worsened and the entire country went into crisis during the 1980s, migration spread from the traditional sending areas in the central states to the periphery. Even indigenous people from the southern state of Oaxaca who did not speak Spanish began joining the migration stream in significant numbers during the 1980s.

In China, the process of cumulative causation in high-migration provinces might cause their relative contribution to the total number of migrants to continue to rise in the short run. But if China follows the path of Mexico, whether by crisis or simply the steady deterioration of rural conditions, we can expect to see the spread of migration to other origin areas, including those poor provinces with large numbers of ethnic minorities.

Another major change in the regional specificity of Mexico–US migration is its spread to non-traditional receiving areas. Between 1990 and 2002, the number of Mexican migrants outside the four traditional receiving states of Texas, California, Illinois and Arizona increased five times, compared with just 87% within those states (Passel 2004). While this spatial diversification requires a level of prosperity in nontraditional receiving areas that China is still far from achieving, already one of the earliest migration streams, originating in the Wenzhou region of Zhejiang province, has begun a 'diffusion path' of migration to small cities after having concentrated in big cities like Beijing (Xiang 2005).

Occupational diversification and education

Mexican migrants to the US during the 1960s worked predominantly in agriculture. They diversified into restaurants and construction during the 1970s and 1980s and were working in every sector of the US economy by the end of the 1990s. A similar occupational diversification is being witnessed in China, from construction and factory work to more jobs in retail and services. Migrants have long provided goods and services to urbanites in the cities, and their variety and sophistication is increasing yearly. Service jobs are especially important for female migrants, with 40% of the female migrants in Beijing working in the service sector in 1997 (Guo & Iredale 2004).

Factory work is likely to become more skill-intensive as China produces more high-technology goods, and factories are already demanding at least a middle-school education for their workers. Returns to elementary and middle-school education were found to be positive for migrants (de Brauw & Giles 2005), and this message is travelling back to the villages as 'migrants write home exhorting their siblings to stay in school' (Murphy 2002:100). Because a larger proportion of women are engaged in factory work, higher levels of education increased the likelihood of the migration of women more than it did the migration of men (Zhang, de Brauw & Rozelle 2004). Thus we see that occupational diversification is related to the gender division of migrant labour, which will be discussed in the next section.

Women and families

The third and fourth of the changes in the Mexico–US migration process—more women and children and more settlement—are of critical importance and are closely related, for it is women who are the foundation and often the motivation for settlement.

While the first phase of Mexican migration to the US was dominated by men, during the second phase there has been a 'feminization of the Mexican migrant flow…accelerating sharply in the 1990s' (Marcelli & Cornelius 2001:111). Similarly, during the early stages of Chinese migration the overwhelming majority of migrants were men, and women were much less likely to engage in interprovincial migration. That profile began to change during the 1990s, between 1995 and 2000 the probability of women's migration doubled relative to men, and for the youngest cohort (16–20) was equal (Zhang, de Brauw & Rozelle 2004).

The reasons that motivate women to migrate are different from those of men. This is especially true in China: in Tianjin female migrants,

> were breaking through the limitations put upon them by men, tradition and the state. The female migrant interviewees shared a common perception that the greatest gains from working in the city were the significant differences they had made in their own lives and destiny (Zhang 1999:38).

For migrants to Shenzhen, 'not that economic reasons were unimportant (but)...these rural young women came for the no less important goals of escaping from parental control and various familial responsibilities' (Lee 1998:73). Young women came to work in Beijing '"because I had nothing to do at home (*mei shi gan*)". This is a common response among married and single young women that...points to the marginalization of young women in the rural economy' (Jacka 2006:133).

The young women working in China's factories are often called *dagongmei*, which 'has the connotation of "maiden workers" who work while waiting to be married off' (Lee 1998:128). Not only does the research by the authors above challenge this assumption, but the second half of the common stereotype—that when these female migrants return they marry, bear children and never migrate again—is no longer true. Jacka (2006:9) notes 'there are thousands of rural women living in Beijing and other cities who are older than the typical *dagongmei*, who are married and have children, and who are either self-employed or who care for their children while their husband earns an income'. One-third of the migrant workers in Beijing, Wuhan, Suzhou and Shenzhen were accompanied by a spouse in 1995 (Knight, Song & Jia 1999), and similar results were found in Shanghai two years earlier (Roberts 2002).

A survey of rural women conducted in 2000 illustrates the diverse patterns of female labour migration, showing that 62% of the female migrants who had returned to Anhui and Sichuan did not engage in their first migration until after the average age of marriage of 21.7, and by this age more than half were married when they migrated for the first time. The proportion who were married on subsequent migrations was even higher, so that of the total of first through third trips engaged in by women, two-thirds were accomplished while they were married. About half of these women migrated alone and half were accompanied by their husbands, indicating that one-third of female migrant returnees in Anhui and Sichuan had migrated as couples (Roberts et al 2004). Since migrant couples are more likely to engage in long-term migration and settlement and thus not to have been included in the rural sample, it is likely that an even greater proportion of all migrants came as couples.

The biggest potential constraint on the migration of married women is their responsibility as mothers. Yet children do not appear to constitute an insurmountable barrier to migration, for four out of five married migrants in the sample had children by the time they took their first trip. The care provided by grandparents was the critical factor that relieved this constraint, with three-fourths of the women who had children by their first migration leaving them with grandparents, most commonly paternal grandparents. In addition, about one fourth of the women migrating with their husbands brought their children with them, contributing to the issue of schooling for migrant children discussed earlier (Roberts et al 2004).

Gender and marital status interact strongly with occupation in the destination. More than half of the single women migrants from Anhui and Sichuan were factory workers, but the probability of working in a factory declined on subsequent trips and for married women migrating with their husbands. This is partly due to the type of accommodation associated with the job, for factories frequently provide same-sex dormitories for workers. A related explanation is that some types of jobs, such as home repairs, vending and food preparation permit couples to work together efficiently and earn more money (Roberts et al 2004).

Overall, the findings above demonstrate a remarkable diversity of migration patterns among rural Chinese women, as opposed to the simple *dagongmei* stereotype. Women are migrating married and single, with and without their husbands and their children. Marriage and subsequent childbearing occur during their early 20s for both migrant and non-migrant women, but these life events no longer form insurmountable barriers to migration. This diversity of migration patterns is in sharp contrast with that of Mexican women whose migration to the US is mainly linked to that of their husbands and other male family members.

Settlement

The last of the trends in Mexican migration is increasing settlement in the destination. While the majority of migrants in Mexico and China do not express an intention to stay, 'settlement has a funny way of creeping up on immigrant workers' (Hondagneu-Sotelo 1995:1). Marcelli and Cornelius (2001) estimate the proportion of the migration stream who returned to Mexico fell 28% from 1980 to 1992, and relate this to the feminisation of migration. Massey, Durand and Malone (2002) calculate that the annual probability of return migration fell from 0.25 to 0.07 between the two major periods of Mexican migration, implying a rise in the median duration from 2.4 years to 8.9 years and a quadrupling of the migrant population resident in the US.

For reasons of autonomy and freedom discussed earlier with regard to young Chinese migrant women, Mexican women enjoy more autonomy in the US than in their rural villages, and are more likely than men to express a preference for staying permanently. Pessar (2003:29), in a recent review of gender and US immigration, says 'research shows consistently that gains in gender equity are central to women's desires to settle, more or less permanently, to protect their advances. In contrast, many men seek to return home rapidly to regain the status and privileges that migration itself has challenged'. These desires translate into reality: 45% of Mexican women stayed in the US more than ten years compared with only 26% of Mexican men (Reyes 1997).

The narratives of Chinese migrant women in the city express a profound ambivalence regarding place of origin: 'while these narratives express a yearning for the countryside of one's past, they also suggest an understanding of the countryside as the past; as a place and a period in one's life that one has lost or left behind' (Jacka 2006:125). While men tend to think of their rural home as the primary locus of their identity, 'migrant women tend to see a future in the city as holding greater potential for development than life in the countryside' (Jacka 2006: 160). For this reason, 'significant, and possibly growing, numbers of migrant women wish to stay away from their "home" in the countryside for as long as possible, despite the discrimination and hardships they face in the city' (Jacka 2006: 141). Of migrants surveyed in Hebei, more women than men envied the urban life, wanted their families with them, and 'were more eager to abandon rural life and settle in the cities' (Song 1999:88). Some single women hoped to find urban boyfriends and eventually settle in the city (Zhang 1999).

The only evidence concerning settlement in the cities of China comes from successive urban floating population surveys that allow comparison of the duration of migrants over time. The duration of stay for Shanghai's floating population was relatively stable between 1988 and 1993, with between 69% and 71% staying less than one year. But the proportion of rural labour migrants staying less than a year fell from 73% to 51% between 1993 and 1997, while those staying from one to five years rose from 24% to 39%, and more than five years from 4% to 10%. Based upon analysis of the entire floating population in these surveys rather than just labour migrants, Liang (2007) concludes 'the increasing duration of residence indicates that substantial portion of migrants are clearly settling in Shanghai'.

Conclusion

It has now been 40 years since the beginning of undocumented labour migration from Mexico to the US, during which the profile of the migration stream has changed in significant ways. This chapter uses the changes in that profile to identify factors at the origin, the destination and the migration process that have affected its evolution over time, and looks to parallel factors in China that might influence the dynamics of migration there. Understanding these dynamics is critical to the development of appropriate policies and will have significant impacts upon some of the most important issues facing China today, including rural poverty, the pace and character of urbanisation, the evolution of the labour market and human rights.

But before the usefulness of the analogy can be appreciated, the reader must be persuaded on two issues. First, is the analogy to international migration generally, and the Mexico–US example in particular, appropriate? The first section of this chapter examined the relevance of the comparison, and is addressed particularly to Chinese scholars relatively unfamiliar with the evolution of western migration theory over the past two decades. A similar argument was made in an earlier paper (Roberts 1997), but was addressed instead to Western scholars trying to understand Chinese migration. Since then, the process has changed considerably.

The second potential objection is that even though labour migration across international boundaries may provide a relevant theoretical model, the factors operating in the two systems are so different that it would be inappropriate to apply the results of one to the other. The reader is conceded this important point: the goal of the analysis is not to say what will necessarily happen, for there are too many variables and actors, but rather to identify particular types of factors that will play a major role in the process, though they might have a different effect in the two cases. The impact of rural factor markets is a case in point: they are relatively developed in Mexico, allowing smallholders to continue agricultural production while migrating, but not in China. If rural factor markets in China become more developed, this will facilitate migration; if not, agricultural production will suffer, carrying its own set of consequences. The development of rural factor markets is thus an important 'marker' for the evolution of migration.

The four major changes in the process of Mexican migration to the US were more migration from more origins to more destinations, occupational diversification and intensification of education and skills, more women and children, and more settlement. Although there are some important differences between Mexico and China regarding the factors at the origin that have influenced theses changes, the overall outcome will probably be the same—fewer workers needed in agriculture, large cohorts entering the labour market and dissatisfaction with farming as an occupation and the village as the locus of one's future plans. Likewise, the migration process is likely to develop in a similar manner, with networks deepening and widening. This too will increase the intensity of migration, and can cause spatial and occupational focusing followed by diversification. Networks can have paradoxical effects, so again it is not the specific prediction that is important, but instead the necessity of paying close attention to the evolution of migrant networks and the role of local and national governments and private recruiters in facilitating or hindering the operation these networks.

Factors at the destination offer the potential for the greatest divergence between the two processes. The comparison drew attention to the interplay of economic and social factors which are very different in the two countries. The US is a 'country of immigrants', so that anti-immigrant groups must find other grounds for opposition, while China has a long tradition of a 'place-embedded social control paradigm' that allows abrupt changes in government policy in reaction to perceived problems. In China's booming economy there is little competition between migrants and locals, but that can change rapidly with economic conditions and with increases in migrants' human capital. Settlement is easy in the US once the border has been crossed, and every child once there is entitled to an education. In China housing and education are the two biggest obstacles to settlement. *Hukou* policy is central to these issues, with recent changes favouring relaxation, the integration of migrants and efficient labour markets.

In one regard, the process in China is moving much faster than it did in Mexico: more women are coming at an earlier stage in the process, more single women are coming to work in industry and more married women are coming without their husbands. This is partly due to differences in the labour markets in the two destinations: if the US–Mexico border area is considered part of the destination, the difference narrows, and the service sector in urban China was non-existent before migrants moved in. But Chinese women seem to have seized the opportunity to change their lives in ways that Mexican women never did. Their desires for themselves and their families will have a major impact upon the future of Chinese migration.

glossary

ACFTA	ASEAN–China free trade area
ACFTU	All China Federation of Trade Unions
ADB	Asian Development Bank
ANZ	Australia and New Zealand
ASEAN	Association of South East Asian Nations
ASSA	Academy of Social Sciences in Australia
CASS	Chinese Academy of Social Sciences
CEGEC	China Expert Group on Economic Co-operation
CGT	Confederation General du Travail
CLB	China Labour Bulletin
CMP	Common Minimum Programme (India)
CROC	Revolutionary Confederation of Workers and Peasants (Mexico)
CROM	Mexican Regional Labour Confederation
CSR Asia	Corporate Social Responsibility in Asia
CTCC	China Tuberculosis Control Collaboration
CTM	Confederation de Trabajadores Mexicanos (Confederation of Mexican Workers)
DGAP	Deutche Gesellschaft für Austwärtige Politik eV (German Council on Foreign Relations)
DIFD	Department for International Development (UK)
DOTS	Directly Observed Therapy Short-course
EPW	Economic and Political Weekly (India)
EU	European Union

EV	Equivalent variation
FDI	Foreign direct investment
GATT	General Agreement on Tariffs and Trade
GDP	Gross domestic product
GTAP	Global Trade Analysis Project
HES	Household economic status
ICSSR	Indian Council of Social Science Research
ILO	International Labour Organisation
IPPR	Institute for Public Policy Research (UK)
IT	Information technology
MIS	Migration information source
NC	Nimingde Chengtuan (pseudonym for firm)
NBS	National Bureau of Statistics (China)
NGO	Non-government organisation
NMG	Nanjing Municipal Government
NPC	National Peoples Congress
NSS	National Sample Survey
NSSO	National Sample Survey Organisation
PRC	Peoples Republic of China
PRI	Institutional Revolutionary Party
RMB	Renminbi
ROW	Rest of the world
SOEs	State owned enterprises
UI	Unemployment Insurance (China)
UK	United Kingdom
UN	United Nations
UNDP	United Nations Development Program

UNESCO	United Nations Educational, Social and Cultural Organisation
UNT	Union Nacional de Trabajadores (National Workers' Union [Mexico])
US	United States
USSR	Union of Soviet Socialist Republics
WB	World Bank
WMG	Wuxi Municipal Government
WTO	World Trade Organisation
XPCC	Xinjiang Production & Construction Corps, or Bingtuan
ZG	Zhizao Gongsi (pseudonym for firm)

bibliography

ADB (Asian Development Bank) 2002, 'The 2020 Project: policy support in the People's Republic of China—final report and policy directions', Manila, www.adb.org/Documents/Reports/2020_Project/default.asp, accessed August 2005.

Andrew, F and S Withey 1976, *Social indicators of well-being*, Plenum, New York.

Appleton, S, J Knight, L Song and Q Xia 2001, 'Towards a competitive labour market? Urban workers, rural migrants, redundancies and hardship in China', paper presented at the American Economic Association Conference.

ASEAN Secretariat 2002, 'Framework agreement on comprehensive economic co-operation between the Association of South East Asian Nations and the People's Republic of China', Phnom Penh, 5 November.

—— 2004a, 'Agreement on trade in goods of the framework agreement on comprehensive economic co-operation between the Association of South East Asian Nations and the People's Republic of China', Vientiane, 29 November.

—— 2004b, 'Joint communiqué: the eighteenth ASEAN labour ministers meeting', Brunei Darussalam, 13–14 May.

—— 2005, 'The economic benefits to ASEAN of the ASEAN–China Free Trade Area (ACFTA)', prepared by R Cordenillo, Bureau for Economic Integration, ASEAN Secretariat, Jakarta.

ASEAN-CEGEC (ASEAN-China Expert Group on Economic Cooperation) 2001, 'Forging closer ASEAN–China economic relations in the twenty-first century'.

Aubert, C and Li Xiande 2002, 'Agricultural underemployment and rural migration in China: facts and figures', *China Perspectives* 41.

Audley, J, S Polaski, DG Papademetriou and S Vaughan 2004, 'Nafta's promise and reality: lessons from Mexico for the hemisphere', Carnegie Endowment for International Peace, Washington.

Bagchi, AK 1972, Private investment in India 1900–1939, Cambridge University Press, Cambridge.

—— 1989, *The presidency banks and the Indian economy 1876–1914*, Oxford University Press, Calcutta.

—— 2002a, 'Dualism and dialectics in the historiography of labour' in Bagchi, AK, *Capital and labour redefined: India and the Third World*, Tulika, New Delhi and Anthem Press, London.

——2002b, 'Wealth and work in Calcutta 1860–1921' in Bagchi, AK, *Capital and labour redefined: India and the Third World*, Tulika, New Delhi and Anthem Press, London.

—— 2004, 'The axial ages of the capitalist world-system', *Review* XVII(2).

—— 2005a, 'Globalization and vulnerability: India at the dawn of the twentieth century' in Cao Tian Yu (ed), *The Chinese model of modern development*, Routledge, London.

—— 2005b, *Perilous passage: mankind and the global ascendancy of capital*, Rowman & Littlefield, Lanham and Oxford University Press, New Delhi.

—— 2005c, 'Rural credit and systemic risk' in Ramachandran, VK and Madhura Swaminathan (eds), *Financial liberalization and rural credit in India*, Tulika, New Delhi.

Bagchi, AK, P Das and S Chattopadhyay 2005, 'Growth and structural change in Gujarat, 1970–2000', *Economic and Political Weekly* 40(28).

Bangkok Post 2005, 'China likely to profit most from ASEAN free trade deal', 10 September.

Barboza, D 2006, 'Labor shortage in China may lead to trade shift', *New York Times*, 4 March.

Bastian, Jens 1998, 'Putting the cart before the horse? Labour market challenges ahead of monetary union in Europe' in Hine, D and Hussein Kassim (eds), *Beyond the market: the EU and national social policy*, Routledge, London.

BDMN (*Bernama Daily Malaysian News*) 2005, 'FTA to strengthen Malaysia–China trade', 12 August.

Beard, J and M Ragheb 1980, 'Measuring leisure satisfaction', *Journal of Leisure Research* 12.

Becquelin, N 2000, 'Xinjiang in the nineties', *The China Journal* 44.

Beijing Review 2005, 'The price of health: many migrant workers struggle with medical expenses in big cities', June.

Bell, DS and B Criddle 1988, *The French Socialist Party: The emergence of a party of government*, second edition, Clarendon Press, Oxford.

Bernstein, R 2003, 'Europe's lofty vision of unity meets headwinds', *New York Times*, 4 December.

Bhalla, AS and Qiu S 2004, *The employment impact of China's WTO accession*, RoutledgeCurzon, London and New York.

Bhattacharya, PC 1993, 'Rural–urban migration in economic development', *Journal of Economic Surveys* 7(3).

Bhattacharyya, A and E Parker 1999, 'Labour productivity and migration in Chinese agriculture: a stochastic frontier approach', *China Economic Review* 10(1).

Blecher, M 2001, 'The working class and governance in China,' paper presented to the Forum on Governance in China, Institute of Development Studies, University of Sussex, 11–13 September.

Boltho, A 1996, 'Has France converged on Germany? Policies and institutions since 1958' in Berger, S and R Dore (eds), *Regional diversity and global capitalism*, Cornell University Press, Ithaca.

Bonnin, M 2000, 'Perspectives on social stability after the fifteenth congress' in Tien H-M and Chu Y-H (eds), *China under Jiang Zemin*, Lynne Rienner, Boulder.

Boyer, R 1984, 'Wage labor, capital accumulation, and the crisis, 1968–82' in Kesselman, M (ed), *The French workers' movement: economic crisis and political change*, George Allen & Unwin, London.

Breman, J 1996, *Footloose labour: working in India's informal economy*, Cambridge University Press, Cambridge.

—— 2002, 'Communal upheaval as resurgence of social Darwinism', *Economic and Political Weekly* 37(16).

Burgess, K 1999, 'Loyalty dilemmas and market reform: party–union alliances under stress in Mexico, Spain, and Venezuala', *World Politics* 52(1).

Cai, F 2001, *Institutional barriers in two processes of rural labor migration in China*, Institute of Population Studies, Chinese Academy of Social Sciences.

—— 2003, 'Removing the barriers to labour mobility: labour market development and its attendant reforms', paper presented at the World Bank Workshop on national market integration in Beijing.

Cai, F and Wang D 2003, 'Migration as marketization: what can we learn from China's 2000 census data?', *The China Review* 3(2).

Cai, F, Wang D and Wang M 2002, 'China's regional specialization in the course of gradual reform', *Economic Research Journal* 9.

Cai, Y 2004, 'Managed participation in China', *Political Science Quarterly* 119(3).

Cameron, D 1995, 'From Barre to Balladur: economic policy in the era of the EMS' in Flynn, G (ed), *Remaking the hexagon: the new France in the new Europe*, Westview Press, Boulder.

—— 2001, 'Unemployment, job creation, and economic and monetary union' in Bermeo, N (ed), *Unemployment in the new Europe*, Cambridge University Press, New York.

Camp, RA 1996, *Politics in Mexico*, second edition, Oxford University Press, New York.

Cao DW, MY Su and YZ Yang 2000, 'Assessment on management of pulmonary tuberculosis cases in temporary residence population on effect of chemotherapy', *Bulletin of the Chinese Anti-Tuberculosis Association* 22 (in Chinese).

Cao, M 1994, 'Labor disputes increase 50%', *China Daily*, 30 May.

Carr, B 1987, 'Crossing borders: labor internationalism in the era of NAFTA' in Gunderson, M, NM Meltz and S Ostry (eds), *Unemployment: international perspectives*, University of Toronto Press, Toronto.

Carruthers, C and C Hood 2004, 'The power of the positive: leisure and well-being', *Therapeutic Recreation Journal 38.*

Carter, CA and AJ Estrin 2005, 'Opening of China's trade, labour market reform and impact on rural wages', *World Economy* 28(6).

Castaneda, JG 1993, 'The clouding political horizon', *Current History* 92(571).

CCT (Concerned Citizens Tribunal) 2002, *Crime against humanity: an inquiry into the Gujarat carnage*, volumes 1 and 2, Citizens for Justice and Peace, Mumbai.

Chai, J 1992, 'Consumption and living standards in China', *China Quarterly* 131.

Chai, Joseph CH and Karin B Chai 1997, 'China's floating population and its implications', *International Journal of Social Economics* 24(7, 8, 9).

Chan, A 2002, 'The culture of survival: lives of migrant workers through the prism of private letters' in Link, P, R Madsen and P Pickowicz (eds), *Popular China: unofficial culture in a globalizing society*, Rowman & Littlefield, Boulder.

—— 2003, 'Race to the bottom: globalisation and China's labour standards', *China Perspectives* 46.

—— 2005, 'Recent trends in Chinese labour issues—signs of change', *China Perspectives* 57.

Chan, KW 1999 'Internal migration in China: a dualistic approach' in Pieke, FN and H Mallee (eds), *Internal and international migration: Chinese perspectives*, Curzon, Richmond.

Chan, KW and L Zhang 1998, 'The *hukou* system and rural–urban migration in China: process and changes', CSDE Working Paper Series, http://csed.washington.edu/pubs/wps/98-13.pdf, accessed 24 April 2003.

—— 1999, 'The *hukou* system and rural–urban migration in china: processes and changes', *China Quarterly* 160.

Chen, F 2000, 'Subsistence crises, managerial corruption and labour protests in China', *The China Journal* 44.

—— 2003, 'Between the state and labor: the conflict of Chinese trade unions' double identity in market reform', *China Quarterly* 176.

Chen, Y and Luo Y 1995, 'Watch your doors and windows—burglary prevention is the focus', *Yangcheng Evening News*, 28 February.

Cheng, T and M Selden 1994, 'The origins and social consequences of China's *hukou* system', *China Quarterly* 139.

Cheng, Y-S and D Lo 2002, 'Research report: explaining the financial performance of China's industrial enterprises: beyond the competition-ownership controversy', *China Quarterly* 170.

Chengzhen qiye xiagang zhigong zaijiuye zhuangkuang diaocha ketizu 1997, [Investigation of urban enterprises' laid-off staff and workers' re-employment situation project group], 'Kunjing yu chulu' [A difficult pass and the way out], *Shehuixue yanjiu* [*Sociology research*] 6.

China Daily 2003a, 'Migrant workers invited to join unions', 8 August.

—— 2003b, 'Helping migrants belong in cities', 28 November.

—— 2005, 'One-yuan apartments for migrant workers', 28 July.

—— 2006a, 'China, Kazakhstan discuss gas pipeline', 11 January.

—— 2006b, 'Migrant workers get more protection', 28 March.

—— 2006c, 'Rural labor resources shortage beginning to be felt in China', 29 May.

—— 2006d, 'Migrants need more protection', 5 June.

—— 2006e, 'Migration drives globalization', 9 June.

China Quarterly 2005, Quarterly chronicle and documentation (January–March 2005), June, 182.

—— 2006, Quarterly chronicle and documentation (October–December 2005), March, 185.

China View 2006, http://news.xinhuanet.com/english/2006-012/26/content_4104676.htm, accessed 17 February 2006.

Chou, K, N Chow and I Chi 2004, 'Leisure participation amongst Hong Kong Chinese older adults', *Ageing and Society* 24.

Chow, N and Xu X 2001, *Socialist welfare in a market economy: social security reforms in Guangzhou, China*, Ashgate, Aldershot.

CIA (Central Intelligence Agency) 2006a, 'Kazakhstan', *The world factbook*, www.cia.gov/cia/publications/factbook/, accessed May 2006.

—— 2006b, 'Tasjikistan', *The world factbook*, www.cia.gov/cia/publications/factbook/, accessed May 2006

Clark, M, P Riben and E Nowgesic 2002, 'The association of housing density, isolation and tuberculosis in Canadian First Nations communities', *International Journal of Epidemiology* 31.

CLB (China Labour Bulletin) 2004, www.china-labour.org.hk/public/contents/article?revision%5fid=18591&item%5fid=4000, accessed 6 June 2006.

Collier, RB 1992, *The contradictory alliance: state–labor relations and regime change in Mexico*, International and Area Studies, University of California, Berkeley.

Cook, S 1990, 'Surplus labour and productivity in Chinese agriculture: evidence and household survey date', *Journal of Development Studies* 35(3).

—— 2000, 'Politics, policy processes and the poor: responding to poverty in China's cities', report on 'The political and social dynamics of poverty in China' project, IDS Poverty Research Programme.

Cornelius, WA 1992, 'From sojourners to settlers: the changing profile of Mexican immigration to the United States' in Bustamante, JA, CW Reynolds and RAH Ojeda (eds), *US–Mexico relations: labor market interdependence*, Stanford University Press, Stanford.

Cornelius, WA and PL Martin 1993, 'The uncertain connection: free trade and rural Mexican migration to the United States', *International Migration Review* 27(3).

CTCC (China Tuberculosis Control Collaboration) 2004, 'The effect of tuberculosis control in China', *Lancet* 364.

Dai, L and Li Y 2001, 'Qiantan jiaru WTO dui jiuye xingshi de yingxiang yu duice', (Superficially talking about the influence of entering the WTO on the situation of employment and how to handle that), *Zhongguo laodong* (*Chinese Labor*) 9.

Daley, A 1992, 'The steel crisis and labor politics in France and the United States' in Golden, M and J Pontusson (eds), *Bargaining for change: union politics in North America and Europe*, Cornell University Press, Ithaca.

Davin, D 1999, *Internal migration in contemporary China*, St Martin's Press, New York.

—— 2000, 'Migrants and the media: concerns about rural migration in the Chinese press' in West, LA and Zhao Yaohui (eds), *Rural labor flows in China*, Institute of East Asian Studies, University of California, Berkeley.

—— 2001, *'The impact of export-oriented manufacturing on Chinese women workers'*, United Nations Research Institute for Social Development, www.unrisd.org, accessed 24 July 2006.

Davis, D 2000, *The consumer revolution in urban China*, University of California Press, Berkeley.

de Brauw, A and J Giles 2005, 'Migrant opportunity and the educational attainment of youth in rural China', unpublished manuscript, Brown University.

de la Garza Toledo, E 2002, 'Free trade and labor relations in Mexico,' International Labor Standards Conference, Stanford Law School, Stanford, 19–21 May.

de Oliverira, O and B Garcia 1997, 'Socioeconomic transformation and labor markets in urban Mexico', in Tardanico, R and RM Larin (eds), *Global restructuring, employment, and social inequality in urban Latin America*, North–South Center Press, Coral Gables.

Devy, G 2002, 'Tribal voice and violence' in Varadarajan, S (ed), *Gujarat: the making of a tragedy*, Penguin, New Delhi.

DGAP (German Council on Foreign Relations) 2004, *Asian migration to Europe and European migration and refugee policies*, http://en.dgap.org/midcom-serveattachmentguid-e5a637e8cb0b11daacdad5d96a230bd70bd7/asian_migration.pdf, accessed 26 July 2006.

Dion, M 2002, 'Mexico's welfare regime before and after the debt crisis: organized labor and the effects of globalization', paper prepared for the Annual Meeting of the Southern Political Science Association, Savannah, 7–9 November.

Du, Y and Cai F 2004, 'China's labour market integration: evidence of manufacturing wage convergence', Institute of Population and Labour Economics, Chinese Academy of Social Sciences.

Duckett, J 2003, 'China's social security reforms and the comparative politics of market transition', *Journal of Communist Politics and Transition Studies* 19(1).

Durand, J, DS Massey and EA Parrado 1999, 'The new era of Mexican migration to the United States', *Journal of American History* 86(2).

Economist 2004, 'China—help wanted', 9 October.

Ellman, M 1987, 'Eurosclerosis?' in Gunderson, M, NM Meltz and S Ostry (eds), *Unemployment: international perspectives*, University of Toronto Press, Toronto.

Eslake, S 2006, 'Catch me if you can: India and China', *Monash Business Review* 2(1).

Fan, CC 2004, 'The state, the migrant labor regime, and maiden workers in China', *Political Geography* 23(3).

—— 2005, 'Interprovincial migration, population redistribution, and regional development in China: 1990 and 2000 census comparisons', *The Professional Geographer* 57(2).

Fan, Z and Z Wang 2002, 'WTO accession, rural labour migration and urban unemployment in China', *Urban Studies* 39.

FBIS (Foreign Broadcast Information Service) 1994, 25 January, from Xinhua [New China News Service], 24 January.

Fei, J and Ranis, G 1965, 'A theory of economic development', *American Economic Review* 51(4)

Financial Times 2004, 'Solomonic ruling on stability pact: the possibility of a sensible eurozone reform is preserved', 14 July.

Fishman, TC 2004, 'The Chinese century', *New York Times*, 4 July.

Florence, Eric 2004, 'Migrant workers in Shenzhen' in Entzinger, H, M Martiniello and CW de Wenden (eds), *Migration between states and markets*, Ashgate, New York.

Frazier, Mark W 2004, 'China's pension reform and its discontents,' *China Journal* 51.

Freeman, RB 2005, 'Does globalization of the scientific/engineering workforce threaten US economic leadership?', National Bureau of Economic Research, Cambridge.

Frost, Stephen 2005a, 'China View', *CSR Asia Weekly* 1(29).

—— 2005b, 'China View', *CSR Asia Weekly* 1(33).

—— 2006, 'China View', *CSR Asia Weekly* 2(5).

Fu, J 2006, 'Housing, education top urbanites' worries', *China Daily*, 24 February.

Gallagher, Mary 1997, 'An unequal battle: why labor laws and regulations fail to protect workers', *China Rights Forum* (Summer).

Gao Yun 2004, *Chinese migrants and force labour in Europe*, International Labor Office, Geneva, July, www.ilo.org/dyn/declaris/DECLARATIONWEB.DOWNLOAD_BLOB?Var_DocumentID=4416, accessed 26 July 2006.

GI (Government of India) 2005, *Economic survey 2004–05*, Ministry of Finance, New Delhi.

Giles, J, A Park and Cai F 2006, 'How has economic restructuring affected China's urban workers?', *China Quarterly* 185.

Gladney, D 2003, 'China's minorities: the case of Xinjiang and the Uygur people', Commission on Human Rights, Sub-Commission on Promotion and Protection of Human Rights, Working Group on Minorities, 9th session, 12–16 May, Paper E/CN.4/Sub.2/AC.5/2003/WP.16, http://193.194.138.190/minorities/ninth.htm, accessed January 2006.

Gong, L 2000, *Kuashiji nanti: jiuye yu shehui baozhang* (*A difficult issue straddling the century: employment and social security*), Yunnan renmin chubanshe, Kunming.

Goodkind, D and LA West 2002, 'China's floating population: definitions, estimates and recent findings', *Urban Studies* 39(12).

Gruber, L 2000, *Ruling the world: power politics and the rise of supranational institutions*, Princeton University Press, Princeton.

Guan, Y 2003, 'Spare-time life of Chinese children', Journal of Family and Economic Issues 24.

Guang, L and L Zhang 2005, 'Migration as the second best option: local power and off-farm employment', China Quarterly 181.

Guo, F and R Iredale 2004, 'The impact of hukou status on migrants' employment: findings from the 1997 Beijing migrant census', *International Migration Review* 38(2).

Gwartney, J, R Stroup and R Sobel 2000, *Economics: private and public choice*, Dryden Press, Fort Worth.

Haggard, S and RR Kaufman 1995, *The political economy of democratic transitions*, Princeton University Press, Princeton.

Hanser, A 2004, 'Made in the PRC: consumers in China', Contexts 3, www.contextsmagazine.org/content_sample_v3-1.php, accessed 4 March 2006.

Hare, D 1999, 'Push versus pull factors in migration outflows and returns: determinants of migration status and spell duration among China's rural population', *Journal of Development Studies* 35.

Harney, A 2004, 'Going home: Chinese migrant workers shun long factory hours and low pay', *Financial Times*, 3 November.

Hart, K 1973, 'Informal income opportunities and urban employment in Ghana', *Journal of Modern African Studies* II.

Hatton, TJ and JG Williamson 1998, *The age of mass migration: causes and economic impact*, Oxford University Press, New York.

Haworth, J and S Hill 1992, 'Work, leisure, and psychological well-being in a sample of young adults', *Journal of Community & Applied Social Psychology 2.*

Heath, J 1998, 'Original goals and current outcomes of economic reform in Mexico' in Roett, Riordan (ed), *Mexico's private sector: recent history, future challenges*, Lynne Rienner, Boulder.

Hemerijck, A and M Schludi 2000, 'Sequences of policy failure and effective policy responses' in Scharpf, FW and VA Schmidt (eds), *Welfare and work in the open economy: from vulnerability to competitiveness*, volume 1, Oxford University Press, Oxford.

Herald Translation Service, Chinalaw Web, www.qis.net/chinalaw/prclaw66.htm.

Hills, P and M Argyle 1998, 'Positive moods derived from leisure and their relationship to happiness and personality', *Personality and Individual Differences 25.*

Hindustan Times 2005, '700 hurt as police lock horns with Honda staff', 25 July.

Hirway, I and P Terhal 2004, *Towards employment guarantee in India*, Sage, New Delhi.

Ho, Brian 2006, 'Is there a migrant labour shortage in China?', *CSR Asia Weekly* 2(8).

Ho, Mary 2006, 'What expose?', *CSR Asia Weekly* 2(12).

Hondagneu-Sotelo, P 1995, *Gendered transitions: Mexican experiences of immigration*, University of California Press, Berkeley.

Howard, P 1991, 'Rice bowls and job security: the urban contract labour system', *Australian Journal of Chinese Affairs* 25.

Howell, C 1992, *Regulating labor: the state and industrial relations reform in postwar France*, Princeton University Press, Princeton.

Hoy, C and Ren Qiang 2003, 'Socioeconomic impacts of Uyghur movement to Beijing' in Iredale, R, Naran Bilik and Fei Guo (eds), *China's minorities on the move: selected case studies*, M E Sharpe, New York and London.

Hu, A 2000, 'Creative destruction of restructuring: China's urban unemployment and social security (1993–2000)', unpublished manuscript.

—— 2001, 'China's present economic situation and its macro-economic policies', Rand-China Reform forum Conference, Santa Monica, 29–30 November.

Huang, P and FN Pieke 2003, 'China migration country study', Regional Conference on Migration, Development and Pro-Poor Policy Choices in Asia, Dhaka.

Huang, P and Zhan, S 2005, 'Internal migration in China: linking it to development', Regional Conference on Migration and Development in Asia, Lanzhou, 14–15 March.

Hugo, G 2004, 'International migration in the Asia-Pacific region: Emerging trends and issues', in Massey DS and JE Taylor (eds), *International migration: prospects and policies in a global market*, Oxford University Press, New York.

Ibraimov, Bakyt 2004, 'Uighurs: Beijing to blame for Kyrgyz crackdown', *Eurasianet.org*, 28 January.

ILO (International Labour Organization) 2001, *The construction industry in the 21st century: its image, employment prospects and skill requirements*, Geneva.

—— 2004, 'Labour migration in East Asian economies', paper presented by Manolo Abella, *Annual Bank Conference on Development Economics*, 10–11 May, Brussels.

Imai, Hiroshi 2002, 'Special report: China's growing unemployment problem', *Pacific Business and Industries RIM* II(6).

Invest China 2005, statistics on Xinjiang's total imports and exports with bordering countries, 1997–2002, www.china.org.cn/chinese/zhuanti/xjbjmy/656364.htm, accessed 4 August 2005.

IPPR (Institute for Public Policy Research) 2006, *Migration between Europe and South Asia: impacts on development?* www.migrationdevelopment.org, accessed 25 July 2006.

Irwin, J 1999, 'Shanghai's migrant millions', *UNESCO Courier*, June.

Jack, W 1999, *Principles of health economics for developing countries*, World Bank, Washington.

Jacka, T 2005, 'Finding a place: negotiations of modernization and globalization among rural women in Beijing', *Critical Asian Studies* 37.

—— 2006, *Rural women in urban China: gender, migration, and social change*, ME Sharpe, Armonk.

Jackson, S, Adrian C Sleigh, Guo-Jie Wang and Xi-Li Liu 2006a, 'Poverty and the economic effects of TB in rural China', *International Journal of Tuberculosis and Lung Disease* 10(10).

—— 2006b, 'Household poverty, off-farm migration and pulmonary tuberculosis in rural Henan, China' in Sleigh, Adrian C, Chee Heng Leng, Brenda SA Yeoh, Phua Kai Hong and Rachel Safman (eds), *Population dynamics and infectious diseases in Asia*, World Scientific, London.

Jackman, R 1998, 'The impact of the European Union on unemployment and unemployment policy', in Hine, D and Hussein Kassim (eds), *Beyond the market: the EU and national social policy,* Routledge, London.

Jiang, X 2001, 'Fighting to organize', *Far Eastern Economic Review*, 6 September.

Kahn, J 2005, 'China to drop urbanite-peasant legal differences', *New York Times*, 3 November.

Kaufman, RR 1986, 'Democratic and authoritarian responses to the debt issue: Argentina, Brazil, Mexico' in Kahler, Miles (ed), *The politics of international debt*, Cornell University Press, Ithaca.

Kernen, A and J-L Rocca 2000, 'Social responses to unemployment and the 'new urban poor': case study in Shenyang city and Liaoning province', *China Perspectives* 27.

Kesselman, M 1989, 'The new shape of French labour and industrial relations: *Ce n'est plus la meme chose*' in Godt, P (ed), *Policy-making in France: from de Gaulle to Mitterrand*, Pinter, London.

—— 1996, 'Does the French labor movement have a future?' in Keeler, JTS and MA Schain (eds), *Chirac's challenge: liberalization, Europeanization, and malaise in France*, St Martin's Press, New York.

Khan, Azizur Rahman and C Riskin 2001, *Inequality and poverty in China in the age of globalization*, Oxford University Press, New York.

——2005, 'China's household income and its distribution, 1995 and 2002', *China Quarterly* 182.

Kirkcaldy, B and A Furnham 1991, 'Extraversion, neuroticism, psychoticism and recreational choice', *Personality and Individual Differences* 7.

Kitschelt, H, P Lange, G Marks, and JD Stephens 1998, 'Introduction' in Kitschelt, H, P Lange, G Marks, and JD Stephens (eds), *Continuity and change in contemporary capitalism*, Cambridge University Press, New York.

Knight, J, L Song and Jia H 1999, 'Chinese rural migrants in urban enterprises: three perspectives', *The Journal of Development Studies* 35(3).

Knight, John and Lina Song 2003, 'Chinese peasant choices: migration, rural industry or farming', *Oxford Development Studies* 31(2).

—— 2005, *Towards a labour market in China*, Oxford University Press, Oxford.

Kuhn, A 2004, 'A high price to pay for a job', *Far Eastern Economic Review*, 22 January.

Kundu, Amitabh and Shalini Gupta 2000, 'Declining population mobility, liberalization and growing regional imbalances: the Indian case' in Kundu, Amitabh (ed), *Inequality, mobility and urbanisation: China and India*, Indian Council of Social Science Research, New Delhi and Manak.

Kung, JK 2002, 'Off-farm labor markets and the emergence of land rental markets in rural China', *Journal of Comparative Economics* 30(2).

Kwan, A 2000, 'Report from China: producing for Adidas and Nike', *Clean clothes campaign: improving working conditions in the global garment industry*, www.cleanclothes.org/companies/nike00-04.htm, accessed 4 March 2006.

Kwong, J 2004, 'Educating migrant children: negotiations between the state and civil society', *The China Quarterly* 180.

Laczko, F 2003, 'Europe attracts more migrants from China', *Migration Information Source*, 1 July, www.migrationinformaton.org/Feature/display.cfm?ID=144, accessed 25 July 2006.

Lague, D 2003, 'The human tide sweeps into Chinese cities', *Far Eastern Economic Review*, 9 January.

Lai, P 2002, 'Foreign direct investment in China: recent trends and patterns', *China and World Economy* 2.

Lardy, NR 2002, *Integrating China into the global economy*, Brookings Institution, Washington.

Latapí, AE, P Martin, PS Davies, GL Castro and K Donato 1998, 'Factors that influence migration' in US Commission on Immigration Reform and Mexican Ministry of Foreign Affairs, *Migration between Mexico and the United States: binational study*, volume 1, Washington and Mexico City.

Laumulin, M 2005, 'China's current policy in Central Asia', *Central Asia's Affairs* 3, www.kisi.kz/old/English/Extpol/04-10-05%20Laumulin_CHINA%20CENTRAL_en.pdf, accessed May 2006.

Leamer, EE 1984, *Source of international comparative advantage; theory and evidence*, MIT Press, Cambridge.

Lee, CK 1998, *Gender and the South China miracle: two worlds of factory women*, University of California Press, Berkeley.

—— 1999a, 'From organized dependence to disorganized despotism: changing labour regimes in Chinese factories', *China Quarterly* 157.

—— 1999b, 'The politics of working-class transitions in China', draft paper prepared for the conference on 'Wealth and labor in China: cross-cutting approaches of present developments', Centre d'Etudes et de Recherches Internationales, Paris, 6–7 December.

Lei, G 2005, 'The State connection in China's rural–urban migration', *International Migration Review*, 39(2).

Levy, JD 2000, 'France: directing adjustment?' in Scharpf, FW and VA Schmidt (eds), *Welfare and work in the open economy: diverse responses to common challenges*, volume 2, Oxford University Press, Oxford.

Lewis WA 1954, 'Economic development with unlimited supplies of labour', *Manchester School*, May.

Li, B 2005, 'Urban social change in transitional China: a perspective of social exclusion and vulnerability', *Journal of Contingencies and Crisis Management* 13(2).

—— 2006, 'Floating population or urban citizens? Status, social provision and circumstances of rural migrants in China', *Social Policy and Administration* 40(2).

Li, Hong 1992, *China Daily*, 10 February.

Li, Q 2003, 'Policy issues concerning the informal employment of rural–urban migrants in China', *Social Sciences in China* 24(4).

Liang Z and W Ye 2001, 'From Fujian to New York: understanding the new Chinese immigration' in Kyle, D and R Koslowski (eds), *Global human smuggling: comparative perspectives*, Johns Hopkins University Press, Baltimore.

Liang, Z 2007, 'Internal migration: policy changes, recent trends, and new challenges' in Zhao Zhongwei and Fei Guo (eds), *Transition and challenge: China's population at the beginning of the 21st century*, Oxford University Press, Oxford.

Liang, Z and Ma Z 2004, 'China's floating population: new evidence from the 2000 census', *Population and Development Review* 30(3).

Lillywhite, S 2002, 'Pursuing corporate social responsibility in China—experiences of a small enterprise in the optical industry', *OECD guidelines for multinational enterprises annual report*, OECD, Paris.

—— 2003, 'Pursuing corporate responsibility in China—supply chain management and labour rights', paper presented at the RMIT - ACESA conference, Melbourne, October.

—— 2005, 'Ethical purchasing and workers' rights in China: considerations for an Australia–China free trade agreement', paper presented at the symposium 'China trade liberalisation and labour: racing to the bottom or building a foundation for labour rights', Australian Council of Trade Unions, Melbourne, 14–15 February.

Lim, LL and G Sziraczki 1993, 'Employment, social security, and enterprise reforms in China' in Gregory K Schoepfle (ed), *Work without protections: case studies of the informal sector in developing countries*, Department of Labor, Bureau of International Labor Affairs, Washington.

Linz, JJ 1975, 'Totalitarian and authoritarian regimes' in Greenstein, FI and NW Polsby (eds), *Handbook of political science, volume 3: macropolitical theory*, Addison-Wesley, Reading.

Linz, JJ and A Stepan 1996, *Problems of democratic transition and consolidation: Southern Europe, South America and post-communist Europe*, Johns Hopkins University Press, Baltimore.

Liu Chenyan 2005, 'What do migrant workers want?', *CSR Asia Weekly* 1(46).

Liu Kaiming 2002, 'Working together to build a sustainable improving model', paper presented to the conference 'Academic meeting on international labour standards and workers' rights, and business and human rights', 25–27 October, Wuhan.

Liu, B 1997, 'The working class speaks out', *China Focus* 5(8).

Liu, J 2003, 'Rural employment' in edited by Rong, Mo, *2002 China employment report*, China Labour and Social Security Press, Beijing.

Liu, W and Cai X 2005, 'City job hurdles cleared for migrants', *China Daily*, Beijing, 21 February.

Liu, Z 2005, 'Institution and inequality: the *hukou* system in China', *Journal of Comparative Economics* 33.

Lovejoy, PE and JS Hogendorn 1993, *Slow death for slavery: the course of abolition in northern Nigeria, 1897–1936*, Cambridge University Press, Cambridge.

Lu, L and C Hu 2002, 'Experiencing leisure: the case of Chinese university students', *Fu Jen Studies: Science and Engineering* 36.

—— 2005, 'Personality, leisure experiences and happiness', *Journal of Happiness Studies* 6.

Lull, J 1991, *China turned on: television, reform, and resistance*, Routledge, New York.

Ma, LJC and Biao Xiang 1998, 'Native place, migration and the emergence of peasant enclaves in Beijing', *The China Quarterly* 155.

Ma, Zhongdong 2004, 'Labor migration as a new determinant of income growth in rural China', paper presented at the annual meeting of the Population Association of America, Boston, 1–3 April.

Machin, H and V Wright 1985, 'Economic policy under the Mitterrand presidency, 1981–1984: an introduction' in Machin, H and V Wright (eds), *Economic policy and policy-making under the Mitterrand presidency 1981–1984*, Frances Pinter, London.

Mackerras, C 2004, 'Ethnicity in China: the case of Xinjiang', *Harvard Asia Quarterly,* 8(1).

Mallee, Hein 2000, 'Migration, *hukou* and resistance in reform China' in Perry, EJ and M Selden (eds), *Chinese society: change, conflict and resistance*, Routledge, London.

Manning, C 2000, 'Labor mobility, business migration and economic development in the APEC Region', paper presented at the conference 'Trade facilitation in the Asia Pacific: new directions and the development challenge', 13–14 September, Singapore.

Manthorpe, J 2005, 'Migration in China spawns urban class of poor outsiders', *Vancouver Sun*, 7 November.

Marcelli, EA and WA Cornelius 2001, 'The changing profile of Mexican migrants to the United States: new evidence from California and Mexico', *Latin American Research Review* 36(3).

Martin, PL 1993, *Trade and migration: NAFTA and agriculture*, Institute for International Economics, Washington.

Massey, Douglas S and Kristin E Espinosa 1997, 'What's driving Mexico–US migration? A theoretical, empirical, and policy analysis', *American Journal of Sociology* 102(4).

Massey, Douglas S, Jorge Durand and Nolan J Malone 2002, *Beyond smoke and mirrors: Mexican immigration in an era of economic integration*, Russell Sage Foundation, New York.

Massey, DS, J Arango, G Hugo, A Kouaouci, A Pellegrino and JE Taylor 1994, 'An evaluation of international migration theory: the North American case', *Population and Development Review* 20(4).

McGranahan, G and Tacoli, C 2005, 'International contribution to the migrant component', CICED Taskforce on Sustainable Urbanisation Strategies, International Institute for Environment and Development, London.

Meng, X 2000, *Labour market reform in China*, Cambridge University Press, New York.

Meng, X, R Gregory and Wang Youjuan 2005, 'Poverty, inequality, and growth in urban China', *Journal of Comparative Economics* 33(4).

Meyer, L 1998, 'Mexico: economic liberalism in an authoritarian polity', in Lindau, JD and T Cheek (eds), *Market economics and political change: comparing China and Mexico*, Rowman & Littlefield, Lanham.

Middlebrook, K 1989, 'The CTM and the future of state–labor relations' in Cornelius, W, J Gentleman and PH Smith (eds), *Mexico's alternative political futures*, Center for US–Mexican Studies, University of California, San Diego.

—— 1995, *The paradox of revolution: labor, the state, and authoritarianism in Mexico*, Johns Hopkins University Press, Baltimore.

MIS (Migration Information Source) 2001, 'United Kingdom: stock of foreign born population by country of birth, 2001', www.migrationinformation.org/GlobalData/countrydata/data.cfm, accessed 23 July 2006.

Morici, P 1993 'Grasping the benefits of NAFTA', *Current History* 2.

Moss, BH 1988, 'After the Auroux laws (AL): employers, industrial relations and the right in France', *West European Politics* 11(1).

MPS 2001 (*Gong'anbu dixi yanjiusuo 'quntixing shijian yanjiu' ketizu* – Ministry of Public Security Fourth Research Institute's 'mass incidents' research group), 'Woguo fasheng quntixing shijian de diaocha yu sikao' (Investigation and reflections on our country's mass incidents), *Neibu canyue* (Internal consultations) 31(576).

Mu, Yi 2003, 'Migrants villages in Beijing', *China Economic Express Weekly* 45, www.people.com.cn/GB/paper1631/10837/984358.html, accessed 9 August 2005.

Murillo, MV 2000, 'From populism to neoiliberalism: labor unions and market reforms in Latin America', *World Politics* 52(2).

Murphy, R 2002, *How migrant labour is changing rural China*, Cambridge University Press, Cambridge.

Naughton, B 1995, *Growing out of the plan,* Cambridge University Press, Cambridge.

—— 1999, 'The Chinese economy through 2005: domestic developments and their implications for US interests', in Library of Congress, *China's future: implications for US interests: conference report*, Washington, September.

NBS & MLSS (National Bureau of Statistics and Ministry of Labour and Social Security) 2004, *China labour statistical yearbook 2004*, China Statistics Press, Beijing.

NBS (National Bureau of Statistics) 1986, *Tabulation on the 1982 census of the People's Republic of China*, China Statistics Press, Beijing.

—— 1991–1992, *China statistical yearbook*, China Statistics Press, Beijing.

—— 1993a, *China statistical yearbook*, China Statistics Press, Beijing.

—— 1993b, *Tabulation on the 1990 census of the People's Republic of China*, China Statistics Press, Beijing.

—— 1994–2001, *China statistical yearbook*, China Statistics Press, Beijing.

—— 2002a, *China statistical yearbook*, China Statistics Press, Beijing.

—— 2002b, *Tabulation on the 2000 census of the People's Republic of China*, China Statistics Press, Beijing.

—— 2003a, *China statistical yearbook*, China Statistics Press, Beijing.

—— 2003b, *Henan Province statistical yearbook 2003*, China Statistics Press, Beijing.

—— 2004a, *China statistical yearbook*, China Statistics Press, Beijing.

—— 2004b, *Shanghai yearbook, 2004,* 'New Shanghainese' www.shtong.gov.cn/node2/node19828/node71798/node71862/node71946/userobject1ai77060.html, accessed 8 May, 2006.

—— 2004c, *China industrial economy statistical yearbook 2004*, China Statistics Press, Beijing.
2005, *China statistical yearbook*, China Statistics Press, Beijing.

New York Times 2003, 'Chinese economy's underside: abuse of migrants', 26 August.

Newland, K and E Patrick 2004, *Beyond remittances: the role of diaspora in poverty reduction in their countries of origin*, Migration Policy Institute, Washington, www.livelihoods.org/hot_topics/docs/MPIDiaspora.doc, accessed August 2006.

Nielsen, I, C Nyland, R Smyth and C Zhu 2005, 'Perceptions of subjective economic well-being and support for market reform among China's urban population', *Post-communist Economies* 17.

Nielsen, I, C Nyland, R Smyth, M Zhang and C Zhu 2006, 'Effects of intergroup contact on Chinese urban residents' attitudes to migrant workers', *Urban Studies* 43(3).

Nielsen, I, R Smyth, and Y Guo 2006, 'Where have all the workers gone? China's emerging migrant labour shortage', *Around the Globe* 3.

Nielsen, I, R Smyth and M Zhang 2006, 'Unemployment within China's floating population: empirical evidence from Jiangsu survey data', *Chinese Economy* 39(4).

Nielsen, I, M Zhang, C Nyland, R Smyth and C Zhu 2005, 'Which rural migrants receive social insurance in Chinese cities? Evidence from Jiangsu survey data', *Global Social Policy* 5.

NMG (Nanjing Municipal Government) 2003, *Circular on deepening the reform of the household registration system*, Nanjing.

Nyland, C, R Smyth and CJ Zhu 2006, 'What determines the extent to which employers will comply with their social insurance obligations? Evidence from Chinese firm-level data', *Social Policy and Administration* 40(2).

O'Neill, M 1999, 'The WTO deal: mixed blessing for mainland workers', *South China Morning Post*, 17 November.

Pan, P 2002, 'Poisoned back into poverty: as China embraces capitalism hazards to workers rise', *Washington Post*, 4 August.

Parker, G 2004, 'Stability pact: European court ruling: verdict satisfies honour on both sides', *Financial Times*, 14 July.

Parker, G and Benoit, B 2004, 'Court attacks deficit breaches', *Financial Times*, 14 July.

Passel, J 2004, 'Mexican migration to the us: the latest estimates', Migration Information Source, www.migrationinformation.org.

Pastor, M and C Wise 1997, 'State policy, distribution and neoliberal reform in Mexico', *Journal of Latin American Studies* 29(2).

PC (Planning Commission) 2001, 'Report of the study group on development of small scale enterprises', Government of India, New Delhi.

—— 2002, 'Report of the special group on targeting ten million employment opportunities per year', Government of India, New Delhi.

Pei, Minxin 1997, 'Citizens v mandarins: administrative litigation in China', *China Quarterly* 152.

Pessar, P 2003, 'Engendering migration studies: the case of new immigrants in the United States' in Hondagneu-Sotelo, P (ed) *Gender and US immigration: contemporary trends*, University of California Press, Berkeley.

Peters, E Dussel 1996, 'From export-oriented to import-oriented industrialization: changes in Mexico's manufacturing sector, 1988–1994' in Otero, G (ed), *Neoliberalism revisited: economic restructuring and Mexico's political future*, Westview Press, Boulder.

—— 2000, *Polarizing Mexico: the impact of liberalization strategy*, Lynne Rienner, Boulder.

PRC (People's Republic of China) 1994, Labour Law.

Qiang, Ren and Xin, Yuan 2003, 'Impacts of migration to Xinjiang since the 1950s' in Airedale, R, Naran Bilik and Fei Guo, *China's minorities on the move: selected case studies*, ME Sharpe, New York and London.

Qiang, X 2005, 'Leaving the blood and sweat factory', *Nanfang Weekend*, 31 October.

Ranis, G and JCH Fei 1961, 'A theory of economic development', *American Economic Review* 51(4).

Rawal, V and K Mukherjee 2005, 'Debt and unfreedom among landless manual workers in rural Haryana' in Ramachandran, VK and Madhura Swaminathan (eds) 2005, *Financial liberalization and rural credit in India*, Tulika, New Delhi.

Rawski, TG 2002, 'Recent developments in China's labor economy', manuscript, Pittsburgh.

Rawski, TG and RW Mead 1998, 'On the trail of China's phantom farmers', *World Development* 26(5).

RBI (Reserve Bank of India) 2004, 'Handbook of statistics on the Indian economy', Mumbai.

Reyes, BI 1997, *Dynamics of immigration: return migration to western Mexico*, Public Policy Institute of California, San Francisco.

Riskin, C 1987, *China's political economy: the quest for development since 1949*, Oxford University Press, New York.

—— 2007, 'Has China reached the top of the Kuznets curve?' in Shue, V and C Wong (eds) *Paying for poverty reduction*, Routledge, London.

Roberts, K 1982, 'Agrarian structure and labor mobility in rural Mexico', *Population and Development Review* 8(2).

—— 1997, 'China's "tidal wave" of migrant labor: what can we learn from Mexican undocumented migration to the United States?' *International Migration Review* 31(2).

—— 2001, 'The determinants of job choice by rural labour migrants in Shanghai', *China Economic Review* 12(1).

—— 2002, 'Female labor migrants to Shanghai: temporary "floaters" or settlers?' *International Migration Review* 36(2).

Roberts, K, R Connelly, Z Xie and Z Zheng 2004, 'Patterns of temporary migration of rural women from Anhui and Sichuan provinces of China', *The China Journal* 52.

Roberts, SR 2004, 'A "land of borderlands": implications of Xinjiang's trans-border interactions', in Starr, FS (ed), *Xinjiang: China's Muslim borderland*, ME Sharpe, London and New York.

Rochlin, JF 1997, *Redefining Mexican 'security'*, Lynne Rienner, Boulder.

Rodrik, D 1997, *Has globalization gone too far?*, Institute for International Economics, Washington.

Rong, Ma 2003, 'Population distribution and relations among ethnic groups in the Kashgar region, Xinjiang Uygur Autonomous Region' in Airedale, R, Naran Bilik and Fei Guo 2003, *China's minorities on the move: selected case studies*, ME Sharpe, New York and London.

Ross, G 1984, 'The CGT, economic crisis, and political change' in Kesselman, M (ed), *The French workers' movement: economic crisis and political change*, George Allen & Unwin, London.

Rothermund, D and DC Wadhwa (eds) 1978, *Zamindars, mines and peasants: studies in the history of a coalfield and its rural hinterland*, Manohar, Delhi.

Rowland, DT 1992, 'Family characteristics of internal migration in China', *Asia-Pacific Population Journal* 7(1).

Roxborough, I 1989, 'Organized labor: a major victim of the debt crisis' in Stallings, B and R Kaufman (eds), *Debt and democracy in Latin America*, Westview Press, Boulder.

Ru, X, X Lu and T Dan (eds), 1998, *1998 nian: zhongguo shehui xingshi fenxi yu yuce* [1998: analysis and prediction of China's social situation], Shehui Kexue Wenxian Chubanshe, Beijing.

Russell, S 2004, 'The economic burden of illness for households in developing countries: a review of studies focusing on malaria, tuberculosis, and human immunodeficiency virus/acquired immunodeficiency syndrome', *American Journal of Tropical Medicine and Hygiene* 71.

Ryder, G 2006, 'China: all that glitters is not gold', *New Perspectives Quarterly* 23(1).

Samstad, JG 2002, 'The unanticipated persistence of labor power in Mexico: the transition to a more democratic corporatism', prepared for annual meeting of the American Political Science Association, Boston, 28 August–1 September.

Sarvekshana 2002, 'An integrated survey of employment and unemployment survey results', NSS 55th round (July 1999–June 2000), 25(2 & 3).

Sassen, S 1999, *Guests and aliens*, The New Press, New York.

Scharpf, FW 2000, 'Economic changes, vulnerabilities, and institutional capabilities,' in Scharpf, FW and VA Schmidt (eds), *Welfare and work in the open economy: from vulnerability to competitiveness*, volume 1, Oxford University Press, Oxford.

Schmidt, VA 1996, *From state to market? The transformation of French business and government*, Cambridge University Press, Cambridge.

—— 1999, 'Still three models of capitalism? The dynamics of econmic adjustment in Britain, Germany, and France' in Czada, R and S Luetz (eds), *Die Politische Konstitution von Maerkten* [The Political Constitution of Markets], Westdeutscher Verlag, Opladen.

Sciolino, E 2003, 'France seeks pension reform, confronting unions', *New York Times*, 9 May.

SCMP (*South China Morning Post*) 2005, 'Labour shortage threatening industrial growth', 26 May.

Seeborg, MC, Z Jin and Y Zhu 2000, 'The new rural–urban labor mobility in China: causes and implications', *Journal of Socio-Economics* 29(1).

Selden, M 1993, *The political economy of Chinese development*, ME Sharpe, Armont.

Sen, S 2005, 'China's finance after WTO', *Economic and Political Weekly* 40(6).

SGMA (Study Group of the Ministry of Agriculture) 2005, 'Migration and employment of rural labour forces: current situation, problems and countermeasures', *Journal of Rural Economic Surveys* 5.

Shah, G, M Rutten and H Streefkerk (eds) 2002, *Development and deprivation in Gujarat: in honour of Jan Breman*, Sage, New Delhi.

Shanghai Daily 2005a, 'Migrant workers are dying to work', 29 October.

—— 2005b, 'Migrants cheated of insurance funds', 2 November.

—— 2005c, 'Shanghai migrants benefit', 9 December.

—— 2006a, 'Shanghai migrant insurance should cover Ayis', 21 January.

—— 2006b, 'Social insurance spot checks begin', 1 April.

Shao, S, I Nielsen, C Nyland, R Smyth, M Zhang and C Zhu 2006, 'Migrants as *Homo Economicus*: explaining the emerging phenomenon of a shortage of migrant labor in China's coastal provinces', *China Information* 20.

Sheehan, J 1998, *Chinese workers: a new history*, Routledge, London.

Shen, JF 2002, 'A study of the temporary population in Chinese cities', *Habitat International* 26.

Shenzhen Daily 2005, 'Social security to cover migrants', 12 April.

Shetty, SL 2005, 'Regional, sectoral and functional distribution of rural credit in India', in Ramachandran, VK and Madhura Swaminathan (eds), *Financial liberalization and rural credit in India*, Tulika, New Delhi.

Shijie ribao [*World daily*] 1997, 8 December.

Sklair, L 1989, *Assembling for development: the maquila industry in Mexico and the United States*, Unwin Hyman, London.

Smith, WR 1995, 'Industrial crisis and the left: adjustment strategies in socialist France and Spain', *Comparative Politics* 28(1).

—— 2000, 'Unemployment and the left coalition in France and Spain' in Bermeo, NG (ed), *Unemployment in Southern Europe: coping with the consequences*, Frank Cass, London.

Soesastro, H 2003, 'Regional integration initiatives in the Asia Pacific: trade and finance dimensions', paper presented at the '15th PECC general meeting- focus workshop on trade', 1 September, Brunei Darussalam.

Solinger, DJ 1991, *China's transition from socialism*, ME Sharpe, Armonk.

—— 1993, 'China's transients and the state: a form of civil society?', *Politics and Society* 21.

—— 1995, 'The Chinese work unit and transient labor in the transition from socialism', *Modern China* 21.

—— 1999, *Contesting citizenship in urban China: peasant migrants, the state and the logic of the market*, University of California Press, Berkeley.

—— 2001, 'Why we cannot count the unemployed', *China Quarterly* 167.

Song, L 1996, *Changing global comparative advantage: evidence from Asia and the Pacific*, Longman, South Melbourne.

—— 1999, 'The role of women in labour migration: a case study in northern China' in West, J, M Zhao, X Chang and Y Cheng (eds), *Women of China: economic and social transformation*, St Martin's Press, New York.

Song, X 2001, *Zhongguo shehui baozhang zhidu gaige* [*The reform of China's social security system*], Tsinghua University Publishers, Beijing.

SPC 2000 (*Guojia jiwei hongguan jingji yanjiuyuan ketizu* – State Planning Commission, Macroeconomic Research Group), 'Jianli shehui baohu tixi shi wo guo shehui wending de guanjian' (Establishing a social protection system is the key to our country's social stability), *Neibu canyue* (Internal consultations) 511.

Sriskandarajah, D and F Hopwood Road 2005, 'United Kingdom: rising numbers, rising anxieties', Migration Information Source, Institute for Public Policy Research, May, http://migrationinformation.com/Feature/display.cfm?id=306, accessed 25 July 2006.

Stallings, B and W Peres 2000, *Growth, employment, and equity: the impact of the economic reforms in Latin America and the Caribbean*, Brookings Institution Press, Washington.

State Council 2002, 'White paper on employment, social security', *Asian Wall Street Journal*, 29 April.

SWB (Summary of World Broadcasts) 1998, FE/3231, 20 May, from Xinhua [New China News Service], 17 May.

Symes, V 1995, *Unemployment in Europe: problems and policies*, Routledge, London and New York.

Tagliabue, J 2003a, 'Protest strike in France interrupts travel', *New York Times*, 4 April.

—— 2003b, 'Militant unions may scuttle a French pension proposal', *New York Times*, 17 May.

Tang, J 2002a, 'The new situation of poverty and antipoverty' in Ru X et al (eds), *2002 nian: Zhongguo shehui xingshi yu yuce* (*shehui lanpishu*) [*Year 2002: analysis and forecast of China's social situation (Blue book on Chinese Society)*].

—— 2002b, 'The report of poverty and anti-poverty in urban China—the poverty problems in urban China and the program of minimum living standard', manuscript, Beijing.

—— 2003, 'Zhongguo chengshi jumin zuidi shenghuo baozhang zhidu de tiaoyueshi fazhan' [The leap forward style of development of Chinese urban residents minimum livelihood guarantee] in Ru Xin, Lu Xueyi and Li Peilin, *Shehui lanpishu: 2003 nian: Zhongguo shehui xingshi fenxi yu yuce* [*Social blue book: 2003 analysis and predictions of China's social situation*], Social Science Documents Company, Beijing.

Tarimi, NT 2004, 'China–Uzbek pact bad news for Uighurs', *Spark*, 30 July, www.Uygur.org/wunn04/07_31.htm, accessed May 2006.

Teichman, JA 1995, *Privatization and political change in Mexico*, University of Pittsburgh Press, Pittsburgh.

Thomas, B 1959, 'International migration' in Hauser, PM and OD Duncan (eds), *The study of population: an inventory and appraisal*, University of Chicago Press, Chicago.

Thompson, G 2001, 'Mexican labor protest gets results', *New York Times*, 8 October.

Tian, B and Yuan J 1997, 'Shanghai xiagang renyuan de diaocha yanjiu' [Investigation research on Shanghai laid-off personnel], *Shehuixue* [Sociology] 2.

Tsui, Yen Hu 2003, 'Uygur movement within Xinjiang and its ethnic identity and cultural implications' in Airedale, R, Naran Bilik and Fei Guo (2003), *China's minorities on the move: selected case studies*, ME Sharpe, New York and London.

UN (United Nations) 2004, *World economic and social survey 2004: international migration*, Department of Economic and Social Affairs, New York.

—— 2005a, *China human development report 2005*, United Nations Development Plan, New York.

—— 2005b, *World population prospects*, Population Division, Department of Economic and Social Affairs, United Nations Secretariat.

UNESCO Courier 1999, 'Shanghai's migrant millions', June.

Varadarajan, S (ed) 2002, *Gujarat: the making of a tragedy*, Penguin, New Delhi.

Varshney, A 2002, *Ethnic conflict and civic life: Hindus and Muslims in India*, Oxford University Press, New Delhi.

Verité 2004, *Excessive overtime in Chinese supplier factories: causes, impacts and recommendations for action*, www.verite.org/research/Excessive%20overtime%20in%Chinese%20factories.pdf, viewed 31 March 2006.

Vicziany, M and Zhang Guibin 2004, 'The rise of the private sector in Xinjiang (Western China): Han and Uygur entrepreneurship', in Cribb, R (ed), *Asia examined: proceedings of the15th biennial conference of the ASAA*, Asian Studies Association of Australia, Canberra, http://coombs.anu.edu.au/ASAA/.

Walder, AG 1984, 'The remaking of the Chinese working class', *Modern China*, January, 10(1).

—— 1986, *Communist neo-traditionalism: work and authority in Chinese industry*, University of California Press, Berkeley.

—— 1987, 'Wage reform and the web of factory interests', *China Quarterly* 109.

—— 1992, 'Property rights and stratification in socialist redistributive economies', *American Sociological Review* 57.

Wang F, X Zuo and D Ruan 2002, 'Rural migrants in Shanghai: living under the shadow of socialism', *International Migration Review* 36(2).

Wang Hui 2005, 'The historical origin of China's neo-liberalism: another discussion on the ideological situation in contemporary mainland China and the issue of modernity' in Cao Tian Yu (ed), *The Chinese model of modern development*, Routledge, London.

Wang, Chunguang 2003, 'The social identities of new generations of migrants from China's rural areas', *Social Sciences in China* 24(4).

Wang, F-L 2005, *Organizing through division and exclusion: China's hukou system*, Stanford University Press, Stanford.

Wang, S 1995, 'The politics of private time: changing leisure patterns in urban China' in Davis, D, R Kraus, B Naughton and E Perry (eds), *Urban space in contemporary China: the potential for autonomy and community in post-Mao China*, Woodrow Wilson Centre Press, Washington.

WB (World Bank) 2005a, *India: re-energizing the agricultural sector to sustain growth and reduce poverty*, Oxford University Press, New Delhi.

—— 2005b, *World development indicators*, Washington.

Weiss, John and Gao Shanwen 2003, 'People's Republic of China's export threat to ASEAN: competition in the US and Japanese markets', Asian Development Bank Institute, Tokyo.

Wen, Premier 2004, 'Premier Wen delivers government work report,' http://english.peopledaily.com.cn/, viewed 16 March 2004.

White, G 1993, *Riding the tiger: the politics of economic reform in post-Mao China*, Stanford University Press, Stanford.

WHO (World Health Organisation) 2005, *Global tuberculosis control—surveillance, planning, financing: WHO report 2005*, Geneva.

Wickramasekera, Piyasiri 2002, *Asian labour migration: issues and challenges in an era of globalization*, International Migration Program, International Labour Organisation, Geneva.

Wilson, F 1985, 'Trade unions and economic policy' in Machin, H and V Wright (eds), *Economic policy and policy-making under the Mitterrand presidency 1981–1984*, Frances Pinter, London.

WMG (Wuxi Municipal Government) 2003, *Circular on deepening the reform of the household registration system*, Wuxi.

Wong, CPW, C Heady and WT Woo 1995, *Fiscal management and economic reform in the People's Republic of China*, Oxford University Press, Hong Kong.

Wong, L 1998, *Marginalization and social welfare in China*, Routledge, London.

Wu HX and Zhou L 1996, 'Rural to urban migration in China', *Asian-Pacific Economic Literature* 10.

Wu, WP 2002, 'Migrant housing in urban China: choices and constraints', *Urban Affairs Review* 38.

—— 2004, 'Sources of migrant housing disadvantage in urban China', *Environment and Planning* 36(7).

Wu, Yan 1999, 'Laid-off workers to get extra pay', *China Daily*, 31 August.

Xiang, B 2005, *Transcending boundaries: Zhejiangcun: the story of a migrant village in Beijing*, Brill, Leiden.

Xiang, B and Shen T 2005, *Does migration research matter in China? A review of migration research and its relations to policy since the 1980s*, Centre on Migration, Policy and Society, University of Oxford.

Xinhua News Agency 2004, 'Labor medal granted to migrant worker for the first time', 22 April, http://wnc.dialog.com/.

—— 2005, 'Interview: Laos seizes ASEAN–China FTA opportunities', 28 September.

—— 2006, 'Three hundred million farmers to enter cities amid urbanization in next two decades', 21 March.

Xinjiang statistical yearbook 2004, China Statistics Press, Beijing.

Xu, L 1995, 'National conference on management of transient population held', *Legal Daily*, 9 July.

Xue, Z 2000, 'Dui xiagang zhigong zaijiuye xianzhuang di diaocha, sikao yu jianyi' [Research, reflections, and suggestions about the reemployment situation of laid-off staff and workers], *Gonghui gongzuo tongxun* [*Bulletin of Trade Union Work*] 7.

Yang, DT and Cai F 2003, 'The political economy of China's rural–urban divide' in Hope, NC, DT Yang and Mu Yang Li (eds), *How far across the river? Chinese policy reform at the millennium*, Stanford University Press, Stanford.

Yang, J 2005, 'Going to Guizhou: some thoughts on migrant workers', *CSR Asia Weekly* 1(11).

Yang, S 1999, 'Zaijiuye yao zou xiang shichanghua' [In re-employment we must go toward marketisation], *Zhongguo jiuye* [*Chinese Employment*] 3.

Yardley, J 2004, 'In a tidal wave, China's masses pour from farm to city', *New York Times Week Review*, 12 September.

Yi, Bin and Yang Jiangtao 2004, 'Problems and policy recommendations: rural labour in Xinjiang', *Xinjiang Rural Survey* 12 http://lib.xjife.edu.cn/qtext\ecl.htm, accessed 22 July 2005.

Yin, X 2005, 'New trends of leisure consumption in China', *Journal of Family and Economic Issues* 26.

Yue, C 2004, 'ASEAN–China free trade area', paper presented at the AEP conference, 12–13 April, Hong Kong.

Zachariah, KC, ET Mathew and S Irudaya Rajan 2003, *Dynamics of migration in Kerala: dimensions, differentials and consequences*, Orient Longman, Hyderabad.

Zelinsky, W 1971, 'The hypothesis of the mobility transition', *Geographical Review* 61(2).

Zhang, HX 1999, 'Female migration and urban labour markets in Tianjin', *Development and Change* 30(1).

Zhang, Linxiu, Alan de Brauw and Scott Rozelle 2004, 'China's rural labor market development and its gender implications', *China Economic Review* 15(2).

Zhang, X 1992, 'Urban–rural isolation and its impact on China's production and trade pattern', *China Economic Review* 3(1).

—— 1994, 'Classification and the dualism of China's industries in the 1980s', *Industry and Development*, United Nations Industrial Development Organisation 34, Vienna.

—— 1999, 'Growth of township and village enterprises and change in China's export pattern', *Advances in Chinese Industrial Studies* 6.

—— 2000a, 'Motivations, objectives, locations and partner selections of foreign invested enterprises in China', *Journal of Asia-Pacific Economies* 5(3).

—— 2000b, 'The tale of two sectors: a comparison between state-owned and non-state-owned enterprises in China', *Asian Thought and Society: An International Review* 25(74).

—— 2003, 'Trends of migrant labourers mobility in western China', http://unpan1.un.org/intradoc/groups/public/documents/APCITY/UNPAN012463.pdf, accessed 22 July 2005.

Zhang, X-S 2004, press release, 12 June, www.chinanews.com.cn.

Zhao C 2002, 'Are you alright? Young workers from outside', *Shanghai Labour Security* 2.

Zhao, S 2000, 'Organizational characteristics of rural labor mobility in China' in West, LA and Y Zhao (eds), *Rural labor flows in China*, Institute of East Asian Studies, University of California, Berkeley.

Zhao, Y 2000, 'Rural-to-urban labor migration in China: the past and present', in West, LA and Y Zhao (eds), *Rural labor flows in China*, Institute of East Asian Studies, University of California, Berkeley.

—— 2001, 'The role of migrant networks in labor migration: the case of China', *Contemporary Economic Policy* 21(4).

Zhou, M 2004, 'Immigrants in the US economy' in Massey, DS and JE Taylor (eds) 2004, *International migration: prospects and polices in a global market*, Oxford University Press, New York.

Zhu, Rongji 2000, 'Zhu Rongji zongli zai wanshan shehui baozhang tixi zuotanhuishang qiangdiao, 'zai jinnian shixian "liangge quebao" di jichushang, jiakuai jianli wanshan di shehui baozhang tixi' [The Premier emphasises in the forum on completing a social insurance system, 'In this year, on the foundation of realising the "two guarantees" (pensions and basic living allowances), speeding up the establishment of a complete social insurance system], *Zhongguo Laodong* [*Chinese Labour*] 7.